Rudolf von Sinner

Public Theology in the Secular State

D1523981

Theologie in der Öffentlichkeit
Theology in the Public Square

herausgegeben von / edited by

Prof. Dr. Heinrich Bedford-Strohm
Dietrich-Bonhoeffer-Forschungsstelle
für öffentliche Theologie,
Universität Bamberg

Prof. Dr. James Haire
Public and Contextual
Theology Research Centre,
Charles Sturt University,
Canberra, Australia

Prof. Dr. Helga Kuhlmann
Institut für Evangelische Theologie,
Universität Paderborn

Prof. Dr. Dirk J. Smit
Beyers Naudé Centre for Public Theology,
University of Stellenbosch,
South Africa

Prof. Dr. Rudolf von Sinner
Postgraduate Programme in Theology,
Pontifícia Universidade Católica do Paraná,
Curitiba, Brazil

Band/Volume 15

LIT

Rudolf von Sinner

Public Theology
in the Secular State

A Perspective from the Global South

LIT

Unterstützt von / Supported by

Alexander von Humboldt
Stiftung / Foundation

This book is printed on acid-free paper.

Bibliographic information published by the Deutsche Nationalbibliothek
The Deutsche Nationalbibliothek lists this publication in the Deutsche
Nationalbibliografie; detailed bibliographic data are available in the Internet at
http://dnb.dnb.de.

ISBN 978-3-643-91208-4 (pb)
ISBN 978-3-643-96208-9 (PDF)

A catalogue record for this book is available from the British Library.

© LIT VERLAG GmbH & Co. KG Wien,
Zweigniederlassung Zürich 2021
Flössergasse 10
CH-8001 Zürich
Tel. +41 (0) 76-632 84 35
E-Mail: zuerich@lit-verlag.ch   https://www.lit-verlag.ch
Distribution:
In the UK: Global Book Marketing, e-mail: mo@centralbooks.com
In North America: Independent Publishers Group, e-mail: orders@ipgbook.com
In Germany: LIT Verlag Fresnostr. 2, D-48159 Münster
Tel. +49 (0) 2 51-620 32 22, Fax +49 (0) 2 51-922 60 99, e-mail: vertrieb@lit-verlag.de

I dedicate this book to my present and former colleagues
in the Discipline Group for Systematic Theology and Ecclesiology
at the Faculty of Theology, Stellenbosch University, South Africa
in deep gratitude for our South-South journeying together:
to Gerrit Brand (in memoriam), Dion Forster, Clint Le Bruyns (in memoriam),
Lisel Joubert, Nico Koopman, Nadia Marais, Sipho Mahokoto,
Henry Mbaya, Retief Muller, Mary-Anne Plaatjies van Huffel (in memoriam),
Dirkie Smit, Ashwin Thyssen, and Robert Vosloo,
and also
to Alease Brown (in memoriam), Marnus Havenga, Marthie Momberg, Carike Noeth,
Selina Palm, Karola Radler, Wilma Riekert, Marita Snyman and Kefas Umaru,
to the whole community of teachers, students, and staff at the Faculty of Theology at
Stellenbosch University in the name of their dean, Reggie Nel,
and to all who seek justice and transformation
in South Africa and beyond.

ENDORSEMENTS

This is a public theology under construction, respecting cultural and religious plurality, involving conviviality, citizenship, liberation, interculturality, and inter-religious dialogue, but also promoting a critical and open dialogue with the processes of secularisation, populisms, and theologies of prosperity. It reflects the presence of Christian traditions in the public sphere, taking into consideration the relationships that emerge in daily life and from counter-argument. Public theology is, indeed, public – open for dialogue and new constructions that strengthen democratic societies.

Prof. Dr Claudete Beise Ulrich, João Dias de Araújo Chair for Public Theology and the Study of Religion, Faculdade Unida de Vitória, Brazil

Public theology has been in the making for the last twenty years in Brazil, seeking to build bridges between the academy, society, and the church and taking seriously the reality of religious pluralism, dialogue between persons and organisations of the Global North and South. This is what this book is about, most timely for a contextual theology.

Prof. Dr Ronaldo de Paula Cavalcante, Mackenzie Presbyterian University, São Paulo, Brazil

In this excellent collection of essays, written over a period of 15 years, Rudolf von Sinner provides a superb set of reflections on the relationship between faith and public life. What makes this contribution so valuable is that it emerges from the lived experience of doing theology from the 'Global South', offering a rich set of theological and ethical insights for the future. I highly recommend this book!

Prof. Dr Dr Dion Forster, Beyers Naudé Centre for Public Theology, University of Stellenbosch, South Africa

Von Sinner's contribution offers important insights into how public theology can look like when it is informed by a rigorous dialogue arising from the realities of the Global South such as Brazil and South Africa. His work demonstrates the fruit of theological reflection and the need for intercultural theological engagement that invites deeper reflexivity in systematic theology. As a global communion of Lutheran churches, we value the Lutheran contributions in Latin America and Africa for our understanding of being church in the public space. This theological conversation calls for a stronger participation from parts of the world such as Asia where the experience of religious pluralism, power and wealth, as well as secularisation both resonates and is distinctive in their respective contexts. Every society in our planet is now even more aware of our interconnectedness as a global pandemic, economic crisis, social conflicts, and climate change affects us. Von Sinner's reflection on the centrality of the people in doing public theology is a timely challenge to any tendency towards an elitist theological posture. As we reflect on being a Church of the people and a Church with the people, I see this as an invitation to uplift the voices of younger emerging voices and female theologians who are playing an important role in shaping our theological responses to public issues that are both liberative and transformative.

Rev. Dr Sivin Kit, Program Executive for Public Theology & Interreligious Relations, Lutheran World Federation, Geneva, Switzerland

Here is a work of significant importance for scholars in the Global North. By collating and translating 15 years of reflection and research on theology and public theology in the Global South, von Sinner has made it possible for those of us who are not multi-lingual to read and engage with his expertise in the Brazilian context. If public theology is serious about inclusion and social justice, it cannot be constructed solely from scholarship originating in English-speaking countries; consequently, this is a much-needed volume without which scholarship in the Global North would be poorer. Drawing on developments in Latin American Liberation Theology and its central principle of a prior option for the poor, von Sinner directs his erudite and critically analytic examination of the notion of public theology to diverse and pressing issues in the Brazilian context including trust, citizenship, and human rights. Whilst examining the visibility of Catholic and Protestant buildings, he highlights the less visible and marginalised African Brazilian religious practices, asking challenging questions such as: whose religion is Christianity; what is Christian and what is Western? Debunking Western beliefs that view Christianity as a religion taken to Africa by European missionaries, he restores the historical direction of travel and draws attention to the contemporary flow of missionaries from Nigeria and Brazil to the Global North. In addition, the relevance of the volume is evident in its critique of populism, the concept of 'the people', and the growing but distorted use of prosperity gospel teaching that presumes

capitalism is the answer to suffering. Throughout the book, von Sinner demands that public theology engages with the social and political realities of the excluded and discarded; indeed, we can only achieve justice by hearing and including the voices of the most marginalised. This is a volume rich in content that rewards the reader with twelve informative and thought-provoking chapters.
Prof. Dr Esther McIntosh, York St. John University, United Kingdom

This collection of essays by intercontextual Swiss-Brazilian public theologian Rudolf von Sinner presents forceful arguments for a public theology especially in the contexts of the Global South. While keenly aware of his own contextuality, von Sinner makes a convincing case for a public theology that accepts the challenges posed by Liberation Theology and decolonial thinking, but also by the prosperity gospel while insisting on the importance of an articulate religious plurality.
Prof. Dr Torsten Meireis, Berlin Institute for Public Theology at Humboldt-University, Germany

TABLE OF CONTENTS

LIST OF ABBREVIATIONS

	English	*Portuguese (if original language)*
AD	Assemblies of God	*Assembleias de Deus*
ANC	African National Council	
BSLK	*Bekenntnisschriften der Lutherischen Kirche* Confessional Documents of the Lutheran Church	
CA	*Confessio Augustana* (Augsburg Confession)	*Confissão de Augsburgo*
CAPA	Centre for Assistance with and Promotion of Agroecology (formerly Centre for Assistance to the Small Farmer)	*Centro de Apoio e Promoção da Agroecologia (Centro de Apoio ao Pequeno Agricultor)*
CEB	Church Base Community	*Comunidade Eclesial de Base*
CELAM	Latin American Episcopal Council	*Conselho Episcopal Latino-Americano*
CESE	Ecumenical Project Coordination Service	*Coordenadoria Ecumênica de Serviço*
CITER	Centre for Theological and Religious Studies	*Centro de Investigação em Teologia e Estudos da Religião*
CNBB	Brazilian National Bishop's Conference	*Conferência Nacional dos Bispos do Brasil*
CONIC	(Brazilian) National Council of Churches	*Conselho Nacional de Igrejas Cristãs (do Brasil)*
COVID-19	Coronavirus Disease caused by the SARS-CoV-2 strain	
CPT	Pastoral Land Commission	*Comissão Pastoral da Terra*

EATWOT	Ecumenical Association of Third World Theologians	
EST	Lutheran School of Theology	*Escola Superior de Teologia/ Faculdades EST*
FLD	Lutheran Diakonia Foundation	*Fundação Luterana de Diaconia*
FMTL	World Forum on Theology and Liberation	*Forum Mundial de Teologia e Libertação*
GNPT	Global Network of Public Theology	
IECLB	Evangelical Church of the Lutheran Confession in Brazil	*Igreja Evangélica de Confissão Luterana no Brasil*
IELB	Evangelical Lutheran Church of Brazil	*Igreja Evangélica Luterana do Brasil*
IJPT	International Journal of Public Theology	
IURD	Universal Church of the Kingdom of God	*Igreja Universal do Reino de Deus*
JE	Evangelical Newspaper	*Jornal Evangélico*
LGBTIQA+	Lesbian, gay, bisexual, transgender, intersexual, queer, asexual and new subjects	
LWF	Lutheran World Federation	
ME	Great Encounter Movement	*Movimento Encontrão*
MEUC	Evangelical Mission Christian Unity	*Missão Evangélica União Cristã*
MST	Landless Workers' Movement	*Movimento dos Tralhadores Rurais Sem Terra*
NGO	Non-Governmental Organisation	

OFM	Ordo Fratrum Minorum Franciscan Order	
PAMI	Missionary Action Plan	Plano de Ação Missionária
PPL	Popular Lutheran Pastoral Action	Pastoral Popular Luterana
PT	Workers' Party	Partido dos Trabalhadores
PUC	Pontifical Catholic University	Pontifícia Universidade Católica
PUCRS	Pontifical Catholic University of Rio Grande do Sul	Pontifícia Universidade Católica do Rio Grande do Sul
RGG	Die Religion in Geschichte und Gegenwart Religion Past and Present	
SOTER	Brazilian Association for Theology and Religious Studies	Sociedade de Teologia e Ciências da Religião
TRC	Truth and Reconciliation Commission	
TRE	Theologische Realenzyklopädie Theological Real Encyclopedia	
UCP	Portuguese Catholic University	Universidade Católica Portuguesa
UFRGS	Federal University of Rio Grande do Sul	Universidade Federal do Rio Grande do Sul
ULBRA	Lutheran University of Brazil	Universidade Luterana do Brasil
UN	United Nations	
UNCTAD	United Nations Conference on Trade and Development	
UNISINOS	(Jesuit) University of the Sinos Valley	Universidade do Vale do Rio dos Sinos

USA	United States of America	
WCC	World Council of Churches	
WEF	World Economic Forum	
YMCA	Young Men's Christian Association	
YMHA	Young Men's Hindu Association	
YMMA	Young Men's Muslim Association	

FOREWORD

Public theology is needed. This affirmation is true for political contexts in which religion and state are closely intertwined. Where religion goes along with state power, critical intervention, based on theological insights, can prevent the misuse of religion for simply legitimising power. Public theology, however, is also needed in secularised contexts in which religion is only one perspective in the pluralism of society, and Christian religion is only one of the various forms of religion. Secular states, which deliberately overcome the promotion of a certain religion through the legal power of the state, are no less in need of normative orientation than any other forms of state. In fact, their liberal character poses the question even more clearly, where such normative orientation can come from.

This book on "Public Theology in the Secular State" gives a persuasive answer to this question. Normative orientation must come from civil society. Churches as institutions with a moral wisdom, handed over from generation to generation through many centuries, must play a central role in it. Rudolf von Sinner can draw from a rich basis of scholarship and experience related to the topic of public theology. He was part of the founding group of the Global Network of Public Theology, which is actually the first address for scholarship in this field. He also developed, in a glocal dialogue, a public theology as "theology of citizenship" for Brazil. His clear awareness of the contextuality of public theology is the reason for his repeated assurance in this book that we cannot speak about "public theology" but always only of "a" public theology.

At the same time, it is very clear for him as well that there is not only a contextuality of public theology, but also an "intercontextuality". One of the great strengths of this book is its embeddedness in an international discourse on public theology, with a special emphasis on the South-South exchange. Groundbreaking scholarship in South Africa, especially done in the "Beyers Naudé Center for Public Theology" at Stellenbosch University, is brought into exchange with scholarship in Brazil. What unites both contexts is the situation of a society in transformation trying to build a democratic culture on the foundation of decades of dictatorship.

One of the most fruitful outcomes of this intercontextual exchange is the account of the continuity between the notion of "liberation theology" and the notion of "public theology". These two notions are not to be pitted against each other, but represent different responses to diverse situations. If those who have developed liberation theologies in a situation of dictatorship have now gained democratic mandates with the possibilities to shape government policies themselves, they need critical accompaniment by public theology, always reminding them of the commitment to the preferential option for the poor so characteristic of liberation theologies.

Another mirror of the contextuality of von Sinner's public theology is his wide account of the impact of Pentecostal and Neo-Pentecostal movements on politics in Brazil. One can describe part of this impact, not least in the massive support for the Bolsonaro government, as a perversion of public theology, since, with the notion of "prosperity gospel", it completely ignores the cross as a decisive basis for Christian public theology and adheres to an insensitive neo-liberal capitalism combined with a conservative moralism in terms of family and sexuality. The destructive consequences of the special liaison between populist political and certain Neo-Pentecostal perversions of Christian theology become very apparent through the analyses in this book. This enlightening result will be helpful for many other contexts and is therefore an intercontextual contribution to public theology scholarship in its best sense.

The contributions to such scholarship in public theology are manifold in this book. Together with our other editors I proudly welcome its publication in our series "Theology in the Public Square".

Bishop Prof. Dr. Heinrich Bedford-Strohm

INTRODUCTION

Public theology is increasingly both a global and contextual venture. It is global in the sense that today we have publications, theses and dissertations, centres, programmes and, not least, actions in all parts of the globe, more or less explicitly under this heading. The *Global Network of Public Theology* (GNPT) has, since its foundation in 2007, expanded and relies on a growing number of member institutions, so far from Australia, Austria, Belgium, Brazil, Canada, China, Germany, India, Indonesia, Ireland, the Netherlands, New Zealand, Nigeria, Norway, Portugal, Romania, Rwanda, South Africa, Switzerland, Tonga, the United Kingdom (UK), and the United States of America (USA). The International Journal of Public Theology (IJPT) is celebrating its fifteenth year with a good number of subscribers and up to 28 fascinating articles published each year. While the English language is certainly dominant – even though often only the second or third language of the contributors – slowly Latin languages are entering the scene, namely French, Romanian and Portuguese, as well as Chinese and Russian.

From the beginning, there has also been critique, which is indeed necessary and, even if sometimes hard to take, healthy for identifying blind spots. One of the repeatedly upcoming issues is the reduced representativity of public theology, especially in terms of gender and race. It is a fact that the majority of those who explicitly call their approach "public theology", and who are generally acknowledged in the discourse – are men, particularly white men. However, from early on, important female theologians like Elaine Graham and Esther McIntosh, and more recently also Claudete Beise Ulrich, to name a few, have made significant contributions to public theology. In addition, from the African continent, colleagues from South Africa and Nigeria also participated from the outset, all of whom were not white, as well as scholars from Rwanda. Furthermore, criticism has been voiced as to, in their perspective, public theology being an "unfriendly takeover", so to speak, of Liberation Theology, seeking to silence it, and to be too harmonious, while considering itself a new universal theology under which all others would have to submit. I hope the following pages show that my way of elaborating "a" – the indefinite article is very important – public theology does not have such pretensions, and that I consider it one – again, "a" –

way of continuing Liberation Theology in a democratic context which I have come to find meaningful.

The most important element, in any case, is not the network and its membership, nor if you do or do not call your theology "public theology". The issue at stake is how to live out the faith oriented by Jesus' gospel in today's world with its challenges. Whenever possible, this happens by participation of churches, faith-based organisations, and academic theologians in the public sphere – no longer, as stated already in the early 1970s by my Heidelberg ethics teacher Wolfgang Huber, in a church-state relationship, but with churches (and other religious and non-religious communities) as part of civil society. To practice, as did Jesus, both *parrhesia* and *kenosis,* which I freely translate as boldness and humility, is, I believe, the order of the day. And public theology is helpful, pointing at the simultaneously necessary analysis of the public and the publics with, from, and for whom theology is engaged, and of drawing on the resources of Scripture, theological tradition, and the diversity of approaches that exist today. In my case, the focus has been and continues to be on a theology of citizenship as public theology, when citizenship is not mainly nationality (which especially in Europe immediately creates exclusions), but the struggle for the conscience and effectiveness of fundamental rights for all, thus seeking to be inclusive. This is what I have learnt as a Swiss by origin in my over 20 years of living, working, learning, and teaching in Brazil. Ordained in the Evangelical-Reformed Church in the Canton of Basel-City in 1994, ten years later, after having done research on my doctorate in Brazil and India and, following its completion in 2001, having worked for two years at an ecumenical development organisation in Salvador/Bahia, Brazil, I joined the ministry of the Evangelical Church of the Lutheran Confession in Brazil (IECLB) and became a professor at its seminary, the Escola Superior de Teologia (EST), known today as Faculdades EST. My inaugural lecture on "Trust and *convivência*" emanates from the perception of a deep mistrust embedded in society and the question for its reasons and possibilities of overcoming it, especially as it touched on the lack of ecumenical communion between the ever-growing diversity of Christian churches in Brazil. This is now Chapter 1 in this collection.

The initial insight for a theology of citizenship came from a seminal article by Hugo Assmann (1994) on "a theology of citizenship and solidarity, or: continuing liberation theology". What brought me to Brazil was Liberation Theology, especially as developed by Leonardo

Boff – who became a much respected and dear friend – and I cannot conceive of any theology that would not have to be liberative and to take up at least two of its main insights, *the preferential option for the poor* and *praxis as an essential part of theology*. At the same time, the Liberation Theology I knew seemed too much taken by a mode of resistance and too little by a mode of construction – especially when, in 2002, the Brazilian population elected a person to the presidency that had come out of the Catholic left and now was the president of all Brazilians: Luís Inácio Lula da Silva. During that decade, on discovering "public theology" when I was at the Center of Theological Inquiry at Princeton and the GNPT was founded, I wrote what is now Chapter 2 of this book and presented its first version to the GNPT meeting at Princeton and later to a group at the Third Global Forum on Liberation Theology (FMTL). At Princeton I was busy completing my study entitled *The Churches and Democracy in Brazil: Towards a Public Theology Focused on Citizenship*, which was subsequently published in 2012 with a very generous and significant foreword by my dear colleague and teacher, the late Vítor Westhelle (1952-2018). One of its case studies was the church I now belong to, the IECLB, which is reflected in Chapter 4. I then began to focus my attention more closely on the Pentecostal churches, a growing segment of Christianity in Brazil, and its possible contribution towards citizenship, even though a more outspoken discourse on this was lacking. I also expanded, thus, my view on theologies in Latin America and organised what I perceived under four headings: theology under the sign of liberation (including public theology), of interculturality and inter-religious dialogue, of the Spirit (Pentecostalism), and of prosperity (Neo-Pentecostalism), now recorded in Chapter 3, originally an invitation to present theology in Latin America today to a German public in the very traditional and widely read *Theologische Literaturzeitung*.

Following the contextual localisation of a public theology in section one, the whole second section of the book is on public theology and religious pluralism, focusing on intercultural theology and the shift of Christianity's "centre of gravity" to the South, in Chapter 5, which is the fruit of being a research fellow at the Lichtenberg-Kolleg of the University of Göttingen in 2011.

Chapter 6 was written originally as a memorial lecture for my dear Heidelberg teacher and fatherly friend – Dietrich Ritschl (1929-2018), reflecting on his perception of theology in the New Worlds and the need for a new theology also in the Old World. I am honoured to have been invited by my dear colleagues Martin Hailer and Friederike Nüssel for that occasion in early 2019, who opted to invite a Ritschl pupil from "the end of the world" rather than another of his most competent flock, once Ritschl's long-standing colleague and friend Wolfgang Huber was unavailable.

Focusing on the enormous religious transformations Brazil and Latin America, Africa, and Asia have been going through, but also, in different ways Europe and the United States (US), Chapter 7 was conceived as reflecting on how these contexts relate to the once universally proclaimed but since highly relativised and contextualised secularisation theory. It was written by invitation of my friend and Munich University host, Reiner Anselm, during one of my stays, and funded by the Alexander von Humboldt scholarship for experienced researchers. Chapter 8 was formulated very recently as a contribution to a Latin American collection on the city and its specific challenges for (and by!) the presence of religions in it, pastorally and theologically, on invitation by my dear friend and colleague, Catholic ecumenist Elias Wolff, who first invited me to join the faculty at the Pontifical Catholic University of Paraná at Curitiba. In 2019, this became a reality, after 16 years at EST/Faculdades EST, and in September I most unexpectedly became the Head of the Graduate Programme when my dear friend and colleague Alex Villas Boas took up the post of research coordinator of the Centre for Theological and Religious Studies (CITER) at the Portuguese Catholic University (UCP) in Lisbon. To call a Lutheran theologian for Systematic Theology and for a function of leadership in a Catholic university is a sign of enormous ecumenical trust and generosity both of the university, represented by its Rector, Waldemiro Gremski, and its Grand Chancellor, the Metropolitan Archbishop of Curitiba, Dom José Antônio Peruzzo. I am honoured and indeed very grateful to them, to my colleagues at the Graduate and Undergraduate Programmes in Theology, to the Dean of the School of Education and Humanities, Ericson Falabretti, and the Vice-Rector for Research, Graduate Studies and Innovation, Paula Trevilatto. I am also grateful to the IECLB for recognising my theological magisterium at a Catholic university as an exercise of my Lutheran pastoral ministry and for having celebrated a formal installation service in PUC's chapel, presided over by my Synodal Pastor and Vice-President of the IECLB, Odair Braun, assisted by Pastor Vera Immich and Father Elias Wolff.

At the time the texts of section I were conceived, it seemed that in the "land of the future" (Stephan Zweig), the future had finally arrived. Indeed, many good things happened, and as poverty was reduced, education and infrastructure expanded. But as the years went on and the shades of the Worker's Party (PT) government grew longer, I realised resistance indeed and again was more than necessary – and since the unjust impeachment of the first woman in the Brazilian presidency, Dilma Rousseff, in 2016 and the election of Jair Messias Bolsonaro to the presidency in 2018 (with a just impeachment that has not happened), this need has become ever more evident. Trying to understand how a majority can elect a person that has always been publicly and outrightly sexist, racist, homophobic, aporophobic and who, even when in the presidency, has consistently shown no real interest whatsoever in the well-being of the people except for his own family and close circle, resulting, among other things, in Brazil's more than half a million deaths from COVID-19, has led me to reflect on populism and "the people" (Chapters 9 and 10). Finally, the interesting but also problematic dynamics of Brazilian Neo-Pentecostal interaction with Africa (Chapter 11) and of migration to and mission from Brazil in interaction with the Old World (Chapter 12) also deserves attention while we deepen an understanding of where the people are, how they move, and by whom and by what they are moved.

The twelve chapters published herein are, then, not new. They were published over a time span of 15 years; most, however, were not available in English to date. They represent a specific moment in time, and I opted not to do a thorough revision, which would result in the writing of a new book indeed, but only for minor corrections and updating. Therefore, they bear their assets and restrictions and are indeed offered here for critical discussion. They all have their specific *Sitz im Leben* as I tried to show in my biography, in my context, and in my interaction with many persons in other contexts from whom I have learned so much. Colleagues from the Discipline Group of Systematic Theology and Ecclesiology at the Faculty of Theology, Stellenbosch University, South Africa, nominated me as professor extra-ordinary first in 2013 and then again in 2016 and 2019, respectively, for another three-year-term. I am deeply grateful for this generous welcome, even at geographical distance, into the fold of professors that are connected to the discipline, most of whom are living in the Global North – but here we have a genuine South-South dialogue. This is why this book, situated as it is in the Brazilian context, but interacting globally and especially with

South Africa, is dedicated to my colleagues at Stellenbosch University and beyond, many of whom have become dear friends.

I would like to thank all those who have made this book possible. First, my wife Helena and daughter Taís, without whose patience, emotional support, conversations, jokes, common movie-watching, meals, and walks I would not have enjoyed so much both the working periods and times of rest. I thank my colleagues from the Graduate Programme in Theology for their substantial financial support towards the translations – so competently done by Alexander Busch, Luis Marcos Sander, and Walter O. Schlupp – through the decentralisation quota of PUC's Research Fund. I thank the National Research Foundation of South Africa for providing me with funds based on my publications towards my research account as professor extra-ordinary at Stellenbosch University, which made the competent and thorough formal and English language revision and editing by Lee-Anne Roux possible. She also compiled the indexes. I further thank my teacher, then colleague and friend Bishop Heinrich Bedford-Strohm who generously agreed to write the foreword to this book, and to him and colleagues James Haire, Helga Kuhlmann, and Dirkie Smit, who analysed the proposal and included it in the Theology in the Public Square series. I also thank the chief lector, Michael J. Rainer, for his always efficient work in seeing the publication through during the whole process, and to the Alexander von Humboldt-Foundation for its generous grant towards the publication costs. Finally, I would like to thank all who have in one way or another interacted with me on the journey towards this book, not least those who kindly accepted to read it and give a word of praise – this is most appreciated! All remaining shortcomings are, of course, my own. I now offer it for discussion, critique, and future interaction.

I. PUBLIC THEOLOGY BETWEEN THE ACADEMY, SOCIETY AND THE CHURCH

Chapter 1

Trust and Convivência: Contributions to a Hermeneutics of Trust in Communal Interaction[*]

We are in Spain, in the most vicious period of the Inquisition. Frequently, one sees the stakes burning with the "heretics", supposedly the enemies of the true faith. In this hell of flames, Jesus returns to earth and walks amidst the people. Everyone recognises him. While he begins to take care of the people, heal the sick and resurrect the dead, the Grand Inquisitor arrives. He immediately orders that Jesus be imprisoned. At night, he visits Jesus in his narrow cell. "Why did you come to bother us?", asks the Grand Inquisitor, and announces that on the next day Jesus will die at the stake as "the worst of heretics". In a comprehensive sermon, the Inquisitor explains, in essence, the failure of the gospel message. Jesus proclaimed freedom, but the people did not know how to deal with it. It was necessary that the church guide the people. The people wanted peace, security, happiness, albeit submissive to the authority of the church. They did not want, nor could they support freedom, because freedom brings insecurity and risk. "Why, therefore, did you come to bother us?" Jesus, however, says nothing. He stays silent to the end. He perceives that it was no longer God who was dwelling in the heart of the Inquisitor, even though he represented the church. In the end, Jesus kisses the Inquisitor's lips. The Inquisitor, with his heart burning, lets him go. "Go and never return, never again!" (DOSTOYEVSKY 1993).

    This story is told by the Russian writer Fyodor Dostoyevsky (1821-1881). It is a very rich story, touching on the deepest aspects of human life and faith, as does the whole book, *The Brothers Karamazov,* from which this story is taken. I wish to highlight only one of its many facets: *freedom*; this deepest characteristic of the human being implies risk, taking responsibility for oneself, and not merely following authority. Jesus shows his trust in the human capacity for freedom, he even makes it a central aspect of his proclamation of God's kingdom (BARTSCH 1983; DAHLING-SANDER 2003). However, the church of the Grand Inquisitor, supposedly Jesus' follower and representative on earth, treats human

---

[*] Originally published in *The Ecumenical Review* 57/3 (2005), 322-341. Used with permission and moderately revised and updated.

beings as if they were infants who need motherly care. The church gives the people what they want: bread and games. But it does not trust in their capacity for using freedom. Jesus, on the contrary, as Dostoyevsky's story clearly shows, trusts human beings and their freedom. And I join this attitude of trust. We will see further on how difficult it is to construct *convivência*[1] and how trust is needed not only in freedom but in the good use of freedom. But we are free beings because of the gospel, both capable and worthy of it. We do not need to be guided by the absolute authority of the church or any other power, but by Christ, the living Word of God. On this basis, the church is indeed the community of free humans in Christ.

At the heart of this text lies the thesis that trust is the basis of any *convivência,* within the family, the church, or society – indeed in any human fellowship. The fundamental importance of trust has come clearly to the fore during my research on the contribution of Brazilian churches to citizenship (VON SINNER 2012a; 2017). The need for trust presented itself to me as a central element of human *convivência* and, thereby as central to democracy and to citizenship. Trust is the indispensable foundation of any communal interaction, be it in the circle of family, church, or society, or in any other grouping of human beings. This is the affirmation that I intend to explore in this reflection, trying to offer some thoughts on what I shall call, following reflections from the ecumenical movement and Dietrich Ritschl's seminal proposal, a "hermeneutics of trust".[2]

This chapter is divided into four sections: After showing the need for and the lack of trust, as identified in various surveys (1.1), I shall identify different aspects of trust (1.2). Thereafter, I will develop contributions for a hermeneutics of trust relying on biblical witness (1.3). Finally, the focus will be on pointing out the possible consequences of this hermeneutic in three areas, namely: ecumenism, inter-religious dialogue, and *convivência* in society (1.4).

---

[1] Literally, "conviviality". However, the connotations of its use in Portuguese are very particular and will be explained below; I therefore opted to maintain the Portuguese word, always in italics.

[2] RITSCHL 2003, especially pp. 179-192 and Chapter 6 below; also BOUTENEFF and HELLER 2001.

1.1 Need for and lack of trust

It may seem just too obvious to affirm that we need to trust each other even in the most basic procedures. Even so, it makes sense to remember this fact to realise the absolute necessity of trust. Thus, on a daily basis, we trust many people, appliances, products, procedures, agreements, and many other items, often without being aware of this. Whenever you rise in the morning and buy your bread for breakfast at the bakery, it is rather unlikely that you would waste time thinking about the possibility of eating bread containing poison. You trust in the inspections of the Health Ministry as well as in the baker's professional ethics. You take for granted that this baker would not want to damage his business and therefore would work at maintaining his clients' satisfaction. When you travel to work by train, you usually trust in the driver, as well as in the company who constructed the train. You would enter the carriage calmly, trusting to arrive at the right place in ample time. As you cross the road, you would expect the cars to stop at the red traffic light. And reaching your workplace, you would normally find it as you left it – with the usual procedures, equipment, colleagues, and so on.

Other items could easily be added to this list. Were it not possible for us to trust so many people and things, our life would be seriously restricted. It would not be possible to live our lives if we could not trust without always being preoccupied specifically with every aspect of our life. Without trust there is no life.[3]

However, opinion polls seem to suggest that trust is virtually absent in Brazil. Among the 17 countries of Latin America periodically surveyed by the organisation Latinobarómetro, Brazil is lowest in this regard. Questioned on "speaking in general, would you say that you can trust in the majority of the people or that one is never careful enough in dealing with others?", only 4% of Brazilian respondents affirmed that they would put their trust in others. The average on the continent is 17%, with Uruguay presenting the highest percentage of trust (36%) (LATINOBARÓMETRO 2003, 26).[4] This does not mean that there is no trust

---

[3] LUHMANN 2001, 148 differentiates between "confidence" and "trust", where the daily, normal would fall under "confidence", while "trust" would presuppose a "previous engagement" and a "situation of risk" which one can enter or avoid. See also LUHMANN 2000.

[4] Also in subsequent research, Brazil consistently comes in last. Even 15 years after the above quoted survey, only 4% affirmed one could, indeed, trust the majority of persons

whatsoever in Brazil, but people seem to be convinced that they cannot trust people they do not know. The same research shows that people trust in persons around them or persons with known capacities – firemen (64% in all of Latin America), one's work or study colleagues (59%), and one's neighbours (50%), but not unknown persons.[5] As for institutions, research done by the World Economic Forum (WEF) in 2002 shows that the list of trust is headed by the churches[6]:

Religious Groups and Churches	65%
Non-governmental Organisations	61%
Armed Forces	59%
Press and Media	58%
Educational System	56%
Trade Unions	53%
Big national companies	53%
United Nations	49%
Multinationals in Brazil	47%
World Trade Organisation	45%
Judicial System	44%
Health System	44%
World Bank	41%
Police	40%
Government	38%
Congress	33%

(LATINOBARÓMETRO, 2018). The average on the continent, however, reached its lowest level since 1996, 14%, with Colombia, Uruguay and Guatemala presenting the highest level of trust (20%) – significantly lower than in 2003. In Scandinavian countries, the trust rate comes up to 75%. The 2010 LATINOBARÓMETRO report sees a possible reason in the constantly low Latin American numbers: "to trust something [or someone] you don't know is not in line with our societies' socially fragmented structure" (p. 71).

[5] Ibid, p. 27. On p. 23, the report says that there is trust *within* groups and segments of society, however, there is no trust *between* groups, segments, and networks.

[6] For this research, 1,002 persons in nine metropolitan regions were interviewed, namely: São Paulo, Rio de Janeiro, Belo Horizonte, Salvador, Recife, Fortaleza, Belém, Curitiba, and Porto Alegre (*O Estado de São Paulo,* Nov. 8, 2002, p. A17). The LATINOBARÓMETRO (2018, 48) report confirmed, on the whole continent, the top ranking of the churches (63%), followed – very distantly – by the armed forces (44%), the police (35%), the electoral justice (28%), the judiciary (24%), the government (22%), congress (21%) and, at the bottom end, political parties (13%). In Brazil, there were even 73% that responded they trusted the churches (ibid, 49).

International Monetary Fund   30%

Such lack of trust in people outside one's own group is, in my view, one of the most important factors that impedes communion among people, churches, religions, and institutions of society. In Brazil, one of the roots of the problem seems to be well identified in the reflections of Brazilian anthropologist Roberto DaMatta (1991; 1997). Thus, a woman or a man is a *person* inasmuch as one belongs to a "family" headed by a "boss" (*patrão*), be this the father, an entrepreneur, a large landowner, a politician, a colonel, or some other person who holds a considerable degree of power. This situation has given rise to the well-known phrase "do you know whom you're talking to?" This phrase intends to identify the person as a member of that "family" and demands privileges, such as jumping the queue at the bank or evading a traffic fine. The law, a basic instrument of any transparent and democratic society, presupposes, however, that all are equal. In this context, it is significant that, in the aforementioned survey, a clear majority opted for the affirmation that claims, as a necessary presupposition for trust in the state institutions, equal treatment for all (LATINOBARÓMETRO 2003, 27). For DaMatta, the subjects of the law are not "persons", but "individuals" defined not by their relationships with a "boss" and other members of the "family", but by their rights and duties before the law – therefore as citizens. The "persons" are going to say: "For friends everything; for enemies the law!" Applying this distinction made by DaMatta to our theme, we can conclude that trust would exist only within the "family of persons" and not outside it, where the human being is abandoned to the cold letter of the law. The "boss" is head of a hierarchy, he gives orders and can give or withdraw privileges as he wishes. But – for the members of the "family" – he is also the father who cares for and protects; and this is precisely the reason why he deserves to be trusted.

Where there is no trust, the thread that binds society together and gives it the necessary cohesion is missing. This is recognised even in the area where competition, on principle an enemy of trust, prevails: in the economy. Francis Fukuyama, author of a controversial book about the "end of history" (1992), where he announced the victory of the democratic and capitalist system of Western society due to the fall of socialism, affirms in his book *Trust:* "One of the most important lessons that one learns upon examining economic life is that the wellbeing of a nation, as well as its capacity to compete, is conditioned by a single, wide

ranging cultural characteristic: the level of trust inherent in the society"
(FUKUYAMA 1996, 21). He goes on to cite a number of examples where
solidarity among the people has led to the preservation of welfare for all
implied: for example, in a German company threatened by bankruptcy,
where all, including the chief executives, substantially reduced their work
hours and their salary to save the company, which they managed to do
without a single redundancy. However, it is not only the economic results
that count: "The reason that these economic actors behaved in this way
was not necessarily that they had previously calculated the economic
consequences; more importantly, the solidarity in their economic
communities became an end in itself" (ibid, 23f.). Therefore, this
economist, a champion in the defence of competition, recognises that
trust and solidarity are necessary as values that work beyond self-interest.
Concluding this section, we can say that there is ample consensus that
any communal interaction is not viable without being based on trust.
Otherwise, we would have "a war of all against all", as Thomas Hobbes
once wrote.[7] But what, after all, is trust?

1.2 Aspects of trust

It is not easy to define trust, as it is not a concept that, upon being adopted,
will result directly in action. Instead, it is an attitude that becomes visible
in action itself. It is only when we act with trust that we can identify it.
Even so, we can plausibly use a general definition to have at least a vague
idea of what we are talking about. I suggest defining trust as an
expectation in relation to the other's behaviour which is to lie in my or
our common interest. The decisive difference can be found in the degree
of certainty I can have that my trust will not be disappointed, i.e. that the
other's behaviour will indeed be to my or our benefit rather than harm us.
I should add that I presuppose that there is only a gradual and not a
principal difference between his or her and our common benefit, and that,

---

[7] HOBBES 2000, 115 and passim. Hobbes assumed that it was wiser to trust *one* person
who, as an absolute monarch, might contain the natural state of universalised war, than
human beings as such. Citizens opting for democracy, however, would – according to
Offe – assume the following: "There is more reason for universalized trust in the
judgement capacity and the benevolence of the entirety of fellow citizens than for trust
in the same qualities of autocratic or party-monopolistic holders of power". I quote and
translate from the shorter and modified German version of this article, which, however,
added precisely this assumption to the English version: OFFE 2001, 265; 1999, 58.

thus, I would not expect a behaviour from the other which would be to my benefit but at his or her expense. I will expound on this further in what follows, focusing on interpersonal trust.

1.2.1 TRUST AS BET

In the first place, trust means to *bet on.*[8] I invest trust when I can expect, with a certain amount of probability, that the other will honour it. When dealing with people with whom I live on a daily basis, such as family members and work and study colleagues, I can observe their behaviour over a long period of time. In this way I accumulate experience about the trustworthiness of each person, and I know in whom I can or cannot trust. However, how can I trust in people I do not know?[9] Trust always implies a risk. My experience and my knowledge can help me judge if an unknown person is trustworthy or not. If someone asks me, as I am getting on a bus, to take a bag for that person's friend who would be waiting for me to pick it up at our destination, my experience will counsel me to refuse. Should the way he or she talks and pleads, his or her appearance and treatment convince me to take the risk by doing what he or she is asking for – even though these perceptions can obviously deceive – I would at least ask for the sender's and receiver's address and check the contents to verify that I would not be taking dangerous or illegal items. It also would depend on the rationale provided by the person, if she or he gave good reasons or not that would justify why the objects could not be sent by mail. In the Brazilian context, it is not unthinkable that the person might be forced by the lack of financial means to try this way of transporting goods, while having to invest trust in me that I would indeed hand over the bag to the receiver. Asking for information to

---

[8] Cf. SZTOMPKA 1999, 25: "Trust is a bet about the future contingent actions of others". For Sztompka, *trust* differs from *hope* ("a passive, vague, not rationally justified feeling that things will turn out to the good (or to the bad)") and *confidence* ("a still passive, but more focused and to some extent justified, faith that something good will happen (or not)") in that it "falls within the discourse of agency: actively anticipating and facing an unknown future" (ibid, 24f.).

[9] This is precisely the focus of OFFE's (1999, 57) contribution, who puts it, among other formulations, in this way: "It is not clear how civic trust emerges among the members of mass publics within a democracy, given the condition of anonymity, diversity, and pluralism".

confirm my trustworthiness might indicate sincerity. Still, the possibility of carrying something illegal could not be ruled out.

More complicated yet is the trust in people I will never meet. Any democratic society can only work in this way, presupposing a minimal level of trust among people who know nothing of the other except that they are citizens of the same state. In this case, much depends on the trust I have in the political and judicial system of the country to place my bet. Trust always means betting on the other, because one is never absolutely certain that one's trust will be honoured.

1.2.2 TRUST AS PRIOR INVESTMENT

Here is a second aspect. Trusting is a *prior investment* that I make unilaterally without certainty about the reaction or the result.[10] With this I make myself vulnerable. However, trust can generate trust precisely because it is unilaterally invested. In advancing trust, I impose a moral obligation on the other to honour it, because we both know that breaking the trust someone invests in me is the worst imaginable betrayal.[11] If someone needs my help after a traffic accident, I feel obliged to help the person because I would expect the same from him or her. If I am the one responsible for the accident, by law I am obliged to give immediate help. It is part of the trust in the values accepted by society to be able to count on, always and quickly, first aid given by the first passing person. When we wander in the woods or walk in traffic or in many other situations that present some danger, we are advancing trust. The expectation is that someone will help me if I need it and will not let me suffer or even die without doing everything possible to save me. However, we know from

---

[10] Hobbes described trust as necessary precisely when, in a contract relationship, one party carries out its part before the other. To be sure, however, this trust is facilitated by the fact that both recognise an independent force of coercion which can, should it be necessary, intervene and punish the perpetrator, see HOBBES, 2000, 122.

[11] OFFE, 1999, 44, distinguishes between "confidence" and "trust", although he concedes that they are often used interchangeably. Whenever my confidence is being disappointed, the reasons for it lie beyond my reach and "must be attributed to *bad luck, chance, or Providence*". However, if I trust someone who is not trustworthy, it is my mistake, and I shall regret "my imprudent assessment of the trustworthiness of the person in question and discontinue my trust relationship with him". In my opinion, the latter is extremely serious, as it hurts twice: Not only do I have to presume the other had bad intentions – he wanted to harm me or gain an advantage for him – but I shall also be regarded as naive because of my possibly light-minded trust.

the story of the Good Samaritan in the Gospel of Luke that this does not always happen, and that the person who ends up helping may be someone from whom we least expect it (Lk 10:30-35).

On the other hand, I also suppose and trust that someone who yells for help does not want to rob me. It is an old trick to fake an accident in order to take advantage of the human impulse of the passerby to run and help, and then assault that person. When this happens frequently, the willingness of people to help diminishes drastically because they are afraid of being assaulted. In this way, the thieves who faked being victims of an accident did not only commit a crime; they affected one of the most important elements of human solidarity: to help someone who is in danger. This, consequently, reduces people's willingness to invest trust in others.

1.2.3 TRUST AS PART OF A GREATER ETHICS

The example of giving first aid in the case of danger shows that the expectations we have of other people's actions depend on ethical principles and moral rules that have been widely accepted. I invest trust because I presuppose that the other shares certain basic concepts with me. One widely known and accepted principle is the so-called "golden rule", which says, in its biblical formulation from the Gospel of Matthew: "In everything do to others as you would have them do to you; for this is the law and the prophets" (Mt 7:12). This principle is the cornerstone of the *categorical imperative* of Kant and is found in many philosophical ethics or religions (KANT 1989; KÜNG 1998). Besides this "minimal ethic" we have greater demands, such as indicated by the Sermon on the Mount itself, from which I extracted the citation of the golden rule (cf. THEISSEN 1999). Here we have a *greater ethic* to be followed.

This is the third aspect of trust, specific to those who adhere to a belief or an ideology that contains ethical demands. Upon meeting a person who follows a greater ethic, this person has the right to greater trust but is also subject to greater demands. "From everyone to whom much has been given, much will be required; and from the one to whom much has been entrusted, even more will be demanded", says Jesus in the parable on watchfulness (Lk 12:48). A church or non-governmental organisation (NGO) that receives donations in the form of money and uses it for purposes other than those intended, does considerable damage not only to its relationship with the specific donor or donors, but as soon as the news spreads, also jeopardises the trust and willingness of donors to contribute in general. People or organisations that aim at working for a just cause, such as fighting poverty, have a high probability of gaining greater trust, since they appeal to the hearts of the people who mobilise at the least a minimal sense of indignation about the millions of people in Brazil and elsewhere who live below the poverty line. Should a donation be channelled to private accounts or be misused in any other way, the betrayal will be even greater, as the donors will have a sense of having been misused in a particularly bad way. The same goes for religious ministers. In general, they are considered worthy of great confidence due to the ethics they adopted which demand from them that they serve others. The confessional secrecy, for instance, is protected even by public law. Consequently, strong disappointment and indignation are caused by the discovery that a minister has, for example, broken the confessional secrecy or committed sexual assault.

1.2.4 TRUST AS A GIFT

A fourth aspect is that trust is a *gift*. It is something freely given, and nobody can be obliged to trust. Accordingly, it can only be given by people who give it with conviction. The voluntary and gift character of trust comes clearly to the fore considering how much time it takes to develop an atmosphere of trust, and how quickly it can be destroyed. Once destroyed, it is very difficult to re-establish it. To illustrate this with an example from another context, I remember the South African Truth and Reconciliation Commission (TRC) (2002). Given the atrocities committed during apartheid, the TRC wanted to contribute towards a new South Africa, for which a new relationship of trust is essential. Reconciliation is the presupposition for this, which in turn presupposes repentance and the acknowledgment of guilt. Those who would speak the truth on political crimes would receive amnesty. And indeed, truth came to light in its unbearable cruelty. However, only partly has it been possible to bring forth repentance and acknowledgment. Like trust, these cannot be imposed. Reconciliation, which can be understood as the re-establishment of trust, is a free gift. It can only be established when at least one of the protagonists, by his or her own will, decides to once again invest trust in the other.

1.2.5 INFORMED TRUST

Finally, trust must not be invested and given naively. It can be fatal to trust the wrong person at the wrong moment. Thus, it is necessary to recognise signals which could indicate danger. Of course, it is not always possible to perceive the other's true intentions. Experience and attentiveness may reduce the probability of a disappointment but cannot totally avoid it. Trust remains a risk, a unilateral investment, a free gift. Furthermore, trust is also necessary among bank robbers, smugglers, drug traffickers, and other criminals. Although this trust may be guided more by self-interest and the despotic law imposed by crime than by the free will of the participants, it is still trust and might, especially among younger criminals, be the only form of trust they have ever come to know and appreciate. Evidently, seen in a wider perspective, this trust serves not the building up, but the destruction of society. Thus, trust as such is not enough, but needs to be inserted into a wider value system directed towards the well-being of all. These values need to be recognised by society so that the trustworthiness of the people can be promoted. To the extent that I can expect others to honour my trust, I will be more willing to invest trust myself. If I were the only one to trust and behave in a trustworthy way, I would alone have to deal with the losses. However, if I can presuppose, on principle, that all will do what is necessary to honour the trust, I will have good reasons to trust in others.

1.2.6 CONVIVÊNCIA

It is appropriate here to introduce a short reflection on *convivência* – literally, "conviviality", but better expressed by "communal interaction". On a primary level, it simply means that, we, as human beings, do not live alone. It is part of our being that we coexist with other men and women in time and space (*convivere,* in Latin). The daily contact with neighbours, study colleagues, workers of the bus company, bakery attendants, teachers, and many other people, is part of our life. It belongs to the *conditio humana* that it is not only a fact that we do not live alone, but it is part of our human nature to seek community in family and other forms of associations in society. Moreover, it is one of the most pleasurable aspects of the human condition to be in relationship with others. Therefore, it is necessary to mould and guide this coexistence for it to become *convivência.* Inspired by reflections that evolved from a

Conference in Rio de Janeiro in 1985, the German missiologist Theo Sundermeier developed the concept of *convivência* (*Konvivenz*, as a German neologism) as "a community of learning, mutual support and celebration" (SUNDERMEIER 1986, 51-59). Paulo FREIRE (2000; see also ILLICH 1989) used the term in his famous *Pedagogy of the Oppressed*, where he particularly emphasised the need for "trust in the people". To that end, a "conversion" is needed which presupposes *convivência* with the oppressed in order to learn to understand their life. What matters is the walking together, and this is not possible without trust. Where there is no trust there will not be *convivência* in the sense described here.

The specific challenge is to go beyond restricting trust to my family, friends, and brothers and sisters of my church, and extend it, on principle, to all with whom I coexist in a certain context, aiming at *convivência*. As this trust can base itself on rules and values accepted by all, whether in writing – in the Constitution and in laws – or by common habit, it will become safer to trust. If I see clearly here, it is basically this generalised trust that is lacking in Brazil. And it is not so just by chance. Bad experiences with authorities and with a variety of people and institutions have accumulated. These experiences, together with cultural factors as described by DaMatta, have left the impression that only those who have "friends", "sponsors" or "godfathers" in the right place can expect to be given due attention. One lacks trust in the reliability of people and institutions, and this constitutes a serious threat to the process of democratisation.

1.3 A hermeneutics of trust

Trust, thus, is a bet, it needs prior investment, it is connected to a greater ethic, it is a gift, and it needs to be informed. What, then, is meant by a "hermeneutics of trust"? As is well known, hermeneutics is the science of understanding and interpretation. It is being applied mainly to texts, and in the case of theology, particularly to the text of Holy Scripture. The reader enters a hermeneutical circle, in which he or she and the Bible come to interpret each other mutually. Thus, the Bible is not only the book that I read, but the Book that reads *me*, as Hans-Ruedi Weber formulated following this African story:

> A village woman used to walk around always carrying her Bible. 'Why always the Bible?,' her neighbours asked teasingly. 'There are so many

other books you could read.' The woman knelt down, held the Bible high above her head and said: 'Yes, of course there are many books which I could read. But there is only one book which reads me' (WEBER 1995, ix).

Hermeneutics is reading, understanding, and interpreting. Two thousand years after being written, we read the Bible with today's eyes, marked by our time and our place. And, in a manner of speaking, it reads our lives: it confronts our world with its message. Hermeneutics is the art of interpretation, like special glasses through which we look at a text and through which, following this metaphor, we are seen. In this sense, there can be a "hermeneutics of liberation", a "hermeneutics of suspicion", and also a "hermeneutics of trust" which makes a particular perspective its own and reads, from there, the text as well as its original and today's context. This, however, does not mean to exclude unexpected, surprising interpretations or even a "creative misunderstanding" (COMMISSION ON FAITH AND ORDER 1998).

In the first place, our hermeneutics of trust is formed by the notion of trust in the Bible. There, it is a central concept, although this is not so obvious, since we normally translate the Greek term for trust, *pistis,* as "faith". In the Old Testament, the equivalent would be the group of words connected to *'mn*, a word which we know from every worship service: "Amen!" "Stay firm!" The verb, in the hif'il stem, means "to remain firm, trust, have faith, believe".[12] Therefore, trust and related concepts are strongly highlighted in the Bible, insofar as they are connected to faith itself. On this, Martin Luther wrote in the Large Catechism, while explaining the first commandment, "you shall have no other gods" (Ex 20:3):

> A god is that to which we look for all good and in which we find refuge in every time of need. To have a god is nothing else than to trust and believe him with our whole heart [*ex toto corde fidere et credere*] [...] For these two belong together, faith and God. That to which your heart clings and entrusts itself [*tui fiduciam et cor fixum habueris*] is, I say, really your God (LUTHER 1959, 365).

Faith as trust is based on the promise of God. The promise is first, and the human answer is faith-trust. Abram, upon receiving the promise of

---

[12] WILDBERGER 1984, 178. In this family of words, one also finds *emuna* (faithfulness, sincerity) and *emet* (truth).

God, "put his faith in the Lord, and the Lord counted that faith to him as righteousness" (Gen 15:6). By faith we are inserted into communion with God. This communion goes far beyond religious, social, and gender boundaries: "There is no such thing as Jew and Greek, slave and free, male and female; for you are all one person in Christ Jesus" (Gal 3:28). Therefore, trust also stretches beyond certain groups and seeks to overcome inequalities, creating a new *convivência* among equals. We know that the church, throughout history, often reinforced inequalities and exclusiveness rather than overcoming them. This was apparent in the story of the Grand Inquisitor. But the church is constantly being challenged by God who calls us to an ethics of mutual trust that presupposes equality. In Paul's words:

> [...] live up to your calling. Be humble always and gentle, and patient too. Be forbearing with one another and charitable. Spare no effort to make fast with bonds of peace the unity which the Spirit gives. There is one body and one spirit, as there is also one hope held out in God's call to you; one Lord, one faith, one baptism; one God and Father of all, who is over all and through all and in all (Eph 4:1-6).

When we speak of the trust between persons and of interpersonal ethics that can facilitate it, we need to widen our concept of hermeneutics. Until now, we have used it to understand aspects of faith-trust in the biblical witness based on contemporary reality. However, hermeneutics of trust also means to understand the *convivência* of people based on trust. Just as I read the Bible and the Bible reads me, I also "read" people and they "read" me. My relationship with other people depends on the perception I have of them. On the one hand, my trust is going to be influenced by people's behaviour. This then would be informed trust.[13] On the other hand, I can learn to see people in a different way, as the image and likeness of God and, therefore, as holders of great dignity. This vision of people, based on faith, creates a greater ethic that guides my behaviour in relationship to people. From this is born the trust that risks the bet, makes

---

[13] Sometimes, one talks of the need for a *hermeneutic of suspicion*. The late Paul Ricoeur (1913-2005) called Nietzsche, Freud, and Marx the "masters" of suspicion, because they questioned the immediate meaning, thus being influenced by the "will for power" (Nietzsche), by the "pulses" (Freud), or by class interests (Marx). Ricoeur himself contrasts this hermeneutics of suspicion with a hermeneutics of trust which would be guided by the future, however, only after passing through the suspicion, in a posture of a "second naïveté"; RICOEUR 1965; 1969. cf. VON SINNER 2001; 2002.

a prior investment, and proves itself as a gift. What does this mean for *convivência*? That is what I will explore in the last section.

1.4 *Convivência* based on a hermeneutics of trust

I would like to apply this hermeneutics of trust to three specific forms of *convivência,* namely: Christian ecumenism, inter-religious dialogue, and society.

1.4.1 TRUST AND CONVIVÊNCIA IN ECUMENICAL COMMUNION

The Christian churches believe in Jesus Christ, Son of God the Father, through the power of the Holy Spirit. This faith is trust in God and unites people as sisters and brothers in the communion of the church. However, instead of trust there is often distrust.[14] Even within a church such as the IECLB with its traditional, progressive, pietistic, evangelical, and charismatic tendencies, there exists tensions, separations, prejudices, and distrust that contradict the principle of trust based on a common faith. How much more so is this true among the various churches! Instead of living in communion, we live in competition; instead of equating ourselves with the vision of the kingdom of God, we equate ourselves with the kingdom of the market. While I was living on the periphery of the city of Salvador, Bahia (2001-2002), this was very obvious: at the time of the worship services, hundreds of *crentes* ("believers", as Pentecostals are commonly called) would go to their churches, of which there is a great variety, and Roman Catholics would go to theirs, but without any contact between the different worshippers. The other is considered less true, less "believing", less missionary, and less moral; in other words, of trust, there was not a trace.[15]

---

[14] Cf. DE SANTA ANA 1987, 227, for whom "it is exactly the lack of trust in faith itself" that "leads to isolationist attitudes that, beyond being expressions of religious narcissism, do not correspond with the dynamics of the Christian faith". *Ecumenismo e libertação,* Petrópolis, Vozes, 1987.

[15] The North American anthropologist JOHN BURDICK registered, throughout his field research in the Baixada Fluminense in the State of Rio de Janeiro, a "cycle of mistrust" nurtured by the prejudice between, in this case, the Catholics from the *comunidade* (base community) and the "crentes", that even impeded their practical cooperation in (secular) neighbourhood associations (1993, 230). Contrary to widespread opinion, the "crentes" can be very active members of such associations, provided these are not dominated by

Paul spent a considerable part of his letters caring for the unity of the church. In 1 Corinthians, for example, he writes:

> I appeal to you, my brothers [and sisters], in the name of our Lord Jesus Christ: agree among yourselves, and avoid divisions; be firmly joined in the unity of mind and thought. I have been told, my brothers, by Chloe's people there are quarrels among you. What I mean is this: each of you is saying, 'I am Paul's man', or 'I am for Apollos'; 'I follow Cephas', or 'I am Christ's.' Surely Christ has not been divided among you! Was it Paul who was crucified for you? Was it in the name of Paul that you were baptized? (1 Cor 1:10-13).[16]

Because of Christ, whose body is one, we may dare to risk the bet on the brothers and the sisters, to invest trust, to be guided by the greater ethic to which we are called, to give, freely, trust as a gift, but always in an informed way, as trust of a "second naïveté" (Paul Ricoeur) or a "second innocence" (PANIKKAR 1993). It is not about trusting everyone, nor accepting everything. But it is necessary to find ways of *convivência* based on our common trust, that is, our faith, for the witness of competition which churches and church movements are currently giving is one of incoherence and damages their mission. A united church – not a uniform church – will have a greater impact on society and will be, in a better and more credible way, able to "answer all who ask the reason for the hope that is in you" (1 Pet 3:15). Besides this, the churches can help each other to have a better hermeneutics of trust in God, thereby deepening and correcting their faith in God. As Dietrich Ritschl (2003, 191) says: "Our ecumenical partners are always only the potential reformers of our own doctrine". This implies "to reckon with the possibility that the Spirit speaks within and through the others" and that "those who interpret the Christian tradition differently each have a 'right intention of faith'", as affirmed in a study done by the World Council of Churches (WCC) on an ecumenical hermeneutics (COMMISSION ON FAITH AND ORDER 1998, paragraphs 8; 30) Ritschl challenges us when he defends that advancing this trust, and based on it, it would be possible to commune together at the Eucharist and recognise each other's ministries, even between churches of the Reformation and the Roman Catholic

---

Catholics. On the other hand, Burdick noticed that the bishop, known as progressive, withdrew his permission to use church premises for the association's meetings, as soon as its leadership became "crente" rather than Catholic (ibid, 206-212).

[16] Cf. WITHERINGTON III 1995, 94-101.

Church. And this without the doctrinal differences having to be previously resolved, as this communion is based in the presence of Christ himself in the immediate present (*christus praesens*):

> The hope on the presence of God in the *christus praesens* ... is the horizontal advance of trust which all groups and confessions which have not yet become partners can and have to invest, because it is ultimately God whom they trust to be able to comprehend the differences between them, intellectually heavy or nearly unbridgeable as they may be (RITSCHL 2003, 57).

Naturally, all depends on the comprehension of what doctrine is (RITSCHL 1990). But there is no doubt that, if one does not "bet" on the other church and advance trust, there will never be ecumenism, nor communion in the faith.

1.4.2 TRUST AND CONVIVÊNCIA IN INTER-RELIGIOUS DIALOGUE

I believe that, following this line of a deeply rooted trust, it should be possible to find a basis for the *convivência* of religions and the necessary dialogue among them, although Christians cannot simply presuppose the presence of the same faith in other religions. Among Christians, we do share Christ as the Word of God being our primary reference, together with his main witness, the Bible – something we only partly share with Jews and Muslims, the so-called "Abrahamic" religions, and not with other religions. In spite of this, there are good reasons in my opinion to bet on the depth of trust even in inter-religious dialogue (HICK 2005; VON SINNER 2003, 316-328). To this end, I find the reflections of the Hispano-Indian Raimon Panikkar helpful, an author who is himself rooted in different religions and engaged within himself in a, as he calls it, "intra-religious" dialogue.[17] He can rightly be counted among the pluralistic theologians of religion, although he occupies a particular position there. This can be seen, for instance, in his modification of the well-known river metaphor – according to which the different religions would be like rivers that meet in a common ocean – to affirm that the rivers of religions will

---

[17] PANIKKAR 1978. For a critical appraisal of Panikkar's theology see VON SINNER 2003, 197-328; KOMULAINEN 2005; NITSCHE, ed., 2005; NITSCHE 2009.

only meet in the clouds.[18] Another metaphor points "downwards": religions meet in the depth of the "cosmotheandric" or "theanthropocosmic reality". In relation to the theme of trust and *convivência,* I find it important and helpful that the uniqueness of religions and, thus, the respect for their alterity is not being dissolved; religions are not being melted into a universal "world religion" or "world theology". At the same time, they are also not simply being juxtaposed as self-satisfied semiotic systems. There is a meeting point, high above in the "clouds" or down below in the "depth", that is in the perichoretic Reality of the interrelatedness of God (*theos*), World (*kosmos*), and Man (*aner, anthropos*).[19] From the constant conversion to this Reality, as it is practiced by the different religions in their respective ways, follows "cosmic confidence".[20] Panikkar's main contribution towards dialogue – and thus towards the *convivência* of religions – seems to me to lie in his ability to combine an irenic attitude of "fundamental openness" (AHLSTRAND 1993), a close look and open ear, a thorough restraint in judgement over people of other faiths and the respect in relation to their alterity with trust in the (tri-)unity of Reality. To speak in the language of the Christian faith: it is the same trust in God which makes possible Christian ecumenism, with the difference that it has a much vaguer conceptual basis. It parts from trust in a God who is *semper maior* than what I can perceive of Godself through biblical witness and my lived faith. This also means that it is necessary to have a modest perception of one's own religion. Trust as a bet and prior investment becomes even more obvious here than in Christian ecumenism. If inter-religious dialogue is to be more than the monologue of two persons which defend

---

[18] PANIKKAR 1988, 92: "'They' [sc. the rivers] meet in the form of clouds, once they have suffered a transformation into vapor, which eventually will pour down again into the valleys of mortals to feed the rivers and the earth. Religions do not coalesce [...] they meet once transformed into vapor, once metamorphosized into Spirit, which then is poured down in innumerable tongues".

[19] Panikkar insists on using "man" for human being, and prefers the Greek *aner* (male) rather than *anthropos* (human), opting for traditional terminology and stating that this does not mean to fall into sexism. In any case, I follow his terminology here as it shows more clearly the elements of his "cosmo-the-andr-ism".

[20] Mainly in PANIKKAR 1985. For a critique from an ethical-political perspective, see KNITTER 1996, and the response of PANIKKAR 1996, 276-284. "Cosmic" confidence is not confidence *in* the cosmos, but the confidence (or trust, as I prefer here) *of* the cosmos, to which we belong through our being; "it is the awareness of our being in and of the universe", ibid, 282.

their particular view, if it is to be thinkable that I can learn from the other, if I am to have more than the option of staying with my own or convert to the other's religion, then there must be "something deeper" which enables such mutual "learning". To trust in this makes dialogue and also *convivência*, which is more than mere coexistence, a viable option. Any worthwhile dialogue must build on this fundament.

For the Brazilian context, these reflections are highly relevant because there is a widespread distrust not only between churches, but also between different religions. This affects especially the religions brought to Brazil by people traded as slaves from Africa, that have developed a significant – in part syncretistic – existence as Afro-Brazilian religions. Under the Portuguese *padroado*, they were forbidden, and their practices had to be disguised as Roman Catholic ones: their feasts were made to coincide with the Catholic saints to avoid censure. As a consequence of this longstanding symbiosis with the Catholic Church, it has become common for many faithful to identify themselves as belonging to both. This fact and the difficulty to get in-depth information on these religions – they do not have a sacred book, and the oral tradition is passed on only to initiated persons, only partly and over a long period of time – probably contributed to the mysterious nimbus which surrounds them and leaves many Christians, Protestants and Catholics alike, distrustful. These religions are being demonised and rejected by many, and too often their installations or members are being attacked verbally or even physically. The opposite position, which does not see any essential difference between Afro-Brazilian religions and Christianity and preaches complete harmony between them, although politically understandable and certainly more prone to foster *convivência* than the former exclusivist attitude, is also not helpful as it tends to rule out the understanding of alterity so crucial for dialogue. Considering these arguments, I believe that trust in a possible unity in "depth" – to take up Panikkar's metaphor again – could foster a real dialogue while accepting difference. This reminder goes, in the first place, to Christians, as they are to blame for the widespread fear, prejudice, and discrimination.

1.4.3 TRUST AND CONVIVÊNCIA IN SOCIETY

We saw above how weak trust is between people as one goes beyond the more intimate circles to which they belong. Picking up again on Roberto DaMatta, we can say that it is necessary to broaden the concept of "person" by a comprehension of the fundamental equality of human beings, without, however, falling into a cold individualism that would disregard human relationships.[21] Democracy and *cidadania* (citizenship) depend on the Constitution and the laws that organise *convivência* and establish rights and duties, precisely to facilitate trust even between people who do not know each other. Where I cannot – or must not – punish a fault, the state takes on this task. This is particularly important when people are so poor that they cannot even decide for or against trust: they have no choice.[22] It is to them that the state should extend its protection in the first place – which, in Brazil, needs to be claimed over and over again against the facts. In order to do this, the state needs the collaboration of all. Not least, this presupposes the state's trust in its own citizens and their democratic capacity, which is growing only slowly in Brazil. On the other hand, it is also necessary that these citizens bet on and invest trust in the state, keeping themselves informed and accompanying it in critical-constructive ways. Certainly, since the original confusion after the end of the military government (1985) until the impeachment of the corrupt president Fernando Collor de Melo (1992) and several unsuccessful economic reform plans, the political landscape has become calmer and more stable. Democratic mechanisms of control are working better today, so that politicians and policemen can no longer do whatever they please with impunity. Even so, the distance between government and the governed continues to be vast, the exercise of *cidadania* continues to be weak and, not least, the social and economic situation of the vast majority of Brazilians has not improved much (see VON SINNER 2012a). The surveys quoted earlier show clearly what this means in terms of interpersonal trust. But it is not only the relationship between the government and the citizens which is at stake. Where society is sustained by a high degree of trust – and also well-being is rated highly, as is the case in Scandinavia, especially in Norway (INGLEHART 1999, 102) – the state will also function better, and its services will be more

---

[21] DaMatta has always underlined the ambiguity of the above-mentioned culture of "person" as against the "individual" and stressed the need for a middle way for which mediation is needed – a task that could be performed also by the church: "We may speak of Brazil as a system of oppositions between blacks and whites with Indians mediating between the two; or between people and the government with the church mediating" (DAMATTA 1995, 281).

[22] Following up on the "World Value Surveys" and other empirical research, see INGLEHART 1999.

accessible to the population because the behaviour of the civil servants has immediate consequences on the functioning of the state.

Christians do not only belong to the church, but are also part of human society. While members of the church, we are also citizens, bringing our contribution to *convivência* in society. I have no doubt that churches have an important role to play in fostering trust among citizens, both in themselves and in others. As we have seen, people in Brazil and Latin America hold the churches in high esteem and trust them more than all other institutions. This trust should not be disappointed or wasted, even more so as our faith, *pistis,* trust gives us very good reasons to honour this trust from within our very belief. Citizenship is something that can, ideally, be taught and practiced within churches, as they reach even the poorest sectors of society. One important element is transforming lives, a particular strength of the booming Pentecostal churches. In this way, people find support for feeling and acting like citizens, they feel themselves to be part of *cidadania*. Another crucial element is the critical-constructive cooperation with the state, as well as with other agents of civil society, on all levels. In doing this, they practice and promote values that encourage people to invest and honour trust, and thus help to build up a democratic and inclusive society.

I hope these reflections might be helpful for encouraging citizens, in Brazil and elsewhere, to live trust, be it in the church environment, among religions or in society, betting on other people, making prior investment of trust, seeking to connect to a greater ethic, granting trust as a gift and always keeping oneself informed. My hope would be that in this way, even with all the disappointments that there will be on the path, future research will show that our trust has increased in the people with whom we live, and *convivência* has become more complete.

Chapter 2

Towards a Theology of Citizenship as Public Theology in Brazil[*]

Liberation Theology has laid the ground for a way of thinking that argues and makes plausible the foundational importance of the contextual aspect of theology, especially in view of its economical, political, and social dimensions. It is a theology from and in interaction with a specific context, while not being restricted to it – it links up to Christian theology as done worldwide, interacts with worldwide Christian bodies, confessional or ecumenical, and with the academy and civil society nationally and internationally. This has rendered its recognition and visibility far beyond national or continental borders. It is, therefore, plausible to focus on this theological line, present as it is in literature and public perception – having become virtually hegemonic in Brazil – and question it in terms of new and further developments within it. In a first step, I shall describe and discuss the most important foundations of Latin American Liberation Theology and its recent developments (2.1). Then, I shall present formulations and argue for what I consider to be one of the most promising and necessary thematic foci today: A theology of citizenship (2.2). Finally, I shall attempt to link up the outline of this theology to the wider, worldwide debate of public theology, which so far has not received much attention in Brazil and Latin America (2.3).

2.1 Liberation Theology: Recent developments

Without a doubt, the forerunners of what came to be known as (Latin American) Liberation Theology, Presbyterians Richard Shaull and Rubem Alves, and the Liberation Theology which was formulated mainly by Roman Catholic theologians in the late 1960s and in the 1970s, most prominently by Peruvian Gustavo Gutiérrez, have provided an important theoretical foundation for social and political action. This theological movement has brought, internationally, "theology in[to] movement"

---

[*]Original publication: "Brazil: From Liberation Theology to a Theology of Citizenship as Public Theology", *International Journal of Public Theology* 1/3-4 (2007a), 338-63; used by permission and moderately revised.

(Juan Luis Segundo), providing the grounds for a major consciousness of theology's overall contextual character and bringing to the fore the "theology coming from the edge", in contact with similar movements on various continents, which originated in the same period (BOFF 1989). They are collectively defined as "Third World Theologies", visible in the foundation of the Ecumenical Association of Third World Theologians (EATWOT) in 1976, which has been providing an important platform for this movement of theological decolonisation (PARRATT, ed., 2006; MÍGUEZ BONINO 2006). "Third World", in this context, was a protest term against the dominance of the so-called "First" (the industrialised West) and "Second" (the socialist East) Worlds, quite in line with the movement of non-aligned countries, as well as a reference to the Third Estate coming to the fore in the French Revolution. But also in the so-called "First World", black and feminist theologies emerged as theologies of liberation from oppression based on ethnicity or gender. Thus, there are "theologies of liberation" in the plural. If I still use the singular here, and with capital letters, I do so because Liberation Theology as developed in Latin America can, despite its diversity, be situated historically, personally, and bibliographically. As it sought to present itself not as homogenous, but as united by a common struggle, and has networked intensively, it seems legitimate to use the singular.[1]

Liberation Theology's backbone is, without a doubt, the "preferential option for the poor", as officially adopted by the second and third continental assemblies of the Latin American Episcopal Council (CELAM) in Medellín (1968) and Puebla (1979) and maintained ever since.[2] As Gustavo Gutiérrez recalls, it is a "preferential" option because of the "universality of God's love that excludes no one" (GUTIÉRREZ 1997, 74). The same universal love of God commits Christians to "give people a name and a face", especially those to whom it is denied, particularly "the poor" (GUTIÉRREZ 1997, 75). "Option", on the other

---

[1] For a comprehensive overview, see ELLACURÍA and SOBRINO, eds., 1993.

[2] Cf. GUTIÉRREZ 1993; the "preferential option" was already present at Medellín, although not in these precise words ("preference to the poorest and neediest", quoted ibid, 239), and explicitly so at Puebla, where a whole chapter of the final document was headed under "the preferential option for the poor". POPE JOHN PAUL II, in his encyclical *Sollicitudo Rei Socialis* (n. 42) formulated it as "the *preferential option or love* of the poor" (quoted ibid, 240), and the Santo Domingo Episcopal assembly in 1992 adopted the language of "advancement" [promoción], a certainly much less radical formula. See also GUTIÉRREZ 1997.

hand, does not mean that it is "optional" in the sense of not being necessary, but the "free commitment of a decision", a "matter of a deep, ongoing solidarity, a voluntary daily involvement with the world of the poor" (GUTIÉRREZ 1993, 240).

The poor are both the main focus of Liberation Theology and their intended subjects, its practical and "epistemological *locus*" from where theology is to be developed, hence the importance of "popular education" in the line of Paulo Freire and the Church Base Communities (CEBs), where this could become concrete. Theologians were to share people's lives and work among them as "organic intellectuals" (Gramsci) or, to use the common expression in Brazil, *assessores*, something like "consultants" or "advisors".[3] They underwent a real "conversion" to the people.[4] Many sought to combine academic work with parish or church base community contacts in poor areas, trying to provide a space where people's suffering was taken seriously and turned into positive action. As Clodovis Boff puts it: "Before we do theology, we have to do liberation", which is, then "pre-theological", and theology is always the "second act" following proper action (C. BOFF 1993, 73). This implies what is called an "epistemological rupture", as praxis is given epistemological priority over theory, herein following Marxism, but also Maurice Blondel's "*l'action*" and the Second Vatican Council's call to pastoral commitment in reading the *signs of the times* (*Gaudium et Spes,* 44). Theology is "a critical reflection on Christian praxis in the light of the Word", Gutiérrez affirms (1988, 11). Although not dismissing it entirely, it takes issue with traditional, deductive theology, namely as identified with scholasticism.

Liberation Theology is a theology that started – and continues to start – from the indignation about the appalling poverty millions of people in Latin America and beyond were subjected to, in sharp contrast with the enormous wealth a tiny minority lived in. The question was "how to be Christians in a world of destitution" (L. BOFF and C. BOFF, 1987, 1). As the poverty of many was seen as the consequence of the wealth of the

---

[3] COMBLIN 1998, 201, affirms, at the end of his treatise on freedom, while often being critical of Liberation Theology, that "the best thing about what the church in Latin America has done during the past thirty years has been that it has set itself up in the midst of the poor, sharing directly in their everyday life, in the midst of great struggles to be able to live more humanly despite everything. [...] Christians (whether conscious or unconscious) who decide to share in this grace [sc. of God which enables to overcome the limits of normal human possibilities] have entered into the struggle for liberation".
[4] See, for instance, BOFF 1981; 1989; VON SINNER 2003, 61-76.

few, this situation was duly called a situation of oppression from which liberation was needed. An important theoretical undergirding became, at the time, dependency theory, which sought to move beyond the then predominant developmentalism. The latter suggested that the developing countries will reach, in due time, the level of the developed countries, and the whole question was about modernising "backward" countries, while the former stated the impossibility of development because of structural dependency in a world divided between "centre" and "periphery" (FRANK 1967; CARDOSO and FALETTO 1979; DUSSEL 1993). The economic and social oppression was further aggravated by the political oppression through military regimes.[5] Resistance against such oppression and utopias envisioning a liberated world facilitated a dialogue between Christians and other thinkers and movements, including Marxists, while it divided Christians among those who supported, consciously or not, the *status quo*, and those who struggled for its transformation.

Possibly the most evident influence of Liberation Theology has been its elaboration of Cardinal Cardijn's methodological tripod of "See – Judge – Act", or, in more technical language, "socio-analytical", "hermeneutical", and "practical mediation".[6] The important shift was from philosophy as the traditional dialogue partner for theology to taking seriously the contribution of sociological and economic investigations. This was meant to help in exploring the context *before* interpreting it in the light of a biblically oriented theology in order to finally contribute toward the transformation of social reality, and thus being inductive rather than deductive, moving away from the predominant Thomistic scholastic model in Roman Catholic theology. For some, particularly theologians of liberation, a specific reading of Marx became important.[7]

---

[5] In Brazil 1964-1985, in Argentina 1966-1973 and 1976-1983, in Chile 1973-1990, and so forth; cf. HAGOPIAN and MAINWARING, eds., 2005, 3.

[6] C. BOFF 1987. The Brazilian Catholic Bishops' Conference (CNBB) added a fourth element: "review", as it suggested the model for a critical preparation and accompaniment of the elections. CNBB 2006, 22-24. Commonly, also "celebration" is added as a fourth element.

[7] DUSSEL 1993, 87, 'Theology of Liberation and Marxism', in ELLACURÍA and SOBRINO, eds., *Mysterium Liberationis,* p. 87, affirms: "First it was Jacques Maritain, then Emmanuel Mounier, and afterward Lebret […], whom we followed. […] But then came Marx, by way of the Cuban revolution (1959), and we began to read, simultaneously, the young Marx and works like those of Che Guevara, Antonio Gramsci, and Lukács. That is, we read a 'humanistic' Marx – as he was called at the time, clearly neither dogmatic, nor economistic, nor naively humanistic".

There are many parallels to European political theology and North American black theology which emerged in those same years. Also, the French *Nouvelle Théologie* was influential (Congar, de Lubac). The articulators of Liberation Theology had been trained abroad, mainly in Europe, where especially the Catholic University of Louvain in Belgium had become a centre for theologians from the Third World, counting on the central contribution of François Houtart.[8] They were cognisant of the theological tendencies there and the thrust given to new developments by the Second Vatican Council (1962-1965). But it was Latin American Liberation Theology that most decisively installed the notion of liberation and undersigned it, so to speak, with its martyrs' blood – not only such famous ones like Archbishop Oscar A. Romero of San Salvador, assassinated at the altar in 1980, but many unknown laypersons and clergy who died for resisting the powers and defending the poor.

Liberation became the central hermeneutical category, and a considerable amount of ink was spent on a *relecture* of traditional concepts through the lens of liberation. Both the production of "small literature" for use in communities and of academic books for use in seminaries has been remarkably comprehensive. Apart from systematic theology, biblical studies became especially important and a decisive vehicle in including laypersons into the debate, for many of which in the Catholic fold the Bible had been virtually unknown. Liberation theologians declined to separate secular history from the history of salvation, as the latter is the very heart of the former: "there is only one history – a 'Christo-finalized' history", says Gutiérrez (1988, 86; cf. ELLACURÍA 1993a). Thus, "building the temporal city is […] to become part of a saving process which embraces the whole of humanity and all human history" (GUTIÉRREZ 1988, 91).

Many of Liberation Theology's authors have suffered repression from the state and/or the church as they criticised all kinds of repressive and hierarchical structures. The Vatican issued two notifications on the Theology of Liberation.[9] Leonardo Boff is certainly a case in point: While

---

[8] Houtart, a sociologist of religion, founded the *Centre Tricontinental* in 1976, facilitating the interaction and study of scholars from Africa, Asia, Latin America, and Europe. It is a "center of research, publication and documentation on the development of North-South relations". Available at: http://www.cetri.be [last accessed August 9, 2021].

[9] Congregation for the Doctrine of the Faith, Instruction, 'Libertatis nuntius', available at

he narrowly escaped direct state repression, the Vatican treated him harshly, which resulted, eventually, in his resignation from the Franciscan order and priesthood in 1992. Others, like Gustavo Gutiérrez, Clodovis Boff and, most recently (March of 2007), Jon Sobrino, came under the Vatican's scrutiny and some suffered measures against their theology and its divulgation.[10]

It was also Leonardo Boff (1986) who most effectively propagated a new *ecclesiogenesis* from the "popular church". However, it was not only the Vatican which sobered high expectations, inasmuch as he did not strongly support the upcoming of a "new way of being the church" (*um novo jeito de ser Igreja*), much less the more radical "new being of the whole church" (*um novo jeito de toda Igreja ser*). Even the CEBs were not able to fulfil the high ecclesiological and political expectations invested in them. It is true that their number is still high and estimated at around 80,000. Their national "inter-ecclesial" meetings also continue to be vibrant and with large numbers of participants: The latest national meeting of CEBs, its 11th edition, was held in Ipatinga in the State of Minas Gerais, in July 2005, and brought together some 4,000 delegates, including 50 Roman Catholic and 2 Anglican bishops. But they no longer have the irradiation they had in the 1970s and 1980s, and there has been a considerable evasion from CEBs to social movements, to Afro-Brazilian religions, and to Pentecostal churches (BURDICK 1993; IRELAND 1991; 1998). Thus, in a certain way, both the base and the once strongly committed church leadership eroded as the democratic transition proceeded and political repression faded.

It has repeatedly been stated, and on principle rightly so, that the events at the end of 1989 have caused a great perplexity among liberation

---

https://www.vatican.va/roman_curia/congregations/cfaith/documents/rc_con_cfaith_d oc_19840806_theology-liberation_en.html, and 'Libertatis conscientia', available at https://www.vatican.va/roman_curia/congregations/cfaith/documents/rc_con_cfaith_d oc_19860322_freedom-liberation_en.html [last accessed August 9, 2021].

[10] The 'Notification on the works of Father Jon Sobrino, SJ: *Jesucristo liberador, Lectura histórico-teológica de Jesús de Nazaret* and *La fe en Jesucristo. Ensayo desde las víctimas*', of 26 November, 2006, and an 'Explanatory Note', became public only in early March of 2007. Available at: https://www.vatican.va/roman_curia/congregations/ cfaith/documents/rc_con_cfaith_doc_20061126_notification-sobrino_en.html   and https://www.vatican.va/roman_curia/congregations/cfaith/documents/rc_concfaith_do c_20061126_nota-sobrino_en.html [last accessed August 9, 2021].

theologians in many respects and made changes inevitable. The utopian vision of an imminent new social order was thoroughly frustrated. Trade-union leader Luis Inácio "Lula" da Silva was, by a narrow margin, not elected to the presidency in Brazil then, the socialist alternative broke down with the Berlin Wall, and Nicaragua did not hold to the Sandinista path. Expectations had been very high, given, in the eyes of many, the considerable achievements civil society had conquered, and CEBs and liberation theologians with it. While it might have been possible to swallow a mere delay, any concrete alternative now seemed to have lost its plausibility altogether. Only a good number of years later could liberation theologians speak more calmly and self-critically about that moment.

However, it would be wrong to either consider Liberation Theology dead after 1989 or to affirm that changes came about only because of the named events, although they certainly served as a catalyst, fostering the adaptation of Liberation Theology to a changed context. For one, the appalling poverty has transformed its face to some extent, and some changes have come about, but it is still there. Globalisation and notably neo-liberal politics have given to many in Latin America the impression of being "below a sky without stars" (*bajo un cielo sin estrellas*, in Spanish), without solidarity, without space for humanity to be realised, as Elsa Tamez affirms, quoting an expression coined by Franz Hinkelammert.

Secondly, the 1980s had in fact already seen considerable shifts in terms of subjects and themes. Subjects, because "the poor" or, more widely, "the oppressed" came to be seen and described more and more clearly as concrete persons with a face rather than as a supposedly homogenous category. Already in the 1970s, Leonardo Boff had written about Mary and the "maternal face of God", striving to take seriously women's seven experiences and their divine source in the Trinity (BOFF 1987; BINGEMER and GEBARA 1989). But it was mainly in the following decade that women began to openly claim their specific role and outcry for liberation. A theology from the experience of African Brazilians also came to the fore, as it did in the case of indigenous peoples. Thus, "the poor" or "oppressed" became more specifically identified, and among them persons who were not all materially poor but still oppressed. As Gutiérrez defined, tentatively, "the poor are the non-persons, the 'insignificant ones', the ones that don't count either for the rest of society, and 'far too frequently' for the Christian churches" (GUTIÉRREZ 1997,

72). It has also become customary to speak about the triple oppression poor black women are enduring.

Other "new subjects" are still struggling to be recognised even among Liberation Theologians, namely lesbian, gay, bisexual, transgendered, queer, intersexual, asexual persons, and new subjects (LGBTQIA+). Gay theology and queer theory are having great difficulty taking root in Latin America compared to North America and Europe where they have already gained considerable, although certainly not unanimous, recognition.[11] Receiving greater recognition by churches and their diaconal sectors, persons with disabilities are also beginning to formulate a specific theology from their experience.

Besides these "new subjects" – which in fact are not new, but are coming to the fore in an explicit self-affirmation and are increasingly recognised and supported in this venture – new themes have also emerged. Again, Leonardo Boff (1997) was pioneering when he insisted on the dignity not only of human beings, namely the poor, but of the earth. The economy, although constantly an issue in Liberation Theology, came to be analysed more thoroughly, as neo-liberal market capitalism became envisaged as a kind of religion in its own right, to be denounced as idolatrous from a Christian point of view (HINKELAMMERT 1986). However, there is a lack of concrete alternatives for effective change. This is also true for concrete politics, and especially law, which have not become a theme of interest among liberation theologians. This is somewhat surprising, given that Liberation Theology is a political theology *par excellence*. However, in not too few publications, the law is seen as itself oppressive, confused with what is perceived as pharisaic legalism, and rejected as if it were still serving only the interests of the powerful.[12] There is, as Ivan Petrella (2006) stated, a lack of a "historical project", precisely what used to most clearly define Liberation Theology.

Petrella identifies three – not mutually exclusive, but still distinct – ways of reaction towards the fall of socialism and the consequent lack of a real existing alternative order: (1) Reasserting core ideas, namely the option for the poor; (2) reformulating basic categories to highlight "humanity", "everyday life", and "civil society"; and (3) denouncing capitalism as idolatry, but liberation theologians do not present a new

---

[11] See the provocative challenge posed by MADURO 2006; ALTHAUS-REID 2000.

[12] See, for instance, TAMEZ 1993. For a more positive perspective see MÍGUEZ BONINO 2004.

project and, indeed, seem to abandon the notion of a historical project altogether. Thus, Liberation Theology is, according to Petrella, giving away what once was most central to it: A concrete mediation of liberation in view of the reign of God for social transformation in order to overcome poverty. Petrella's own proposal is not to provide a new historical project, but to pave the way for it. He follows Roberto Mangabeira Unger's (1996; 1998) reflections within critical legal thought. He thus suggests that Liberation Theology "must" follow these three steps: "theorizing society as frozen politics, recognizing the variety of capitalisms, and incorporating critical legal thought's process of mapping and criticism" (PETRELLA 2006, 111). By "frozen politics", he refers to the political and economic institutions as "the result of contained political and ideological strife", presupposing that society is heterogeneous and institutions are not simply a given. Thus, it is "institutional imagination" that has to prevail in its specific context, which leads to a "step-by-step process" rather than an "empty imaginative leap between a monolithic capitalism to an equally monolithic socialism or abstractly defined participatory democracy" (ibid, 107).

Indeed, Liberation Theology should deal with concrete problems of society in order to contribute to their solution. Apart from pointing to shortcomings of an incomplete democracy and an excluding neo-liberal market economy, and the danger of idolatry in its religious features, Liberation Theology should, in interdisciplinary cooperation not least with political scientists and specialists of law, look for possibilities of alternatives in society, while at the same time continuing to strive for reform within the church. As Maclean's earlier study on *Opting for Democracy?* (1999) very aptly showed, liberation theologians were slow in adapting to the changing context and were well behind the political left in terms of finding more pragmatic approaches and building new alliances, which led to their isolation in the 1980s. Nearly a decade later, Petrella is right in pointing to continuous shortcomings in Liberation Theology's adaptation to the new political situation, especially following the 1989 events. There is an as yet unmet need for constructive proposals. At the same time, to speak of a "historical project", as Petrella does, seems to me to reinforce an either/or alternative, a change of "the system" as such. Such either/or alternative, however, is precisely what Petrella wants to avoid, as he emphasises a "step-by-step process" and "mapping and criticism". His concrete positive examples, such as to reshape property rights through "associational networks" and to include the population in political decisions through major popular mobilisation before election (something which seems rather on the decline in contemporary Brazil, but also in many other countries, including Europe and the USA) and through more referenda and plebiscites (here's an interesting proposal for something really new), are noteworthy, but imply a number of factors – social, political, educational – that are not to be drawn up in a specific "historical project". I thus think that Leonardo Boff (1988, 117-142), in being rather generic in terms of what he says on democracy, is right from a theological standpoint, which however should not prevent him or others from discussing concrete institutional frameworks that might correspond better with theology's ideal. Christian values should be brought into the discourse in politics, civil society, the academy, the media and, of course, the churches themselves to see what contribution they could make, and from there enter into dialogue on concrete political issues. Social sciences should come in, as Petrella is right in reminding us, not only in the analysis of the situation, but also in the practical section. This means that theology and politics, as well as theology and the social sciences, are to be correlated in a creative tension, not being identical, nor mutually exclusive, nor simply complementary. What is lacking, then, is not only a more concrete spelling out of how a liberative theology could contribute to concrete politics, law, and the public space, but also a fresh look at how, under the present circumstances, theology and politics are to be related.

One promising way of recontextualising Liberation Theology in light of what has been said on the importance of citizenship in Brazil is the move toward a "theology of citizenship", which I shall present and discuss in the following section.

2.2 Towards a theology of citizenship

Citizenship has become the key term for democracy in Brazil, although there are considerable differences as to what this precisely means.[13] In general terms, it can be said that citizenship is about the "right to have rights" in a situation of "social apartheid" (DAGNINO 1994, 105) where

---

[13] There is more debate as to deficiencies in citizenship and its (non-)functioning than on the concept, and not much is available in English. Anthropological studies have contributed a great deal toward understanding what is at stake, see HOLSTON and CALDEIRA 1998; CALDEIRA 2000; BIEHL 2005.

exclusion prevails. Thus, a major challenge of effective citizenship is for all people to realise that they indeed *do* have rights, that they *are* citizens.[14] This may sound obvious, but it is not in a society with millions of people struggling for mere survival, living with less than two or even one US dollar a day to spend, in appalling contrast to the income and wealth of a small number of very rich people. It is not obvious in a country where there are people whose first photograph ever is taken on the day of their death, where many newborns are not registered and thus do not exist legally, where people suffer total social abandonment, and where the police are known to be corrupt, incompetent, and violent. It is also not obvious in a country with a traditionally strong patriarchal and clientelistic social and political organisation, where it is not the law that defines or even protects relationships.

This being the case, the concept of citizenship must be broader than just indicate the rights – and duties – foreseen by (national) law. It must include the real possibility of access to rights and the consciousness of one's duties, just as the attitude over against the constitutional state as such, and also the constant moulding and extension of the citizens' participation in the social and political life of their country. It is a way of overcoming the distinction between "them" and "us", making people feel they are part of the story, and if others are not doing their part, especially those in public office, they have all the right to denounce that and press for improvement. Aspects of the citizen's effective participation are, then, becoming central, as does the political culture by which such participation is encouraged or hindered. It is not least in this area, I contend, that churches can make a difference.

There has been some repercussion of this in Liberation Theology. Thus, José Comblin (1998, 122) states that "the greatest flaw in Latin American nations is the lack of citizenship", adding that political participation is restricted to a tiny minority. As an important move forward, he mentions Herberto "Betinho" de Souza's "Citizenship's Action against Hunger, Misery and for Life", and insists on the importance of the people of a nation pursuing their common good: "The nation becomes strong and united when its citizens are able to understand

---

[14] Reference is usually made to MARSHALL 1965, with his distinction of civil, political, and social rights. According to DE CARVALHO 2001, the major challenge lies in the ineffectiveness of civil rights due to patronage, clientelism, social disparities and violence, not least by the police; see also O'DONNELL 2005.

and assume together the common tasks entailed in shared life, striving to get along with one another and thereby establishing the 'national project'" (COMBLIN 1998, 123). Where society is split between the elites and the "popular masses", however, nation-building becomes utterly difficult.

Like Comblin, other authors spoke about citizenship through concentrating on the city, given the massive rural exodus that occurred over the last fifty years. More than others, Comblin (1998, 91) underlines the possibilities of freedom found by the people there, even if under poor conditions: "The new content of liberation consists of learning to be a citizen, a member of the city". The rural poor, according to Comblin, opted for the city and preferred "to live in a shantytown [...] than on a plantation [...]. Despite everything, they have more freedom" (ibid). He is, therefore, critical of models of liberation and community that still reflect rural models of life and, not least, a community centred around a powerful priest rather than made up of autonomous lay people. Rather than a theology of liberation in the previous moulds, a "theology of freedom" is needed. He cites a number of challenges to be met, among them citizenship, but does not develop a specific proposal.

Also, Protestant authors follow in locating citizenship primarily in the city. For the IECLB, this is especially important, as their traditional model were the immigrants and their descendants living as small farmers. As urbanisation has not left the IECLB untouched, "urban pastoral action" (*pastoral urbana*) has become urgent. From his experience as a Lutheran pastor in the metropolitan area of Porto Alegre and his membership in the PT, Evaldo Luis Pauly has reflected on "Citizenship and Urban Pastoral Action" (1995). In a rather unusual combination of references, he ventures into "the house" as a hermeneutical key to the city, while analysing its heavy habitation deficits; into psychoanalysis to retrieve the subjectivity of citizens; into the 1988 Constitution and its importance for the churches and the city; into urban technology and how it could be fruitfully used by churches, to finally present urban pastoral action from a theological and ecclesial point of view. Pauly adopts a deeply pastoral attitude[15] in trying to retrieve people's citizenship in a

---

[15] Among others, he points to the importance of listening and pastoral care, PAULY 1995, 69-73. This branch of theological training had to defend itself from being too individualistic and not liberative enough, but has in the meantime flourished, at least at the Lutheran School of Theology in São Leopoldo (Faculdades EST), with specialisation courses invariably booked out. Beyond this, themes like subjectivity,

democracy, reviewing what the new Constitution had to offer and, not least, showing what society expects from the church. This call for citizenship is also radically applied to the church itself, as "of this half citizenship [i.e. what many are, *de facto*, living in], urban pastoral action heads toward the ecclesial, political, social and cultural construction of double citizenship" (PAULY 1995, 173), that is, citizenship in society as well as in the church through the fostering of the laity, their autonomy and responsibility – and, not least, their wishes [*desejos*], which Liberation Theology had oftentimes forgotten to take seriously. As he retells stories from the parish where he served as a minister, Pauly makes plain that striving for political changes often did not come through the correct discourse, but through encouraging lay people to make their own decisions. Among others, he counts that, as a pastor, he tried to introduce a materialist reading of the Gospel of Mark in a Bible reading group. He was disappointed that the group wanted to go to a pietistic evangelistic meeting, despite the class discourse he had introduced which was at odds with pietism. He agreed, however, to join them and, after that, the persons in the group became more honest – they told the pastor that they thought if they did something against his will, he would no longer come to see them. The group then passed from a materialist to a moralist and directive reading of Mark, seemingly contrary to the liberation message and its class discourse. The pastor let them do it and continued to visit them. Shortly after that, they started to organise a group, together with the neighbourhood association, pressing for access to school. Without liberationist discourse, they did what liberationists were striving for. Pauly concludes: "Their discourse was moralist only in my ear. For them, it was liberating" (ibid, 60).

One of the most challenging essays of Liberation Theology in the 1990s was an article by Roman Catholic theologian and professor of education Hugo Assmann (1994, 13-36), where he claimed the continuation of Liberation Theology as a "Theology of Citizenship and Solidarity". His criticism of "classical" Liberation Theology included the lack of a perception of who the poor – or rather the excluded, the discarded, as they now should be called more realistically – in fact are, having held an idealised view of them as subjects of their own liberation while not perceiving their genuine desires and aspirations. Thus, he

---

embodiment *(corporeidade),* and resilience are in the air, seeking to combine personal identity and strength with citizenship. See, for instance, HOCH 2001.

counts among the pendent challenges "a theology of the right to dream, to pleasure [*prazer*], to fraternal tenderness [*fraternura*], to creative life [*creativiver*], to happiness", summed up in the concept of "embodiment" (*corporeidade*).[16] At the same time, as the poor have become "discardable" by the dominant neo-liberal market capitalism, they only come into sight for those "converted to solidarity". Thus, he has consistently worked on the necessity of educating for solidarity. Assmann further insists that it is necessary to "join values of solidarity with effective rights of citizenship" (ibid, 33). Presupposing the lasting presence of a market economy, there is need for the compensation of the logic of exclusion's effects, combining market and social measures by democratically installed institutions. Assmann does not elaborate further on this, but he criticises the exaggerated emphasis given by Christians – and, one should add, many liberation theologians insisting on the notion of community – "to the communitarian relationships, as if they were a sufficient – although indispensable – basis to make solidarity effective in large, complex and accentuatedly urbanized societies. [...] there's a dangerous non-observance of the use of law as the weapon of the weakest [...], especially a fallacious anti-institutional stance" (ibid). Theology, then, is obliged to think about the social aspect of conversion, which goes beyond individual conversion, although the latter is a precondition of solidarity. While Assmann situates his argument more in the economic sphere, I would add that the new situation of political participation, rather than a changed economic situation, makes another kind of theology possible and necessary, precisely as a theology of citizenship.[17]

A few years later, Assmann's (2000) self-critical balance at the Brazilian Association's for Theology and Religious Studies (SOTER) annual congress took up many of these aspects again, even in its title, looking for a "humanely healthy theology". Assmann asks whether theology, namely Liberation Theology, has been a "healthy phenomenon". Has it helped "many people to 'be in tune' with their own life and to irradiate social sensitivity"? Has it been, effectively, a "source

---

[16] ASSMANN 1994, 30-31. *Fraternura* and *creativiver* are neologisms created by Leonardo Boff and Hugo Assmann, respectively.

[17] I developed this further in my writing project at the Center of Theological Inquiry on *Churches and Democracy in Brazil: Towards a Theology of Citizenship as Public Theology*, for which previous research was funded by the Swiss National Science Foundation; I am thankful to both for their invaluable contributions. The result was published as VON SINNER 2012a.

of solidary energy"? Without giving a straightforward answer, Assmann affirms that the "negativism" often present in "progressive" ideas is "humanely harmful". And he justifies why he feels more at ease now in education than in theology: "Against the backdrop of the emergence of a learning society, with market economy and changing ways of employability, there is no doubt that to educate is to struggle against exclusion. In this context, to educate means to save life" (ibid, 130).

Methodist theologian Clovis Pinto de Castro (2000) has dedicated a major study to the theme of citizenship, in which he claimed a *pastoral da cidadania* (pastoral action for citizenship) as a "public dimension of the church". His central concept is an "active and emancipated citizenship", which he develops based on Hannah Arendt's *vita activa*, Marilena Chauí's (2000) reflections on Brazil's foundational myth – which fostered paternalism and messianism, contrary to a democratic and participatory notion of citizenship – and Pedro Demo's critique of a paternalising (*cidadania tutelada,* as in a liberal state) or social assistance based citizenship (*cidadania assistida,* as in a welfare state), in favour of an emancipated citizenship (*cidadania emancipada*), in which the effective participation of the people is being central to democracy (DEMO 1995). De Castro also refers back to the "new political theology" of Johann Baptist Metz and Jürgen Moltmann. Theologically, he grounds the *pastoral da cidadania* on God as the one who loves justice and right, on the commandment to love one's neighbour, good works and justice according to the witness of the New Testament, on the concept of *shalom* ("peace") as comprehensive well-being, and finally on the notion of God's kingdom. From there, he deduces the church's mandate to live not (only) its private, but its public dimension (*pastoral*), oriented towards human beings in their daily, real life, and not only towards the church's members. Faith conscious of citizenship (*fé cidadã*) is oriented by the three dimensions of faith as confession (knowing God), as trust (loving God), and as action (serving God), of which none must be absent, all being of equal value. Although the *pastoral da cidadania* emphasises the aspect of action, the other two are present concomitantly. This *pastoral* has to be, furthermore, a "*meta-pastoral*", i.e. a dimension of all pastoral action. Its non-renounceable aspects are the dimensions of action, the formation of subjects of citizenship (*sujeito cidadão*), participation of Christians in democratic administration of cities, and finally the missionary paradigm of *shalom*. In this way, de Castro adopts a position somewhere in between Liberation Theology (of which he includes a good number of aspects) and a "postmodern mystical religion", in which the action dimension is underestimated or misunderstood in an individualistic manner. He thus avoids separating faith and action, while not fusing them either. While de Castro does not offer any specific insights as to what concretely such a pastoral citizenship might imply, he lays out a theological basis for it. This is especially noteworthy in a church where strong charismatic sectors tend to overstate faith in detriment of (transforming) action, and gained a majority in the 2006 General Council, which decided to withdraw from all ecumenical institutions where the Roman Catholic Church is present. As ecumenical and social engagements have been very close in Brazil and Latin America historically, and in fact received many insights from Methodist theologians, they appear as synonymous in the perception of supporters and adversaries alike.

Citizenship, then, has etched its way into theology, namely those who follow the basic insights of Liberation Theology. Economic exclusion has made it urgent, political change has made it possible. It is pressing to engage more concretely and decisively in issues of citizenship, both theologically and practically, inside and outside the churches, which I see as an adequate recontextualisation of Liberation Theology's insights. It is somewhat surprising that this aspect has not gained its own "citizenship" in Brazilian theology, despite the cited attempts to implant it right there. A reason for this might be, apart from the general lack of concrete proposals in Liberation Theology as identified above, that theologians who take the challenge seriously tend to pursue citizenship in other fields, like education and anthropology, or through engaging in NGOs rather than in the churches. The latter are contributing to this situation by being apparently more concerned about their own survival than about a new type of theology, linked with "Liberation Theology" or "ecumenism", which both have a negative connotation for many clergy and lay people. Sadly, this means that both theology and the churches are being deprived of important challenging voices.

It is noteworthy that a similar insistence – but similarly isolated – can be identified in Asian, namely South Korean theology as developed by Anselm K. Min (2002; 2004), who insists that citizens themselves have to be the focus of attention, "agents" rather than "agendas", overcoming "tribal" tendencies in Asian traditional culture and a simplistic blame of poverty and corruption on outside forces alike. Min urges a recontextualisation in *Minjung* theology, understanding that its logical continuity in a changed context would be the "theology of the citizen", which is essentially a theology of solidarity to others which overcomes "tribal", i.e. closed, group-centered solidarity. Like in Latin America, however, theology in Korea or Asia on the whole has not taken this up as a central point to date (see LIENEMANN-PERRIN and CHUNG 2006, 327-330).

With all setbacks, I believe it is fair to say that democracy in Brazil has advanced to a degree where new forms of popular participation, as well as an insertion of churches into civil society's quest for an effective citizenship and accountability in government's instances, have become possible.[18] Thus, a wider term than "liberation" is needed. Public theology seems to me to be useful to this end, but is too unspecific. Therefore, I would opt for a theology of citizenship *as* public theology. In the following section, I shall explore in what way the debate on public theology might be useful, and how the international and contextual dimensions can be linked.

2.3 A public theology for Brazil?

Within the constraints of space and given the only incipient debate on public theology in Brazil, let me tell six short stories to situate and visualise potential *loci* for the debate of public theology. I shall not discuss the stories as such, but use them to show that public theology is an issue in Brazil, although the term is not commonly used. Of course, the examples do not refer to a univocal concept of public theology; each one of them could be discussed as to its specific bearing on an admittedly diverse concept.[19]

a) In 1931, the statue of *Cristo Redentor,* Christ the Redeemer, was inaugurated. In the midst of 50 bishops and archbishops, Cardinal Sebastião Leme boldly stated that "either the State [...] will recognize the

---

[18] For more on this, see, among others, AVRITZER 2002. I remind the reader that this text was originally written in 2007 and reflects the very positive perspectives for the Brazilian future as they were visible at the time.

[19] For an overview on the debate on public theology and similar concepts, see BREITENBERG 2003.

God of the people or the people will not recognize the State".[20] He said this in the presence of the head of the provisional government, Getúlio Vargas, who indeed learnt to respect and construct a close partnership with the Roman Catholic Church. Leme was the architect of the renewed massive influence of his church on the state and public space, usually called Neo-Christendom. This is public religion, made visible to this day by a 38-meter statue (including the 8 metre pedestal), inaugurated on the day of the national patron saint, Our Lady of the Conception who Appeared (*Nossa Senhora da Conceição Aparecida*), 12 October.[21]

b) In the early '70s, a group of Dominican friars was arrested by the military regime for their critical stance against it. They had to share a cell with atheist Marxists, around 40 people altogether. The priests started to celebrate the Eucharist with juice and whatever there was to eat, and this became the celebration of the whole cell, with everybody partaking. At some point, the priests said: "Let's do that celebration only among us, we have no right to force non-believers to partake in it". But then, the Marxists protested and said: "This is no longer your celebration, it is the whole cell's celebration". The Eucharist became public.[22]

c) In the same period, the military government created compulsory "Moral and Civic Education" in schools, and a National Commission of Morality and Civility to oversee this programme. The Commission issued a "Prayer for Brazil": "O almighty GOD, principle and end of all things, infuse in us, Brazilians, the love for study and work, so that we may make of our FATHERLAND a land of peace, order and greatness – watch, LORD, over Brazil's destinies!" Historian Thales de Azevedo (1981, 134) called this a Brazilian "civil religion", instrumentalised by the regime to assure loyalty and obedience.

d) In 1995, again on the national patron saint's day, Bishop Sérgio von Helde of the Neo-Pentecostal Universal Church of God's Kingdom

---

[20] Quoted by DELLA CAVA 1976, 14, who takes the quote from Margaret Patrice Todaro, 'Pastors, Prophets, and Politicians: A Study of the Brazilian Catholic Church, 1916-1945' (Ph.D. dissertation, Columbia University, New York, 1971).

[21] This day is also Columbus' day on the whole continent, remembering his arrival in the Caribbean, in 1492, as DELLA CAVA 1976, 13, recalls. On 12 October, 1717, fishermen are reported to have found the statue of Our Lady in the waters of Guaratinguetá, Minas Gerais. In 1929, Pope Pius XI declared her "Queen of Brazil" and the national patron saint. At Pope John Paul II's visit to Brazil in 1980, the military regime declared 12 October a national holiday.

[22] Testimony by Ivo Lesbaupin, a former Dominican friar, theologian, and sociologist, in VON SINNER, ZANETTI and GONDIM, eds., 2002.

(IURD) kicked a statue of Our Lady in a programme of the church's own TV network, the country's third largest. The incident created an enormous uproar, not only among Catholics but also among many *evangélicos*, who distanced themselves from the IURD. The church was subject to a defamation campaign by its main competitor, TV Globo. However, after the dust settled, the church continued to mark a strong presence in city centres, in the mass media (radio, TV, weekly journal), and through its elected congressmen (cf. GIUMBELLI 2002; 2003; also Chapter 11 below). A public church, defying and defied.

e) More recently, the Landless Workers' Movement (MST) performed a public manifestation in Rio de Janeiro, where they put up a cross and spread around dashes of red colour to symbolise blood. They thus used Christian symbols to point to their suffering and hope for a different future alike. But there was no priest or pastor present. Are movements and NGOs in Brazil, many of which originated under the umbrella of the Catholic Church, developing their own "civil society's religion" (cf. BIRMAN, ed., 2003, part I, 25-146)?

f) On April 7, 2005, President Lula flew to Pope John Paul II's funeral in Rome. In his airplane, commonly called the "Aerolula", he took with him representatives of ecumenical bodies and non-Christian religions.[23] During the travel, they had an ecumenical celebration, and national TV interviewed some of these representatives. A public recognition not only of religion, but of religious pluralism with their

---

[23] These included Roman Catholics Archbishop João Aviz of Brasília, Bishop Odilo Scherer, secretary-general of the CNBB, Fr. José Ernanne Pinheiro, advisor to the CNBB; Lutheran Rev. Rolf Schünemann, representing the National Council of Churches (CONIC); Sheikh Armando Hussein Saleh, for the Muslim communities, and Rabbi Henry Sobel, for the Jewish communities. Mother Nitinha de Oxum (73) should have been representing the African Brazilian communities, but after deliberating whether she should go or not she missed her plane, and a later connecting flight could not be paid for because she had no bank account – and administrative rules would not allow for the deposit to be made on her son's account. An interesting example of differing priorities in the organisation of life and of bureaucratic endurances, especially for people in poor neighbourhoods, as is the case of Mother Nitinha. See 'Lula chama até mãe-de-santo para funeral de João Paulo 2°', *Folha de São Paulo* of 7 April, 2005. Available at: http://www1.folha.uol.com.br/fsp/mundo/ft0704200511.htm, and 'Mãe-de-santo perde vôo presidencial', *Folha de São Paulo* of 8 April, 2005. Available at: https://www1.folha.uol.com.br/fsp/mundo/ ft0804200513.htm [last accessed August 9, 2021].

public contribution – in many respects significant in what is still the country with the largest Catholic population in the world.

As stated before, "public theology" is not a term commonly used in Brazil. There is only one place I know of which has made it one of its programmes: The Humanitas Institute at the Jesuit University in São Leopoldo (UNISINOS). Founded in 2001, the Institute organises yearly symposia, publishes books and articles under the heading of "Teologia Publica", with a very wide range of topics, mainly in the systematic field (inter-religious dialogue, ecology, ethics, theology at the university, method in theology, etc.).[24] According to the programme's website,

> [T]he Public Theology Programme aims at resituating theological discourse in the academic environment and promote the active participation of theology in the debates which develop in the public sphere of contemporary society. In this perspective, it proposes a theological reflection which, in dialogue with the sciences, seeks to contribute to the elucidation of the principal questions of our time and in the search for responses for the same.[25]

Somewhat ironically, this programme is located at a university which originated from a seminary founded at the outset of the 20th century by German Jesuit missionaries, but does not host a theological faculty. It is, then, the Humanitas Institute which guarantees more explicitly the presence of religion and theology in the environment of a private, confessional university with some 30,000 students.

In 2004, the institute organised an international symposium on "Theology at the University in the 21st Century", with David Tracy, Michael Amaladoss, Andres Torres Queiruga and John Milbank among its speakers, and paid homage to the centenary of Karl Rahner's birthday. This underlines the two main aspects of public theology as understood by the institute: a theology in dialogue with contemporary society and, more specifically, with the scientific community.[26] It is important to remember

---

[24] This includes two major works by Jürgen Moltmann, but surprisingly not his *God for a Secular Society: The Public Relevance of Theology* (1999).

[25] The programme's website was thus formulated and could be viewed at: http://www.unisinos.br/ihu/index.php?option=com_programas&Itemid=25&task=cate gorias&id=5 [accessed March 20, 2007; the link is no longer active and the content has been reformulated].

[26] This is also the general thrust of the collection of interviews, many of which were made around the above-mentioned symposium, in NEUTZLING, ed., 2006.

that theology and religious studies have only recently (1999) been recognised as a subject-matter also on the bachelor's level by the Brazilian Ministry of Education, which is expanding its visibility. However, only one public university has to date installed an undergraduate course in theology or religious studies, and only two postgraduate courses in religious studies are located at public universities. Theology is, thus, virtually exclusively left to private, confessional institutes of higher education, including seminaries and universities like the Pontifical Catholic Universities (PUCs) in various parts of the country. In 2007 there were a total of 93 courses in Theology recognised or authorised by the Ministry of Education on the bachelor's level, and 12 programmes for master's and doctoral studies, seven in Religious Studies and five in Theology.[27] There is an ongoing debate on how to train teachers for Religious Education, which is constitutionally mandated and, by law, has to be funded by the state, but must be taught by licensed teachers, and the Ministry of Education has not authorised any licentiate course in theology.

As stated before, public theology currently is not a common term in Brazil and Latin America. It is rarely mentioned, and if so, *en passant.*[28] One important reason for this is certainly its origin in the English-speaking part of the world,[29] with which especially theology has

---

[27] All of these are Christian, with the exception of the "Umbandist Theological Faculty", which had its course authorised in 2004, cf. http://www1.folha.uol.com.br/folha/educacao/ult305ul4756.shtml [accessed February 22, 2007]. Anthropologist Darcy Ribeiro, although himself an agnostic, wanted to install a course of theology at the University of Brasília already back in the early 1960s, but the military regime in power from 1964 prevented this from happening, as former government minister and now secretary-general of UNCTAD, Rubens Ricupero recalls. Ricupero clearly advocates the study of theology at universities, in NEUTZLING, ed., 2006, 52.

[28] L. BOFF and C. BOFF 1987, 85-7, speak of a "Public and Prophetic Theology", pointing to Liberation Theology's presence in the media and among politicians to the left and to the right alike, but not exploring the concept. It is interesting to note that VÖGELE 1994, 421, note 158, could find only this very reference in German (!) theological literature between 1972 and 1992, when Wolfgang Huber came back to the concept he had elaborated on in the early 1970s, as he wrote the preface to the first volume of the series "Öffentliche Theologie" (1992); cf. HUBER 1991.

[29] This differs notably from post-transition theology in South Africa, cf. DE GRUCHY 2004, 45, and the foundation of the *Beyers Naudé Center for Public Theology* in Stellenbosch in 2002, see

not interacted much, partly due to language restrictions and partly due to resentments as to the USA's role in supporting some of the military regimes and, in general, anti-communist tendencies. Another reason points to the same argument which used to be brought forward against liberalism and "liberal democracy": the concept sounds too bourgeois, not radical, or not specific enough (cf. MACLEAN 1999). However, as with democracy, I believe that public theology could become a useful term for theology in Brazil as it intends to (1) address issues of contemporary society, (2) confirm its place at the university, and (3) be communicable to the scientific, the religious, and the political community, namely civil society, but also to the economy.[30] By qualifying it more specifically as a *theology of citizenship*, as indicated above, the main actual challenges can be addressed, while holding the concept open to other and new challenges in society. Citizenship might, at some point in time, become a less burning issue, which would be the case when most or, ideally, all citizens can understand themselves and act effectively as such. Public issues, however, will always be there to be addressed by the churches and theology. In a new context where a "critical-constructive" approach (ALTMANN 2000, 82) has become plausible, rather than a (merely) conflictive view, it seems promising that, as formulated in South Africa, "Public theology [viz. as different 'from liberation, political, black, feminist, African and other particularistic theologies'] has more of a dialogical, cooperative and constructive approach" (KOOPMAN 2003, 7), without, however, being naively too positive about democracy and, indeed, a neo-liberal capitalist market economy.[31]

As we look at the Brazilian context, we have to be clear that while religions, namely Christian faith communities, abound in an ever more diversified religious field often characterised as a religious market, thoroughly academic reflection on it is a relatively young phenomenon. In general, only 16% are enrolled in higher education in Brazil, and, as already mentioned, theology has only recently made its way into a recognised field of higher education.[32] It is true that public universities in Brazil, possibly due to French influence, have a tradition of strong

---

<http://academic.sun.ac.za/tsv/Centres/beyers_naude_sentrum/bnc.htm>   [accessed May 20, 2007].
[30] Cf. the four publics named in STACKHOUSE 1997, 166-167.
[31] As in Brazil, similar criticism against too harmonious and potentially "Western" theology is to be found in South Africa, cf. KUSMIERZ and COCHRANE 2006, 220.
[32] See the country profile at <http://www.worldbank.org> [accessed January 17, 2007].

reservations against religion and theology, and thus a more qualified communication with them is needed. But the even greater challenge, in my view, is to ensure communication between faith communities, namely churches, among themselves and between them and society.[33] Religious competition and the strongly exclusivist character of Pentecostal and most historical Protestant churches on the one hand, and the still hegemonic behaviour and self-consciousness of the Roman Catholic Church on the other, makes such communication enormously difficult.

One interesting result of the recognition of theology by the Ministry of Education is that many ministers holding a seminary degree are now looking for booster courses to obtain a recognised diploma. It might be, thus, that academic formation can provide a more thorough mediation between the churches' clergy and wider society than church-run seminaries tend to do, and incipient higher studies undertaken by Pentecostal theologians could lead to a yet increased awareness of the churches' role and task in the public sphere. By insisting on rational, communicable, and pluralist reflection, such formation forces students to engage with colleagues from other traditions and with different positions, breaking the ghetto-like homogeneity they tend to experience in their own church. There is, of course, no guarantee of making a lasting difference, but it is a promising space for testing alternative visions on the churches, their task and activity in the public sphere.

---

[33] This is especially urgent as it has become common to invite a variety of religions to an "ecumenical" event on public holidays, inaugurations, or at graduation ceremonies. This is certainly a positive move, as in earlier times only Roman Catholic priests or bishops were invited to such public acts. However, invitations seem to be sent out at random, and there is no time for proper preparation among the participants. In the worst case, the result is that every religion is granted, say, two minutes to speak, which is not rarely used as a platform for propagating their own religion or denomination. In the best case, representatives are sensitive to the event as such and to the other religions, and might even suggest a common religious language, like the Afro-Brazilian representative who invited all to pray the "Our Father", which they did. I take the example from a forthcoming declaration of the IECLB on inter-religious dialogue, elaborated by the presidency's advisory committee on ecumenism.

Chapter 3

Theology in Latin America – New Developments[*]

> *"[...] right in the midst of God's funerals and the requiem on religion,*
> *a rain of new god's has begun to fall*
> *and a new religious aroma has filled*
> *our spaces and our time."*
> (Rubem Alves, 1933-2014)

Theology in Latin America was a popular topic in the 1960s, 1970s and 1980s, when Liberation Theology received much attention, but it was also the subject of controversy, both in Roman Catholic and Protestant theology. It reached its climax before and throughout 1992, during the 500th anniversary of the conquest, that is, the "discovery" of America by Christopher Columbus and the subsequent colonisation with its devastating consequences, especially for the original inhabitants. After that, however, interest rapidly declined in Germany and Europe, although Liberation Theology has continued to be the subject of reflection both in Latin America and elsewhere. For example, Minjung theology in South Korea, Dalit theology in India, black theology in South Africa and the USA, and feminist theology worldwide, to mention just a few prominent examples, which, however, in keeping with their contextual character, are also in the process of formulation and reformulation. Liberation theologies emerged as a response to political, economic, social, gender, religious and ethnic oppression, and, from the theological point of view, draw their strength from the rediscovery of basic liberating elements of biblical theology, such as the Exodus and the practice and preaching of the historical Jesus. Even after overcoming military dictatorships and the economic boom of many Latin American countries – but also after the setbacks in politics and economics, as seen today in Brazil – Latin American Liberation Theology is by no means dead, as seen for instance in the various editions of the World Forum on Theology and Liberation,

---

[*] Originally published as "Theologie in Lateinamerika – neuere Entwicklungen", in: *Theologische Literaturzeitung* 142/6 (2017), 589-602, and in Portuguese as "Teologia na América Latina: desdobramentos recentes", in VON SINNER 2018, 121-140, translated from the Brazilian Portuguese by Alexander Busch and revised by the author. Used with permission.

which usually takes place along with the World Social Forum – such as in 2016 in Montreal, Canada. Its organisation is largely under the responsibility of Professor Luiz Carlos Susin, from PUCRS in Porto Alegre – that is, the same city where the World Social Forum was founded as counterpoint to the WEF that meets in Davos.[1]

But the theology made in and from Latin America is not just Liberation Theology. This has previously been the case, but now it has become more visible. Roman Catholic theology on the continent generally had conservative stances from a moral, political and social point of view, which were disclosed in some countries, such as Argentina, e.g. the support given to the military dictatorship. In contrast, the churches in Chile and especially in Brazil, although not predominantly progressive, had a more supportive attitude towards the poor and were more critical towards the dictatorships, especially because, later, the repression likewise broke in against the Roman Catholic Church. Mention should also be made of *evangélico* groups, which, in general, advocate a conservative theology alien to commitment for social justice and transformation. There are among them, however, positions that include social concerns arising from the context, because the distressing poverty in Latin America – and elsewhere in the world – simply cannot be ignored. Indeed, Latin American representatives such as René Padilla (1932-2021), an Ecuadorian who was living in Argentina, and Valdir Steuernagel, from Brazil, at the 1974 Lausanne Congress on World Evangelisation, insisted upon a holistic evangelisation, comprising not only the salvation of the soul, but also of the body. Hence the concept of "integral mission", particularly around the Latin American Theological Fraternity, created in the 1970s.[2]

Originally, Pentecostal churches, which have grown vigorously in the past thirty years, had only rarely produced their own theology in writing and even less in academic style, but the situation has changed since then (e.g. DE ARAÚJO 2007; GILBERTO, ed., 2008). To contextualise this observation, it is necessary to mention that academic theological formation in Latin America belonged, in the beginning, to the seminaries of the Catholic orders and was later gradually extended to the dioceses.

---

[1] Available at: <http://justicepaix.org> [accessed August 31, 2016]; ALTHAUS-REID, PETRELLA and SUSIN, eds., 2007; GETUI, SUSIN and CHURU, eds., 2008; BOODOO, ed., 2016.
[2] Cf. SANCHES 2009; ZWETSCH 2008, 146-206.

These seminaries were, to a certain extent, integrated by pontifical universities organised as private institutions. In Latin America, there are many private higher education institutions and universities, where most of the academic students are enrolled – in Brazil, this figure stands at 75%. Theology courses exist only in private institutions, for the most part with denominational – mostly, but not exclusively Christian – ties. North American Protestant missionaries have endeavoured, since the second half of the nineteenth century, particularly for the formation of the elites, to win them over to Protestantism by establishing private schools and institutions of higher education. In some countries, such as Brazil, there are undergraduate and graduate theology courses recognised by the state. Since 2016, curricular guidelines have been in effect in Brazil, which meanwhile registers 162 undergraduate theology courses recognised by the state as intra-ecclesiastical formation courses for clergy (BRASIL 2014; 2016). Compliance with these guidelines is an indispensable prerequisite for granting or renewing accreditation. Pentecostal churches are also increasingly seeking academic formation of scientific nature.

Liberation Theology itself has continued to grow in diversity, as it unfolds as indigenous, Afro-American, intercultural and inter-religious theology, as well as public theology. In this regard, Liberation Theology remains, according to my perception and reading, faithful to its vocation as a contextual theology and, in a broad sense, catholic, that is, meaningful to the worldwide church as it resumes biblical and theological traditions. However, it needs to be tested and reformulated in new and changing contexts. New developments, such as those just mentioned, whether they explicitly recognise themselves as liberation theologies or not, contribute to this reorientation.

In what follows, I intend to expose a limited but, in my opinion, representative selection of present trends of the most recent published theological literature in Latin America. In this sense, I must add, to be more precise, that I will refer mainly – although not exclusively – to Brazil, which occupies, as it were, a continent within the continent. The linguistic frontier between Portuguese and Spanish is very perceptible in cultural and political terms; thus, I must admit that, even when using bibliography originally published in Spanish, my point of view is located on this side of the border. As a Swiss citizen who has lived in Brazil for more than 17 years, I am, in a certain way, a twofold stranger in relation to that universe, which gives an idea of my own location. In my opinion, there are four trends that stand out when trying to understand the current theological theory and its religious and contemporary background. As these are trends that respond to specific challenges and convey certain basic theological concepts, I mention them as trends which, in each case, are "under the sign of": the *sign of liberation* (3.1), starting from more recent develop*ments in Liberation Theology; the s*ign of interculturality and inter-religious dialogue (3.2); the *sign of the Spirit*, particularly insofar as it is developed within the framework of Pentecostal churches (3.3); and the *sign of prosperity*, from the inclination for prosperity of the health and wealth gospel, which is also noticeable elsewhere (3.4).

3.1 Theology under the sign of liberation

Liberation Theology continues to be very much alive in publications, lectures, and congresses. It made several self-reflective evaluations and definitions of its location (e.g. ELLACURÍA and SOBRINO, eds., 1990). A text by Hugo Assmann (1994) – which, in my opinion, continues to be of central importance – entitled "Theology of solidarity and citizenship – that is: continuing liberation theology", points out the necessary innovations insofar as liberating theology aims to contribute to the formation of solidarity – understood as something not innate – and to the demand of concrete rights. Thereby a counterpoint is established to the idea, derived from the experience under military dictatorships and, from this perspective, comprehensible, that the law is unjust and, therefore, cannot contribute to promote better justice (e.g. TAMEZ 1993; 2016). Therefore, in democratic times the intention is to build a liberating theology which seeks to help the real poor, the excluded, the "disposable" of society that are no longer needed even to produce wealth for others so that they may reach full citizenship. In this context, poverty is not only a social and economic category, but also a political one.[3] This means, among other things, the ability to perceive one's own legal subjectivity and legal rights, the knowledge of the law and its institutions, a basic sense towards the state and the collectivity, to which all citizens belong, and, certainly, a legal system available not only to the elite of owners, but to the entire population, providing protection and compensation. On that basis, a *public theology* has emerged, especially since the turn of the century, invigorated, among others, by the experiences and theological reformulations in South Africa, which considers a recontextualisation of

---

[3] Cf. ZWETSCH 2015, 86, quoting MARIA CARMELITA YASBEK.

Liberation Theology to be essential. Public theology follows Liberation Theology regarding the preferential option for the poor – understood, in a broad sense, as people who are on the margins of society in a position of subordination – and to the essential importance of praxis not only for the application of theology, but also its formulation. A public theology realises the need to consider the change implied in the transition to democratic state forms and, therefore, basically legitimate insofar as it considers, in a noticeably constructive and cooperative way, which legal, political, and economic transformations contribute to an effective improvement of the standard of living, especially among the poorest of the poor. It is also concerned with religious plurality and diversity, which requires permanent negotiations, also and precisely between Christian denominations. What kind of presence is feasible and makes sense, in religious terms, for religion and, particularly, religious communities constituted in a democratic public sphere in a secular and pluralistic state? In this context, it is important to mention that many Latin American states, influenced by the Spanish and Portuguese colonial powers, adopted, long before the European countries, a secular constitution and abolished the state religion (see Chapter 12). Even so, the Roman Catholic Church remains a very strong presence in society and politics; since the church lost its privileged position at the end of the 19th century – but also because of its decline – it has clearly sought to increase its influence. Today, however, Brazil is not only the most Catholic country on the planet, but also the country most strongly marked by Pentecostalism, which highlights and documents the enormous changes in the religious field (see VON SINNER 2012b).

At the international level, new models are being sought for Liberation Theology that creatively arise from praxis and are developed for it (cf. COOPER, ed., 2013). In this context one can locate a Theology of the City, as particularly and substantially demanded by the Roman Catholic theologian José Comblin (1923-2011) and, meanwhile, reinforced by extensive research and studies (1991; SANCHEZ 2013; ECKHOLT and SILBER, eds., 2014). In the face of the massive urbanisation process of a traditionally rural continent, which occurred within only a few decades, and of the chaotic situation marked by visible contrasts between rich and poor and the prevalence of drug trafficking gangs in certain areas of the cities, this it is more than timely. Mexico City and São Paulo are among the largest population agglomerations and cities in the world. Luiz Carlos Susin (2014) proposes a Theology of the City as a political theology of and in the public space, which must be seen from the perspective of the eschatological vision of the New Jerusalem and, which needs, as a concrete city in history, a prophetic word, because Jerusalem is also – as in Isaiah, for instance – the city destroyed by corruption and the right of the strongest. A new approach is required precisely in view of the necessary pastoral and practical dimension of a reconfigured systematic theology that is able to explicitly proceed from this new location of faith and consider it in the light of tradition. Thus, within the framework of a reinterpretation of the "signs of the times", but also of the "signs of the places" (WESTHELLE 1990; 2012), the question about the "who" or "what" of God shifts to the question about the "where" of God, which was already likewise a prominent question in Liberation Theology and now, in the face of suffering, has to be urgently answered (ZWETSCH, ed., 2014; SANDER 2015). Discovering God in the city – and this too and precisely in the "bewildering locations of God's presence" (in the words of Hans-Joachim Sander) – thus means a new access to the *saeculum*, to a theology of the relationship with the world that is integrated to a plural, diverse, mobile and even fluid city in which churches continue to play an important and central role for many people, but in which they have become one among many religious and non-religious options.[4]

Post-colonial and decolonial theories comprise another important element in the redefinition of liberating theology. Decolonial theories emerged from a contextual and Latin American critique of and complement to post-colonial theories as proposed by Anglophonic scholars (cf. WESTHELLE 2010a; PANOTTO 2016). The importance of human rights discourses in Latin America since the 16th century, for example, were largely neglected for a long time, as well as the participation of the colonial powers in the violation of human rights in the colonies, while in Europe itself one already spoke about "universal" rights of humans and citizens. The term "human rights" itself was already used by Bartolomé de las Casas (1484-1566) by the mid-16th century (DE LAS CASAS 1996, 82). One of the main exponents of decolonial theory is Walter Mignolo (2012), an Argentine who teaches in the USA and reflects on the historical experiences in the Latin American continent in critical dialogue with European philosophy and African and Asian

---

[4] SANDER 2015, 132, talks about topologies as processing "waves of spatial relativization" (130, note 8) and exposing oneself to heterotopias, "strange places"; the reference to "streaks of the presence of God that cause strangeness", is on 132.

scholars and their post-colonial thinking. His reflection does not aim to move to a form of Latin American essentialisation, but, quite the opposite, to focus attention on the elements that cause disturbance, insecurity, the rupture lines and searching movements. Like other continents, Latin America is searching for its identity or identities (plural) that are present within itself. This search includes a critical confrontation with history, its wounds and the dependencies that exist in Latin America.

3.2 Theology under the sign of interculturality and inter-religious dialogue

Another line of thought – but only partially different from the previous one because it is also decidedly under the sign of liberation – is the attempt to reflect on ways of thinking and life that are clearly different from those of the West and to introduce them into an intercultural dialogue. The Swiss Roman Catholic theologian Josef Estermann (2006; 2012), for instance, who spent many years in the Andes region, wrote extensively on religion and theology in the Andean context of Latin America. Among others, he presented his research and ideas under the title "Religion and Theology in the Andean context of Latin America" in the book series "Theologie interkulturell" [Intercultural theology] of the Faculty of Catholic Theology at the University of Frankfurt. Intercultural theology begins with experiences of strangeness (FORNET-BETANCOURT 2007; ZWETSCH 2015). So, for example, it is said that in the colonial era, the Inca Atahualpa would have held the Bible handed to him by Father Vicente Valverde to his ear and then tossed it on the floor, saying: "It does not speak". Valverde understood this reaction as proof of Atahualpa's paganism and as justification for the violent submission of the Incas that followed. From the subsequent asymmetrical and yet creative encounter between Catholicism and the forms of expression of the Andean religion, multiple forms of syncretism emerged. At first, this is not surprising, especially if one understands – as Pannenberg (1967) has already done – Christianity in general as a syncretistic phenomenon. Moreover, it is perfectly understandable to imagine the survival of the Andean religions through its accommodation of elements of the Roman Catholic religion which has empowered the local population to resist the faith imposed upon them. Thus, the "Mother Earth", Pachamama, who grants and sustains life, has periods of untouchability. Since the encounter with Christianity, these periods have been part of Holy Week. According to the Andean belief, during Holy Week Pachamama is mourning because of the death of her partner; Pachamama – in Christian terms, the "Virgin Mary" – and Jesus – in the Andean conception, the protective spirit *Apu Taytayku* – are not mother and son, but husband and wife. It would be possible to consider this belief contrary to the orthodoxy of the Christian faith and, thus, try to fight against it. According to Estermann (2012, 57), however, a deeper understanding should be taken into consideration: "[...] the ideal of living a good life (called in the Andes 'living well' or *vivir bien*) is in danger when the fundamental relationship of complementarity is disturbed or unviable, as symbolically represented during Holy Week. Or, to put it in more Western terms: redemption is only possible when heaven and earth come together, the mountain peaks and Pachamama, Jesus and Mary". Indeed, in the meantime *buen vivir* (*Sumak Kawsay*), which was even included in the national constitutions of Bolivia and Ecuador, was also taken up with debates in Liberation Theology and discussions about alternatives to the economic model of late capitalism (ZWETSCH 2015, 120). According to Roberto Zwetsch, the "productive communitarian social economic model" of Evo Morales, Bolivia's first indigenous president, based on the *buen vivir* principle was quite successful (ibid). This notion, originally from indigenous communities, of living a good life – more an utopian horizon than a concrete programme – is based on the principles of equality, such as respect for diversity and community reciprocity, including the environmental ecosystems. It is in this context that an intercultural dialogue or "polylogue" – a concept employed by Estermann and others, which stems from the Austrian philosopher Franz-Martin Wimmer – can and must take place. The "polylogue" concept consists, from the very beginning, in seriously taking notice of these unknown and, for many people, at first, perplexing voices.[5]

Meanwhile, it is well known that Latin America is no longer simply a "Catholic continent", although it still has the largest percentage of the world's Catholic population. The growth of Pentecostal churches speaks for itself. Other universal religions, such as Judaism, Islam, Buddhism, and Hinduism are also present in several places, and some are growing, even though their numbers are still quite modest. However, the discovery

---

[5] Cf. the journal *Polylog*, published since 1998. Available at: www.polylog.net [last accessed August 9, 2021]; GMAINER-PRANZL 2012.

of the indigenous religions as described above based on the approach of Josef Estermann, and of the various syncretisms resulting from the diverse forms of encounter with the European-Latin Catholic religion, is of great importance. African-American religions should also be mentioned. These forms of religion and their multiple developments are difficult to investigate as they are not religions with publicly accessible scriptures, and their religious self-understanding or doctrine and practice are only partially accessible in public form.[6] The tendency of Roman Catholic theologians, in particular, is to set aside Christian ecumenism – strictly speaking, more plausible in terms of necessity – and to engage in an inter-religious dialogue and a theology of religions (see, for instance, TOMITA, VIGIL and BARROS, eds., 2006). This is evident in the book *Theology of Religious Pluralism* by José María Vigil (2008), a Spanish Claretian priest who has lived in Latin America for decades, first in Nicaragua and then in Panama. The book, structured according to the well-known "see, judge, act" method of Liberation Theology, based on academic theology, but unfolded in 24 group meetings for adult education courses, intends to confront the meaning of the factual existence of religious pluralism for religion itself – in this case, its Roman Catholic version. The book starts from the concrete life reality of the participants and offers subsidies for a deepened understanding through information and reflections. Its fundamental thesis is that all religions are true (Chapter 15). In this sense, taking up John Hick's (2005) idea of "the Real", it presupposes a unity of reality to which the different religions have access, each in its own way. They complement each other. Parallel to the missionary conception of "inculturation" (*inreligionisación*), the Spanish theologian Andrés Torres Queiruga (1997; 2007; cf. SOARES 2003), who has a wide influence among Roman Catholic authors in Latin America, speaks of an "inreligionation". The subject's religious experience is inserted in his culture and religion and can be enriched by experiences and perceptions of other religions. "To be religious means to be inter-religious" (Kuncheria Pathil, quoted by VIGIL 2008). On this account, an "ecumenical movement" in a broad sense is emerging, which in Latin America has also been called, since the Assembly of the People of God held in Quito in 1992, "macroecumenism", a term coined by

---

[6] There are now most interesting moves to develop an Afrotheology, like in the work of SILVEIRA 2019, and also of new religions with indigenous roots as well as Christian elements in the Santo Daime religion, cf. VICENTINI 2021.

Bishop Pedro Casaldáliga (1928-2020), a Spanish priest settled in Brazil for decades who maintained intensive contact with indigenous people and practiced deep solidarity for their cause. By focusing on the kingdom of God – which was already a central emphasis for Liberation Theology – that is, a "kingdom-centric" theology, the struggle "for the cause of Jesus, for the kingdom of God", which brings "life, truth, justice, peace, grace" (VIGIL 2013, 348), is understood as a macroecumenical task par excellence. It can be inferred that religion is the genuinely human element, and vice versa, since the commission to and mission for God's kingdom is something deeply human. One aspect that draws attention to this approach is that indigenous religions are seen as partners in dialogue – African-American religions, however, are hardly mentioned – and, beyond that, the persistence of the inter-religious dialogue that occurs worldwide with the so-called universal religions, which, apart from Christianity, have minimal presence in Latin America, as mentioned above. At the same time, the extremely necessary dialogue within Christianity, which in itself is immensely diverse in Latin America, is hardly addressed. What theologies do we find in these new forms of expression of Christianity?

3.3 Theology under the sign of the Spirit

In Brazil and Latin America in general, Pentecostal churches have become a considerable force. According to the 2010 Census, 13% of the Brazilian population declared themselves as Pentecostals and 5% are classified as being "[ecclesiastically] undetermined *evangélicos*", of which the majority should probably also be counted as Pentecostals. In addition, there are vigorous charismatic movements within the historical churches, so the number of Pentecostals must be even greater. Among them, however, there are considerable differences, which are not possible to examine more closely here.[7] I will limit myself to the Assemblies of God (*Assembleias de Deus* – AD, specifically those that are part of the General Convention, based mainly on a first systematic theology

---

[7] Cf. ROBECK and YONG, eds, 2014; SHAULL and CESAR 1999. In this and in the next section I had the help of the doctoral student Raphaelson Steven Zilse, who is originally from the Assemblies of God, but has so far studied at Lutheran institutions and is currently working on Schleiermacher's theology, as well as decolonial and Latin American approaches. I am immensely grateful for his contribution to this text.

specially geared towards the AD in 1996 (GILBERTO, ed., 2008). Despite being founded by Swedish missionaries and shortly after being taken over by Brazilian leadership, the theological influence in the AD is clearly of North-American origin. In fact, the Swedish missionaries went first to the USA and thereafter came to Brazil. Nels Lawrence Olson (1910-1993) exerted great influence with his dispensational theology, which stresses the existence of several phases of eschatology carried out in relation to historical events, with particular reference to Nebuchadnezzar's dream and its interpretation by the prophet Daniel (OLSON 1994; cf. HORTON, ed., 1994). However, the Book of Revelation also plays a central role, in addition to other prophets such as Ezekiel, Isaiah, Zechariah, and Habakkuk. Central beliefs of the Pentecostal faith are the expectation of the end times, the millennial kingdom brought by the Lord as the last dispensation before his second coming, the rapture of the believers, the judgement of Jesus according to their deeds and, consequently, the believers' rewards (cf. ZIBORDI 2008). From a hermeneutic point of view, the Bible is understood in a literalistic way as "God's revelation to humanity. Its author is God himself. Its real interpreter is the Holy Spirit. Its central subject is the Lord Jesus Christ" (ANDRADE 2008, 26). In line with this, several eschatological elements gain prominence, such as Jesus' judgement of believers, the Great Tribulation (Mt 24:21), the end of the kingdom of the Antichrist, the judgement of the nations after the battle of Armageddon, the Final Judgement after the last rebellion and judgement of the devil, as well as the new heaven and the new earth. Israel's rise is an important sign or indicator of the coming end-time, which is the reason for the uncritical benevolent treatment of the Israeli State. Israel is also an object of support and a tourist destination, while the Palestinians are unilaterally blamed for its current problems. Also, the devastating tsunami of 2004 is (by reference to Lk 21:25) considered to be a sign of the approaching end time, as well as the increase in poverty, epidemics, etc. For a long time, the expectation of the imminence of the end time meant that Pentecostals were not involved in politics, but that changed with the redemocratisation and the 1986-1987 Constituent Assembly. Nowadays, in Brazil and also in other countries, like Guatemala – which has, in percentage terms, the greatest presence of Pentecostal churches – it is not possible to do politics without these churches; the Evangelical Parliamentary Front (a supra-party grouping of evangelicals), dominated by the AD, is a powerful association present in both houses of Congress. Furthermore, Pentecostal churches are by no means inactive in fighting against poverty and diseases as the position above might suggest. In this and other areas, *de facto* transformations are taking place (CORTEN 1996; DE OLIVEIRA, DE VASCONCELOS FERREIRA and FAJARDO, eds., 2017). The importance of healing and specifically spiritual healing in many Pentecostal churches (and beyond) should not be underestimated, and one of the emphases of the Neo-Pentecostal churches that came from them (see below) is healing here and now. Still, millennialism continues to play a considerable role in Pentecostal churches. In the chapter that deals with pneumatology in the book *Pentecostal Systematic Theology*, "changes" are described in a critical tone as something characteristic of the time of the Antichrist, to which Liberation Theology, the prosperity gospel and the ecumenical movement belong and are framed in negative terms. For this reason, Pentecostal churches expect opposition from the world, as they seek not to conform to the world (by reference to Rm 12:1ff.). Being counterculture already had its roots in the church model founded by the North-American missionaries – for example, the abstinence from smoking and alcohol, but also dance and worldly music – but now Pentecostal churches take a counterpoint stand through the "gospel explosion", its music, dance and many other practices, which, so to speak, are "baptised" and introduce worldly elements into ecclesial practice (cf. CUNHA 2007). In this area, therefore, we have a huge diversity, which continues to grow with no defined limits, constantly expanding, changing, and permeating society in different ways. A special case within the Pentecostal movement is the Neo-Pentecostal churches, which I will deal with next.

3.4 Theology under the sign of prosperity

In Brazil, Neo-Pentecostal theologies emerged in the 1970s and gave rise to several churches that are now very influential. Among them, the Universal Church of the Kingdom of God (*Igreja Universal do Reino de Deus* – IURD) deserves special mention, since in the meantime it is already present in more than 80 countries. Neo-Pentecostal theologies, however, are a trend also found in many other churches, including Pentecostal and historical churches. It is particularly characterised by the "gospel of health and wealth", the "prosperity gospel", which has, among its central purposes, personal prosperity, and integral health. Although churches recognised as Neo-Pentecostal have relatively few professed members – the IURD, for example, does not even make an effort towards creating and edifying a church community, but is an "event-driven" church – its public visibility is very high, mainly due to a strong presence in the media and large temples located in central areas, such as the "Temple of Solomon" in São Paulo.[8] According to the founder and supreme bishop of the IURD, Edir Macedo Bezerra, "this is not a denominational, much less a personal project. But, from a spiritual point of view, something so glorious that it transcends reason itself. Certainly, it will awaken the sleeping faith of the cold or lukewarm and throw them into a national, and then, global awakening".[9] A clear pretension, with not the smallest political overtones.

Among the fundamental categories of Edir Macedo is the dualism between "natural" or "emotional" faith, on the one hand, and "supernatural" or "rational" faith, on the other. In his book *Are We All Children of God?* he writes that the question in the title must be answered with "no". Children of God are only those who overcome their feelings by use of reason, who conquer the flesh by the spirit, who do not live under the power of emotions and feelings (including depression, of which Edir Macedo suffered in the past), but live as people reborn by the Spirit. People baptised in the Spirit "have the same capacity and the same conditions to perform the deeds of the Lord Jesus and even greater ones" (MACEDO 2003, 64). God created life "to be lived in abundance, that is, with all its rights and privileges, without any form of affliction, anguish or anxiety" (ibid, 71). The true children of God must take possession of the fullness of life and should not live as beggars, because life in all its fullness also includes financial well-being. In this sense, eschatology is projected into the present time: it is here and now that the believer must change his/her life for the better and remove what prevents happiness. The kingdom of darkness and the kingdom of God are in conflict right now in this world and in this present time. Being a child of God means to be willing to offer sacrifices, that is, as an expression of a strong faith, generously donate money to the church. Thus, in this respect, the following verse from the prophet Malachi has a central role (not only in the IURD): "Bring all the tithes to the treasury, so that there is food in my

---

[8] See http://otemplodesalomao.com/ [last accessed August 9, 2021]; cf. ORO, CORTEN and DOZON, eds., 2003.

[9] Available at: <http://www.otemplodesalomao.com/#/otemplo> [accessed November 14, 2014].

house; and prove me in this, says the Lord of hosts, if I do not open the windows of heaven to you and pour out a blessing without measure" (Mal 3:10). In this regard, faith is something to be accomplished: faith is the prerequisite for true baptism and must be confirmed by verifiable changes in the way of life. These are precisely the fruits of the Spirit highlighted in opposition to the classical Pentecostal churches. Moreover, speaking in tongues is considered an illusion. In hermeneutical terms, Edir Macedo holds on to a literal biblicism which presupposes the divine inspiration of every specific author's writings and, above all, understands God's promises in a literal sense, applicable to the present time. Both in this understanding of the Bible and in the practice of the church, there is no room for doubt. Like other literalisms, however, the choice of the individual biblical passages is very selective, as one can notice in the worship services of the IURD. During preaching there is no sequential explanation of the biblical text, but the dissemination of the fundamental message of the IURD based on a relatively small number of biblical references.

As a rule, in academic research the literature about Neo-Pentecostalism is more often referred to than the Neo-Pentecostal authors themselves, due to the fact that there is little self-reflection, and the existing texts are of a non-scientific, programmatic, and popular character. In contrast to this, here I deliberately gave the word to a prominent exponent of the Neo-Pentecostal movement. Edir Macedo's statements, however, need to be compared with scientific studies and with his and his church's actual public performance. It is also necessary to consider that he often aims to position himself in a distinctly different way from the Roman Catholic Church and, at the same time, as leader within the so-called "evangelical" churches – a term which, in this case, refers especially to Pentecostal churches. Therefore, with regard to moral issues of broad consensus among the churches, both Catholic and other evangelical churches, Edir Macedo can take a divergent position – such as, for example, in the case of abortion, in which he adopts a quite liberal stance, and, therefore, finds sympathy among politicians, doctors, and jurists.

Therefore, the picture that emerges of theology in Latin America, whether as explicit academic theology or, by contrast, as popular and spiritually rich theology, is a very diverse and even contradictory picture. It outlines the enormous religious mobility also known in Africa and with which it has effectively certain connections. Nowadays we have access to primary literature, which was not the case until recently, and it is thanks to this circumstance that an overview such as the one in this article is possible. Critical and self-critical reflection are underway mainly in classical Pentecostal churches, such as the AD. A central distinguishing feature that calls for greater theological observation and reflection is eschatology, which sums up everything – on the one hand, a millenarianism averse to the world to an eschatology projected into the present, and, on the other hand, an inter-religious kingdom-centric theology (on this, see also below Chapters 11 and 12). Thus, theology in Latin America remains instigating and full of tensions.

Chapter 4

Lutheran Contributions for Citizenship in Brazil[*]

"[O] povo da igreja [é o] chão em que
um agir público responsável deve ter
suas verdadeiras raízes."
Lindolfo Weingärtner[1]

Lutheran churches are a tiny minority in Latin America. They have emerged primarily through migration – especially in the Cono Sur, the southernmost part of the Americas with Argentina, Brazil, Chile, Uruguay, and Paraguay. The Central American churches are local foundations and have a special, differentiated history; they are all very small. The largest Lutheran presence is in Brazil, which I will focus on below.

The Evangelical Church of Lutheran Confession in Brazil (*Igreja Evangélica de Confissão Luterana no Brasil* – IECLB) is today the second largest nationally constituted historic Protestant church in Brazil, after the Seventh-day Adventists, with approximately 670,000 members (BUSS 2017a). It is also the oldest, if one allows its existence to begin with the migration that started in 1824. Local congregations first began to form in Nova Friburgo, near the imperial summer residence of Petrópolis in the mountainous region of Rio de Janeiro, and in São Leopoldo, Rio Grande do Sul, and spread to other areas, especially Espírito Santo, northeast of Rio de Janeiro, through further migration and mainly German immigration. From 1886 onwards, the congregations joined together regionally to form synods, which in 1949 formed a Synodal Union, which finally became a national church in 1968. Of the four synods in the union, only one was decidedly Lutheran, the others

---

[*] Originally published as "Die Evangelische Kirche Lutherischen Bekenntnisses in Brasilien", in *Jahrbuch Sozialer Protestantismus* vol. 11, Leipzig: EVA, 2018: "Globale Wirkungen der Reformation", 121-141, translated by Walter O. Schlupp and revised by the author. Used with permission.
[1] "The members of the Church [are] the soil in which responsible public action must have its true roots", (WEINGÄRTNER 2001, 6).

were de facto united [*uniert*]. However, a moderate Lutheran confession prevailed. Thus, the confessional basis of the IELCB, as it has been called since 1954, is the Holy Scriptures, the early church confessions (Apostolic and Nicene-Constantinopolitan), the *Confessio Augustana* (CA), and Luther's Small Catechism. In 1998, a reorganisation took place that divided the church into 18 synods.[2] It was also there that it was decided that the CA should be the (more purely Lutheran) *invariata*. At the same time, a model of "shared ministry" (*ministério compartilhado*) was adopted, according to which pastors, deacons, catechists, and missionaries, despite different emphases, are equally theologically trained, ordained, and qualified to exercise congregational leadership, including preaching and administering the sacraments.

There is also the Evangelical Lutheran Church of Brazil (*Igreja Evangélica Luterana do Brasil* – IELB), which was founded in 1904 through missionary activities of the Lutheran Church – Missouri Synod as a separate district among German immigrants and their descendants; today it has about 240,000 members (Buss 2017b). In addition, there are a number of free Lutheran congregations. In the 2010 Census, just under one million people reported being Lutheran.

In this chapter, I will first discuss "Lutheranism" and Protestantism in Brazil and Latin America in the 16th–18th centuries (4.1). Then, from the beginning of German immigration in the 19th century until today, I will present the three phases of what I call the struggle for the IECLB's citizenship (4.2– 4.4), as well as describe today's situation within religious pluralism (4.5).

4.1 "Lutheranism" in Latin America

Nestor Beck (2014, 629) wrote a few years ago that despite great efforts over two centuries, Luther's theology "has had no notable impact in Latin America, not even in Brazil". The almost revolutionary attention that the 500th anniversary of the Lutheran Reformation has received, both in a wide range of Protestant churches – so-called historical as well as Pentecostal – and in many Catholic congregations, seminaries, and universities, as well as in the general public through lectures, services, commemorations, publications, special stamps, dedication of statues, shows, concerts and media coverage, seems to paint a different picture.

---

[2] Information on the structure can be found at http://www.luteranos.com.br.

The enthusiastic statement of a young Lutheran woman: "Luther is 'show'", which I overheard, points both to Luther's suitability as a media event – historically and contemporarily – and admittedly also to the fact that the interest relates more to the person of Luther and the religious, social, linguistic and educational changes initiated by him than to Lutheran theology and the Lutheran church.[3] Nevertheless, the great response is likely to give members of the two Lutheran churches a sense of pride, attention and recognition, as was clearly felt at the major events, for example, the spectacle "Roots and Legacy of 500 Years of Reformation" in the packed Araújo Vianna Theatre in Porto Alegre.[4] At the same time, it must also be said that theological insights gained in the environment of Lutheran theology, and scientific theology in general, are of political, scientific, and thus, cultural significance in Brazil, far beyond Lutheranism and Protestantism. In that jubilee year, we should also mention a series of publications, some of which are ecumenical in nature[5], as well as the 2017 annual congress of the primarily Catholic Brazilian Association for Theology and Religious Studies (*Sociedade de Teologia e Ciências da Religião* – SOTER), which was dedicated to the topic of the Reformation (in a broad sense of reform processes), having specifically invited Lutheran, Pentecostal, Jewish, and Muslim speakers.[6]

---

[3] However, this certainly came up in the reports, such as in the broadcast of one of the major Brazilian television networks TV Bandeirantes titled: "The Greatest Revolution in the Church: 500 Years of Reformation". Available at: https://www.facebook.com/jornaldaband/videos/729142690623819/ [accessed November 2, 2017]. The recordings were made at the IECLB main church [in Porto Alegre] and the Lutheran High School (*Faculdades EST*) in São Leopoldo, as well as the Lutheran University (ULBRA), and featured university teachers Walter Altmann (IECLB) and Ricardo Willy Rieth (IELB), as well as the local pastor of IECLB, Maurício Haacke. On the topic as a whole, see GERTZ 2004.

[4] See, for example, the excerpt at https://www.facebook.com/anilindner/videos/1935638576462955/ [accessed November 2, 2017]; the "Kyrie" is sung, composed by colleague Rodolfo Gaede Neto and now known worldwide through the WCC; dancers gesturally "nail" theses. The event was conceived and coordinated by the well-known Brazilian actor, Lutheran Werner Schünemann.

[5] For example, RIBEIRO and ROCHA, eds., 2017; CAVALCANTE and BONOME, eds., 2017; CAVALCANTE 2017; VIANA 2017; BITUN, ed., 2017; ARAÚJO, ed., 2017; CHAVES 2017; HOFFMANN, BEROS and MOONEY, eds., 2017.

[6] The topic was: "*Religiões em Reforma – 500 anos depois*" ("Religions in the Reformation – 500 years later"). Available at:

Overall, it seems to me that one of the important contributions of Protestant, and especially Lutheran theology in Brazil today, besides profound theoretical and practical contributions to diakonia and social justice, is a solid, methodologically and epistemologically responsible reflection that should and can be carried out in contextual creativity, academic freedom, evangelical commitment and awareness of public responsibility (see VON SINNER 2012a, 198-239; cf. Chapter 12 below).

At the time of the "discovery" of Brazil at Easter 1500 and the following 16th century, this was by no means the case, though. The Counter-Reformation spread to the New World through Jesuit missionaries and gradually led to the view that the North was reserved for the heretical Luther and the South for the true Catholic faith. There were practically no Lutherans or other Protestants here at that time. The writings of the Reformers were hardly accessible in the New World; inquisition trials against Protestants were extremely rare (BASTIAN 1995, 55; PRIEN 1977, 333-344). Nevertheless, the name "Luther" and the designation "Lutheran" served as a cipher for all kinds of heresy, indeed the greatest of them. The Mexican chronicles referred to Luther as *archihereticus maledictus in Germania* (MAYER 2004, 123). The New World became the antithesis of Central Europe, which was riddled with Lutheran heresy, and the privileged place of God's providential action, the heresy-free America. New Spanish paintings showed Luther, Calvin, and other reformers being overrun by the triumphant chariot of the Roman Church or drowning in the sea in the face of the victorious Catholic ship. Not least for this reason, Marian devotion was specifically promoted by exalting the Virgin of Guadelupe in Mexico and stylising Luther as her antipode. Iberian culture, South American soil and Catholic religion formed a unity in this conception. The idea that the Protestants (and other heresies) were "sects" that were religiously, culturally, and politically alien to South America was still propagated deep into the 20th century. At the time of the independence movement in 19th century Mexico, the Inquisition even identified Luther with the leader of the insurgents, the priest Miguel Hidalgo, who, of course, clearly distanced himself from that (SCHMIDT 2004, 151). Liberal Mexicans saw Protestantism as a hope for economic recovery and progress. The same is true of Brazilian republicanism in the late 19th century. This alliance

---

<http://www.soter.org.br/eventodinamico/index.php?evento=11> [accessed November 4, 2017].

between liberal Catholics, Positivists, Freemasons, and Protestants also led to the creation of legally secular states in South America in the 19th century, even before secularisation happened in Europe.

One of the first Lutherans we know to have set foot in the southern part of the New World was the Hessian Hans Staden (1525-1576), a mercenary hired by the Portuguese. Before his journey to America, he probably fought for Philip of Hesse in the Schmalkaldic War. Staden also dedicated his book, published in 1557, to Landgrave Philip, in which he describes the nine months of his captivity among the Brazilian Tupinambá, as *Wahrhaftige Historia und beschreibung eyner Landtschafft der Wilden, Nacketen, Grimmigen Menschenfresser Leuthen, in der Neuenwelt America gelegen* ["True History and Description of a Country of Savage, Naked, Fierce Man-Eaters, Situated in the New World America"] (STADEN 1557/2008). The book became an early bestseller. Staden escaped being eaten by the so-called cannibals several times. He reports that, although he constantly feared for his life, he was always able to skilfully convince the Tupinambá that his God was stronger. In his fear, he also prayed and sang Luther's song *Aus tiefer Not schrei ich zu dir* ["Out of the depths I cry to you"].

Later, Huguenots from France and Reformers from Geneva set out for Brazil and found "Antarctic France", among other things, as a refuge for the oppressed Protestants. The colony soon perished. Apart from the presence of Dutch Reformed with the West India Company on the north-east coast of Brazil in the 17th century, from 1630-1654, there was no notable Protestant presence until the 19th century. Until then, non-Catholics were barred from staying in Brazil.

4.2 Immigration and the obtainment of civil rights

In Brazil, the immigration of non-Catholics was made possible by the constitution of the empire (1824), which was now independent of Portugal. Although it continued to regard the "Catholic religion" as the state religion, other religions were permitted, provided believers gathered in private houses that did not look like churches – i.e. did not have a bell tower, for example. Immigrants, among them many Protestants, came mainly from Germany, but also from Switzerland, Austria, Luxemburg, and Russia, among them mainly Lutherans, but also United and Reformed Protestants. In those countries, poverty and disproportionate population growth prevailed at the time, so that governments were interested in emigration without return, and partly also financed it. Religious interpretations shaped emigration for some. For example, one song compared the migrant families to Abraham and his calling by God to move to a new land. The song ended with the words, "We also trust firmly in God, his holy word, so we now leave for Brazil" (PRIEN 1989, 30). Other songs were more mundane, probably closer to the concrete dreams – usually bitterly disappointed after arrival: "We are going to another country. There we'll find gold like sand. We'll go to Brasilia, hurrah, hurrah. Only debts we leave behind" (ibid, n. 20). For its part, the Brazilian Empire was interested in the entry of white immigrant families: Some replaced African slaves in the coffee plantations of São Paulo because the slave trade had already become too dangerous and expensive. After the revolutions of the Afro-Americans in Haiti (1804) and in the *malês* rebellion in Bahia (1807-1810), the descendants of European immigrants feared a more widespread uprising of the Afro-Brazilian population, which already constituted the majority of Brazil's inhabitants. With the aim of "whitening" society, European settlers were therefore invited into the country, who were not to live on the usual large estates of coffee and sugar cane plantations, but were to practice subsistence farming as a family on small plots of land – without slaves, i.e. with the necessity of producing many descendants. Companies like the *Hamburger Colonisationsverein* [Hamburg Colonisation Association] vigorously advertised the "paradise" in the New World – an expectation that was soon frustrated, as the land first had to be made fit for cultivation, since it was heavily forested and had many swamps. The hard work, along with diseases like malaria and invading predators, claimed their victims daily (cf. CUNHA 2004; HASLER 1988).

The ban on erecting bell towers was not much of a problem at first, because the congregations met mainly in the communitarian schools founded by the immigrants, whose teachers also performed pastoral tasks. This grassroots congregational model, which implemented the priesthood of all believers in its fullness, was soon transformed into a more clerical model by the arrival of pastors trained in Germany and sent out by missionary societies. The previous lay preachers were denigrated as "pseudo" and *schnapps* ["brandy"] pastors. In terms of civil rights, it was problematic that there were no public cemeteries and no civil registry office for registering births and marriages, as these official acts were in the sole hands of the state church. This forced the Protestants to set up their own cemeteries. Since they were neither legally baptised (i.e.

Catholic), nor legally married, they were considered second-class citizens. Thus, the 19th century, until the full guarantee of religious freedom following the founding of the Republic in 1889, can be considered a time of struggle for the civil rights of immigrant families. I call it the First Phase of the Struggle for Citizenship (*cidadania, citoyenneté, Bürgerschaftlichkeit*).

In their then largely homogeneous, rural communities with family subsistence farming, the immigrants cultivated their culture and language, for which the church provided the social framework, so that it was known early on as the "German church" or the "church of the Germans" – it is sometimes still referred to as such today. Like the German Catholic immigrants, their Protestant counterparts probably kept to themselves more for practical than ideological reasons and understood themselves as Germans. The same phenomenon can be observed among others, for example, Italian Catholic immigrants; "Brazilians" were the Portuguese-speaking others.

With the expanding pan-Germanic tendencies of the now constituted German Empire, the congregations and synods became increasingly connected to the central church bodies in Germany. From this point on, a clearly demonstrated Germanism emerged, as Martin Dreher elaborated in his already classic Munich dissertation (1978; cf. SPLIESGART 2006). Not a few advocated that the "Protestant Church and Germanness must remain indissolubly linked" – "for us, *Volkstum* [ethnicity] and Kirche, Germanness and Gospel belong closely and indissolubly together" (quoted in FISCHER 1970, 163; cf. PRIEN 1989, 299-462).

The two World Wars severely restricted contacts with Germany and even the public use of the German language in Brazil, so that the Lutheran churches were increasingly left on their own and also had to found their own college to train pastors, later also female pastors and other ministers. Until then, there had only been a "proseminary", which offered graduates a classical humanistic education before they studied theology in Germany and attended the seminary for preachers. Thus, in 1946, the Escola de Teologia in São Leopoldo, now Faculdades EST, came into being (HOCH, STRÖHER and WACHHOLZ, eds., 2008). This phase heralded the Second Phase of the Struggle for Citizenship: the clear positioning of the church as a Brazilian church.

4.3 Towards a Brazilian ecclesial identity

The Second World War had cut the umbilical cord to Germany and the soon-to-be-named IECLB had to orient itself completely towards Brazil. The first General Council of the Synodal Union took place in São Leopoldo in 1950 and emphasised: "the Synodal Union is the Church of Jesus Christ in Brazil, with all the consequences that flow from this for the proclamation of the Gospel in this country and the co-responsibility for shaping the political, cultural and economic life of its people" (quoted in FISCHER 1970, 167). At the same time as this decidedly Brazilian identity and citizenship, the nascent IECLB joined the WCC as early as 1950 and the Lutheran World Federation (LWF) two years later. The theological college was still largely dominated by German professors and their linguistic approach; from 1968, however, the chairs were gradually taken over by theologians with doctorates in Germany, Switzerland, and the USA (the first was Gottfried Brakemeier), and later also by women theologians, and teaching was increasingly given exclusively in Portuguese. At the same time, the proportion of German pastors declined rapidly: while in 1965 almost 58% of the pastors were from Germany, by 1967 the figure was only 20.5%, with the number of pastors increasing by around 50% in the same period (SCHÜNEMANN 1992, 65).

When a military regime took power on 1 April 1964 in a coup called "revolution", this was clearly welcomed by almost all of the churches, because the widespread anti-communism had great misgivings about possible left-wing movements. Lutherans were mainly politically conservative or abstinent; the Lutheran middle class profited from the "Brazilian economic miracle" of the late 1960s; in the highly patriotic climate the church probably did not want to be tagged by criticism as being "foreign" (cf. BRANDT 1973, 44; PRIEN 1977, 219). However, the relocation of the 5th Assembly of the LWF, originally again planned for Porto Alegre, to Evian, a relocation demanded not least by German delegates, had a catalytic effect, leading to a new attitude. The LWF was rightly concerned because at the time the highest level of state repression had been reached and, according to LWF usages, the President of the state would have addressed the Assembly. For the IECLB, the postponement came as a shock; as a protest reaction, only two delegates attended in Evian, who read out a disappointed statement in which the church stated, among other things: "if the church feels called to exercise its political guardianship, then expertise and an unbiased attitude are two indispensable prerequisites".[7]

Already existing, more critical sectors – there had already been a commission for political, economic, and political affairs in the IECLB since 1968, in which namely prominent members of the faculty of the theological seminary were involved – gained prominence in the course of these events. In the same year, the General Council in São Paulo, where the Synodal Union was transformed into a national church, had also declared that it saw itself as "co-responsible [...] for the shaping of public life in our country".[8] There were rumblings in the IECLB, especially among the pastors, for whose critical attitude the theological college was largely responsible, so that it even came under the radar of the police.[9] Bonhoeffer's (2010) *Letters and Papers from Prison* was the reading of the time, as was Richard Shaull's (1966) *Profound Transformations in the Light of an Evangelical Theology*. Shaull, a Presbyterian US missionary who worked in Colombia and Brazil, had spoken on "the revolutionary challenge to church and theology" (SHAULL 1967) at the famous Geneva Conference on Church and Society in 1966. The same can be said abouts Jürgen Moltmann's (1993b) *Theology of Hope* (cf. DREHER 2008, 61). The 1962 Northeast Conference sponsored by the WCC on 'Christ and the Revolutionary Process in Brazil' radicalised many Protestant theologians, including Lutherans. The spirit of the Second Vatican Council and the vigorous revolutionary mobilisation of many Catholics did their part.

Church President Karl Gottschald had called on the congregations to celebrate the Fatherland Week and in particular to hold services for Independence Day on 7 September, preferably ecumenically. Several pastors refused; they also refused to position national flags in their churches and openly and critically discussed the compulsory subject "Moral and Civil Education" in schools (cf. DE AZEVEDO 1981). These

---

[7] LUTHERAN WORLD FEDERATION, 1971, 124; the entire declaration 123-125.

[8] Quoted in FISCHER 1970, 186. Fischer notes that the church "[has] not made frequent use of the opportunity to address the congregations with a special word" (ibid, 185). This was to change after 1970, as we shall see.

[9] According to historian Dreher, there was a police dossier that read, from the pen of Lutheran General Ernesto Geisel: "In a seminary in Rio Grande do Sul, in São Leopoldo, there was a strong leftist infiltration promoted by German pastors. Like many Catholic priests, they too cannibalized the problem of land reform, land distribution, and poor settlers"; DREHER 2008, 64.

neuralgic points, as well as human rights violations, especially torture, were to form the central elements of the "Curitiba Manifesto". The Manifesto was adopted at the General Council of the IECLB in October 1970. It had been prepared by the aforementioned commission for some time. Gottschald was to hand it personally to the current President of the Republic, General Emílio Garrastazú Médici, the following month.[10] For the celebration of the 150th anniversary of independence, the question once again became particularly urgent; the Theological Commission under the leadership of the then Rector of the Theological Faculty and later Church President, Gottfried Brakemeier, wrote "Considerations for a Sermon in the Fatherland Week".[11] With the first Lutheran president of Brazil, of German descent, General Ernesto Geisel (in office 1974-1978), the government-controlled and so-called "slow, gradual and safe" transition began, which only came to an end in 1985 with the installation of a civilian president and the subsequent Constituent Assembly. The IECLB now took a more frequent and increasingly critical stance on issues of democracy and civil rights, land reform, economic and social issues, human rights, violence, and ecology.

4.4 From the Curitiba Manifesto to the present day

With the Curitiba Manifesto and the following statements of the General Councils or the Church's Presidency, but also many individual initiatives and those of groups and Lutheran or ecumenical organisations, the phase began which I call the Third Phase of the Struggle for Citizenship, now no longer (only) in the members' or the church's own interest, but in commitment to the whole of society. The cooperation has intensified with sectors of the Roman Catholic Church, namely the Rural Pastoral Commission (*Comissão Pastoral da Terra* – CPT), as well as other critical and progressive circles of Protestant churches, especially Methodists, Anglicans, and dissident Presbyterians; the issues and positions were practically the same. Nevertheless, a distinct theological rationale can be discerned in the Lutheran positions.

The Curitiba Manifesto argued along lines that can also be found in later documents. I summarise them as follows: (1) While salvation and

---

[10] An English version can be found in LISSNER and SOVIK, eds., 1978, 38f.
[11] BRANDT (1973, 47f.), who was working as a systematic theologian at the seminary in São Leopoldo, was also asked for a statement.

history (or "the world") should not be mixed or confused, and while priority is always due to God, the witness of faith is addressed to the world. Speaking to the world is therefore part of the mission of the Church. (2) The Church's proclamation is directed to the well-being of all humanity and therefore includes social, economic, political, cultural, and physical aspects. In order to contribute to this well-being, the root causes must be recognised and "eradicated". (3) The Church cooperates with other parts of civil society and also with the state in its effort to build certain relationships through ethical principles stemming from its proclamation. (4) A kind of two-regiments doctrine is found at the base of the argument that while church and state are to be distinguished, they cannot be considered separate and independent from each other. Both spheres are under the power of Christ, which secular rulers may not claim for themselves (cf. Mk 12:17). Believers are "Christ's disciples" and "citizens of their country". (5) The Church therefore has a critical role to play, as "guardian" and "conscience of the nation" in a "co-responsible" partnership, so that solutions can be found for society. This gave rise to the specific points of criticism already indicated: (a) Christian worship should be protected from excessive presence of patriotic symbols (e.g. flags in churches); (b) Christian education should not be replaced by "moral and civil education"; (c) human rights must be respected; torture specifically is an "inhuman method" that cannot be justified even by "exceptional circumstances". Thus, the IECLB officially expressed itself in this direction even before the Brazilian Catholic Bishops' Conference (*Conferência Nacional dos Bispos do Brasil* – CNBB) did so in all clarity (from 1973; cf. VON SINNER 2012a, 149-197). This was despite the fact that the IECLB was much more vulnerable as a minority church, in addition to being considered "foreign" by many. Some protection may have come from international relations, notably with the LWF and the WCC, which were very sceptical of the Brazilian military government and able to mobilise world opinion, which the military feared. On the other hand, the IECLB, being a small church and existing at that time almost only in the south and in the state of Espírito Santo, was indeed critical, but by no means revolutionary, and would hardly cause major problems for the regime. Nevertheless, it should be noted that according to Protestantism expert Paul Freston (1994, 27), the Curitiba Manifesto was the "only public statement by a Protestant church that criticised the regime". According to Schünemann, the new phase in the IECLB only really began with the document "Our Social Responsibility" of 1975-

1976 (LISSNER and SOVIK, eds., 1978, 41-45). From 1978 onwards, the new church leadership under Augusto Kunert was much more open to such ideas than the previous one.

Elsewhere, I have undertaken an in-depth study of documents from the General Council, the Church Council, the Presidency, some empirical studies and articles in the monthly *Jornal Evangélico* (JE, "Evangelical Newspaper"), which has been published since 1971 as a merger of two earlier newspapers and became the organ of the church leadership from 1989. The expectation that the JE would reflect the opinions of the church members or congregations had to be corrected, however. Rather, it represented the opinions of a progressive leading group in the IECLB (FIEGENBAUM 2006; VON SINNER 2012a, 217). That this line has never been shared by the whole church is hardly surprising and was already described by Hermann Brandt (1973). In the following, I will limit myself to theological argumentation patterns present in the documents, namely, on: (1) democracy and citizenship; (2) the relationship to the state; (3) the relationship to society; and (4) the relation between political and church citizenship.

(1) In the documents studied, democracy and citizenship are clearly affirmed in their importance, and democracy is described as the best and most appropriate political system. Theologically, reference is made to human dignity, the common good, discipleship and "Christ's commandment" or "God's commandment" in a broad sense. Although the content of this commandment is rarely explicitly mentioned, it is considered the foundation of human action according to God's will and Christ's example and commandments to love and serve. Such service is understood to be directed to all, not just to oneself or to one's own church members, and the church cannot therefore escape its public responsibility. Church President Kunert based his argument on the central doctrine of Lutheran theology, justification by faith, a faith that "seeks fellowship" and "knows itself to be united with the brethren". Christ came precisely to save that which was lost (Lk 19:10). "So God loved the world that he gave his only begotten Son" (Jn 3:16), faith becomes concrete in loving one's neighbour (Mt 22:37-40) and this is a responsible love according to the new commandment (Jn 13:34). This means that the gospel is to be lived in the context, since "the life of one is bound up with the life of others", which should guide the preaching of the Church. In the whole of the text, Kunert argues that Christ is Lord over all, humans in their totality as well as over church and state, so that "the state,

government, politics are part of the responsibility of the evangelical citizen" (KUNERT 1982, 242). On the 500th anniversary of Luther's birth in 1983, church historian Martin Dreher spoke on "Lutheranism and Political Participation" at the Federal University of Rio Grande do Sul (UFRGS); he referred to Luther's writing "To the Christian nobility" and mentioned the concept of "improvement", which meant more than reform (DREHER 1984). The Lutherans who had come to Brazil had been "apolitical"; but this is no longer the case, he noted, referring to documents of the church leadership – which was, certainly, also a message to the military government, whose days were counted. "Political engagement, the pursuit of the common good, the defence of justice are commandments of God and a way to serve people and the Creator. The attempt to circumvent this important task is to violate the commandment of love", wrote Church President Brakemeier in his 1988 pastoral letter on "Church and Politics" (BRAKEMEIER 1997, 16). Church, or faith, and politics are seen there as dialectically related to each other as church and state. In this, the underlying view of the nation is somewhat reduced because it does not sufficiently consider the difference between state and society, namely as far the latter is represented by civil society. This probably still reflects the earlier dual antagonism under military rule when there was no organised civil society. The importance of freedom is also emphasised. Church President Kunert noted in the progress of the democratic transition under the last military President, General Figueredo, the importance of a growing awareness of democracy as a form of government among church members, "because democracy is the system that bears respect for the human person, the freedom of the person and of society itself. [...] In its prophetic task, the church must proclaim to the Christian community, to the world and to the state that freedom is a characteristic of the 'Regnum Dei'" (KUNERT 1982, 227). Although Church President Brakemeier does not explicitly mention freedom in a pastoral letter on the 1989 elections, democracy is praised as the best system at present because it "holds the citizen in high esteem and at the same time makes them responsible" (BRAKEMEIER 1989). This is only conceivable if freedom to act and free choice can be taken for granted for the adult citizen. Indeed, the letter mentions a "counting [literally: a bet] on the maturity and responsibility [sc. of the voter]". This reflects the Protestant principle of the universal priesthood, in which there is no ontological difference between Christians and citizens, between laity and pastors.

(2) In his programmatic lecture at the theological seminary in São Leopoldo, Church President Kunert emphasised:

> They [viz. church and state] are different entities, but at the same time given to the individual. [...] We cannot [...] separate the relationship between church and state into a spiritual and political (secular) sphere, as if there were no communication between the two spheres for the citizen. [...] Luther, to speak in today's language, protested, in a contextual reality, against the totalitarianism of the state, he protested and raised his voice against the intention of the state to want to determine all spheres of human life and to dominate the human being entirely (KUNERT 1982, 224f.).

Kunert concluded by saying that whenever the state reaches its limits, the church must protest and take up its "prophetic" role. At the same time, it must not forget that it must also know and observe limits itself. He referred to Articles XVI and XVIII of the CA, which teach subordination to secular authority and laws, but are limited by the *clausula Petri* (Acts 5:29) and the use of free will. Further, Luther's writing on authority is cited. In a self-critique, it is said that the IECLB had "closed in on itself" and kept away from the "public and political life of Brazil" because of a wrong interpretation of CA XXVIII [on the distinction between spiritual and secular authority], which had led to an improper separation of the spiritual and the secular and an "actual quietism" (ibid, 228).

Even if, as Prien noted in 1977, an explicit two-kingdoms or two-regiments doctrine was hardly explicitly effective in the IECLB, it was implicitly present at many moments, first in an uncritical attitude toward the German or the Brazilian state. In contrast, criticism came from followers of Karl Barth and the Barmer Theological Declaration. Reading the two kingdoms or regiments doctrine through Barth's theology and drawing directly on Luther's writings, Walter Altmann stated that "the so-called two kingdoms can be distinguished regarding their tasks and their means, but they overlap in time and space. Furthermore, they have a common foundation – God is the Lord of both – and a common goal – human well being" (ALTMANN 2000, 71). Like Brakemeier in his pastoral letters and church leadership as a whole during the period studied (1985-2002), Altmann relies on Scripture and Luther's writings rather than on Lutheran confessional teaching, that is, on Luther rather than Lutheranism, possibly in an effort similar to the liberation theologians (and the Reformers!) to return to the sources rather than their magisterial or confessional interpretation.

One of the important aspects here is that the two regiments must be distinguished, but not separated, precisely because God in Christ rules over both. So Brakemeier (1989) could then say that "politics is also under the divine claim. It is not a neutral field, alien to faith [...] rather it pertains genuinely [sc. to the church] to recall publicly the will of God, which applies to Christians as well as non-Christians".

These are strong words, as they can probably only be uttered in a country with a large majority of Christians. Of course, this was also true for Luther in his time, but he had nevertheless paved the way for a certain restriction of the church's action by also admonishing it to stick to its actual task. The state, for its part, had to guarantee the free exercise of religion, which, as is well known, led to the territorial principle *cuius regio, eius religio* and not yet to religious freedom. Ironically, the much more influential Brazilian Roman Catholic Church is significantly more reserved in its statements on the nation or society as a whole.

Further, it is noteworthy that the IECLB defines its attitude from the inside out: it contributes to "peace in society" and stands in "solidarity with all who suffer injustice" precisely because it adheres to the "primary commandment, which is to bear witness to the work of God and to learn to believe, hope and love" (BRAKEMEIER 1992, 6). In this sense, the Church's action in the public sphere is part of its mission, as the Curitiba Manifesto already emphasised and the Mission Plan (*Plano de Ação Missionária* – PAMI) of 2000 maintained.

(3) While at first it seemed as if the IECLB positioned itself simply as a counterpart to the state in a church-state model, it later clearly emphasised its involvement in the ecumenical movement by highlighting its "sister churches" and ecumenical organisations such as the National Council of Churches (*Consalho Nacional de Igrejas Cristãs* – CONIC) and the Ecumenical Project Coordination Service (*Coordenadoria Ecumênica de Serviço* – CESE). The 1993 pastoral letter on "Law and Power" clearly stated that "we invite the congregations of the IECLB and its sister churches to ally themselves with the corresponding movements" (BRAKEMEIER 1993). The Church also clearly declared itself to be at the service of society, "heir to the prophetic tradition of the Bible, committed to peace and justice", in a "partnership with all people of good will", echoing a common phrase in the Roman Catholic Church. The church is "co-responsible for the well-being of society", the church president's

report to the 1992 General Council said. Thus, a critical-constructive stance was now integrated into a network of churches and movements with the same or similar goals. Although there were Lutheran politicians, the church never supported them as such. Unlike the progressive circles of the Roman Catholic Church, it also never favoured a particular party, not even indirectly through the criteria for voting which it regularly published before elections, although quite a few pastors and theologians became members of the Workers' Party (*Partido dos Trabalhadores – PT*). Others joined the Pastoral Land Commission (*Comissão Pastoral da Terra – CPT*) in the struggle for a just distribution of land. Probably the IECLB, traditionally composed of small farmers, has been the most effective in contributing to social transformation in this area, in a practice that has gone beyond plain assistance services, and also beyond documents, namely through its Assistance Center for Small Farmers (*Centro de Apoio ao Pequeno Agricultor* – CAPA). More recently, the Lutheran Diaconia Foundation (*Fundação Luterana de Diaconia* – FLD) has also sought to provide professional and effective assistance for concrete, transformative projects. Admittedly, these organisations are still largely dependent on grants from abroad.

(4) The IECLB is certainly a church in which the internal, democratic structure is closely connected with the desired democratic structures of state and society. In accordance with the principle of the universal priesthood of believers (1 Pet 2:9) through baptism and the constitution of the church as the congregation of believers ("the assembly [*congregatio*] of all (true) believers and saints", BSLK 62), there is no reason to assert other than functional distinctions within such congregations. Although matters of faith cannot simply be subjected to majority votes, in the IECLB processes for verifying the faithfulness of ministers are also democratically organised, i.e. through regulated processes requiring justification and involving lay persons at all levels. In principle, there is no reason why the citizen should act differently as a member of the church or as part of society, even though the two affiliations are by no means identical. The church emphasises that faith affects all areas of life, and that the church's message must be credible both internally and externally. In the early 1980s, Church President Kunert (1982, 242) maintained that "the IECLB must always keep in mind that its public actions must not deviate from its internal actions. It has the duty to proclaim the Gospel of Jesus Christ, which applies to the Christian community as well as to the whole of society". Church

President Altmann's (2006) letter on elections and the country's "political project" begins with a reference to the experience of elections as it would have been gained in the church, from where it would radiate into elections at the local, state, and federal levels. In fact, the IECLB has a long experience in democratic organisation, since the congregations had no other form of self-organisation and had to provide for school and spiritual care themselves, through persons who later, unfortunately, would be called "pseudo-pastors", as they had no formal education in theology. In fact, the structure of the church is organised from the bottom up, with a considerable amount of autonomy of the parishes, synods, and finally, the General Council and the Church Council. This in itself is an education in citizenship, with an emphasis on rights and duties and the responsibility that goes with them.

4.5 The IECLB in religious pluralism

At its 2004 General Council in São Leopoldo, where it celebrated 180 years since the beginning of immigration and the first founding of congregations, the Church made a very positive self-assessment:

> 180 years after the emergence of the first congregations [...] we celebrate and emphasize that we are a Church of Jesus Christ in this country, an inclusive, solidary and citizen [*cidadã*] Church. We have walked our way with a commitment to peace, justice and the integrity of all creation, practicing mission, diakonia and public responsibility in our congregations in favour of social inclusion and overcoming poverty and misery (IECLB 2004, 1).

One may certainly want (and need) to discuss the extent to which this positive evaluation corresponds with reality. However, historian René Gertz rightly emphasises that the "actual importance [of the Lutherans] is greater than their numerical weakness would suggest", not least because of their long tradition and high quality of schooling and higher education, which is widely recognised, especially in Rio Grande do Sul (GERTZ 2004, 166). It is arguably the most academically productive and ecumenically engaged evangelical church in Brazil and on the continent. In terms of numbers, however, it is stagnating and lagging far behind the growth rate of the general population. Ethnic origin is a hindrance to outward growth; at the same time, it is this origin that has given the church a certain stability and allowed it to become Brazil's only

"*Volkskirche*" in the sense described by Schleiermacher (see below, Chapter 10). According to a 1987 survey, 92.5% of IECLB members were of German descent, although many had immigrated several generations earlier, and, according to 1991 census data, 94.6% were white (KLIEWER 2005, 320).

In addition to the growing religious pluralism in Brazil (cf. VON SINNER, BOBSIN and BARTZ 2012) – which, in absolute numbers, is still the most Catholic country on Earth, but at the same time also the most Pentecostal – there is also considerable diversity within the IECLB. Various movements are courting church members, theology students, the attention of church leadership and the public, among them the Evangelical Mission Christian Unity (*Missão Evangélica União Cristã* – MEUC), established in 1927 by mission of the *Gnadauer Bund* in the pietist tradition, which also runs a theological college in São Bento do Sul (state of Santa Catarina). Under the influence of US missionaries, the evangelical "Great Encounter Movement" (*Movimento Encontrão* – ME) emerged in the 1950s, which also runs a theological college in Curitiba (state of Paraná). On the other side of the spectrum, there is the "Lutheran People's Pastoral" (*Pastoral Popular Luterana* – PPL), which follows a progressive, socially, and politically committed line. Somewhat in between is the "Martin Luther Fellowship" (*Comunhão Martin Lutero*), which is particularly concerned with preserving the Lutheran heritage. More recently, there has also been a "movement of spiritual renewal", of charismatic Pentecostal character, with which there was a break when pastors began to rebaptise themselves and others.

Under the presidency of Huberto Kirchheim (1995-2002), restructuring took place in 18 synods and special attention was paid to congregational reality. The congregations were to be strengthened and encouraged to engage in missionary activity within the framework of the "Plan of Missionary Action" (*Plano de Ação Missionária* – PAMI), according to which "no congregation without mission – no mission without congregation" applies. The concept of mission is broad, including diakonia and solidarity, but also evangelisation, ecumenism, education, and administration. This missionary activity, albeit with strong ecumenical-international networking, was also continued by church president Walter Altmann (2003-2010), the then chairman of the central committee of the WCC (from 2006-2013). In his opening address to the 2006 Mission Forum, he said that the IECLB is a "church in transition" that cannot be based on ethnic and regional origins, but whose members "[need] reasons of conviction and passion [to] belong to and remain in the IECLB". It should be missionary, but not participate in the general religious competition.[12] Also under the presidency of Nestor Paulo Friedrich (2011-2018), special attention was paid to mission, again in that broad sense, as well as to the sustainability of church administration and financing, and to ecumenical cooperation. In 2018, the first ever female president was elected, Sílvia Beatrice Genz.

---

[12] Available at: <http://www.ieclb.org.br/noticia.php?id=8101> [accessed July 7, 2007]. Another minister, from the *Encontrão* movement, cited by the document, mentioned explicitly a concept of "integral evangelization which joins faith, diaconia, and citizenship".

II. PUBLIC THEOLOGY AND RELIGIOUS PLURALISM

Chapter 5

Christianity on Its Way to the South: Intercultural Theology as a Challenge to Systematic Theology*

"Whose Religion is Christianity?"
Lamin Sanneh (2003)

The Roman Catholic Leopold Sédar Senghor (1906-2001), former president of Senegal (from 1960 to 1980), one of the leaders of the *négritude* movement, said precisely half a century ago:

> So low was the level to which the *black soul* had been reduced at that point that we accepted that we were a 'tabula rasa': a race, almost a continent, that for 30,000 years thought nothing, felt nothing, wrote nothing, painted or sculpted nothing, sang or danced nothing. A *nothingness* at the bottom of the abyss, unable to do anything but beg and receive: a soft wax in the hands of the white God with pink fingers and sky blue eyes (SENGHOR 1962, 216, quoted from JEFFERS 2010, 230, italics in original).

This major provocation leads directly to the concern that underlies this contribution and that will be justified and discussed in it, namely, that despite the variegated, more or less successful cultural contacts with the *Global South*, for instance, through mission, colonialism, globalisation and migration, the autonomous, particularly cultural contribution offered

* Republished with permission from Peter Lang GmbH, Internationaler Verlag der Wissenschaften, from "Das Christentum auf dem Weg nach Süden: Interkulturelle Theologie als Herausforderung an die Systematische Theologie," in Franz Gmainer-Pranzl and Judith Gruber (eds.), *Interkulturalität als Anspruch universitärer Lehre und Forschung* (Salzburg, 2012), 215-237; permission conveyed through Copyright Clearance Center, Inc. Translated by Hedy L. Hofmann and Luís Marcos Sander. First published in English in Perumalla, Victor and Rao, eds., *The Yobel Spring. Festschrift for Chilkuri Vasantha Rao* (Delhi: ISPCK, 2013), 198-222. Used with permission. The text has been elaborated originally during a sabbatical as fellow of the Lichtenberg-Kolleg at the University of Göttingen, Germany, in 2011, for which I am greatly thankful.

by the South, still goes practically unnoticed by the *Global North*.[1] Especially in German systematic theology, which is what I have in mind here, Christianity and theology in non-Western cultures is effectively not considered important; at most, it is seen as an exotic complement, but not as something from which Western theology could also learn. Unchallenged facts are the huge growth and transformation of Christianity in Africa, as well as in Latin America and in certain parts of Asia. While Western Christianity struggles with the different forms taken on by the phenomenon of secularisation and increasingly empty churches, it appears that in other places Christianity is flourishing. What is the result of these facts for the identity of such global and pluriform Christianity? Does the displacement of its so-called centre of gravity southwards also mean an inversion of the power of definition?

It is known that, already in early times, Christianity was strongly represented in North Africa, mainly in Ethiopia and in Egypt, before it was pushed back by Islam.[2] Thus, it was not in the 20th century that Christianity went South for the first time; its origin lies in the South, more precisely, in the area of the Mediterranean centred in Palestine. Philip Jenkins (2007a, 19) considers that Europe began to be the centre of gravity of Christianity only in the year 1400, whereas up to that time its presence had been stronger in Africa and in Asia. After 1500, worldwide Christian missionary activities began, in which mostly the Jesuits played a central role. Beginning in the 18th century, Protestant missionary societies also began their work. However, there has always been – and with greater intensity than is generally perceived – a strong agency of the people reached by the missions themselves, and even a genuinely autonomous Christianisation, as in the case of the Kingdom of Kongo in the 15th century. Its ruler Afonso I (Mvemba Nzinga, 1506-1543) corresponded regularly with the King of Portugal Dom Manuel and with the Papal Curia in Rome (KOSCHORKE 2009, 196-207; THORNTON 1984).

---

[1] I use these terms because they are usual and useful in heuristic terms, since they designate real breaks that occur between different groups of countries with their religious, economic, and political specificities. However, they should be understood in metaphoric terms rather than in real geographic ones, especially because the "South" also exists in the "North", and vice versa. Certainly, the intention here is not to provide essentialist attributions and much less to eternalise them.

[2] Christianity in (North) Africa is so ancient that "it can rightly be described as an indigenous, traditional, and African religion" (MBITI 1969, 229, quoted in S. KIM and K. KIM 2007, 63).

Other examples of autonomous evangelisation and growth could also be added, including the "exportation" of Christians among the slaves shipped to America. Christianity gradually found its way back to the "South" and even penetrated completely new regions. A growth spurt of unprecedented dimensions took place during the 20th century mainly in Latin America and in Africa, and in relatively smaller proportions – but in equally considerable absolute numbers – also in Asia. Thus, it can now be said, as formulated by Dana Robert, that "the typical late twentieth-century Christian was no longer a European man, but a Latin American or African woman" (ROBERT 2000, 50).

Christianity, therefore, is on its way to the South. Or rather: it is already there, in the form of manifestations that have long been autonomous, as a "synthesis of global and local elements that has its own integrity" (ROBERT 2000, 57) and it is returning from there to the North through migration and mission (cf. WÄHRISCH-OBLAU 2009; cf. Chapter 12 below). This fact arouses, for instance, the following question from actors in the South: "Whose religion is Christianity?"[3] Analysts in the North ask, both fascinated and concerned, whether a "next Christendom" is arising in the South, which would set the tone for the coming decades, showing the way to traditional Christianity of the North – perceived by many as decadent – and facing Islam. A few associate this with hopes,[4] others with fears, yet others simply ignore the challenge. The possible significance of this fact for general perception, especially for an intercultural and systematic Christian theology, is the object of this contribution. Initially, I shall try to describe this global transformation more precisely as "the way to the South" (5.1). In a second step, I will discuss the intercultural theology that arose from missiology and attempt to understand and interpret this movement (5.2). Then I will talk about

---

[3] Lamin Sanneh is a convert from Islam, born in Gambia, and has for many years been a professor at Yale. Like others, he emphasises that mission in no way was or is a simple import. It requires recognising the agency of local people and groups. A sign of this is, for instance, the rapid growth of Christianity in Africa, which in this process creates indigenous forms of its own.

[4] See, for instance, USTORF (2010, esp. 63ff.), who shows that it was not only in recent times that the Christianity of the South has fed hopes of compensation among missionaries and ecumenists of the North, which may be repeated in an exemplary manner by the unilateral contrast between "liberal Christianity" in the North and a new *corpus Christianum* in the South proposed by Jenkins. However, I dare doubt that the dreams of hegemony are an exclusively Western invention (see ibid, 68), as they are apparently being formed also in the South.

the relationship between contextuality, intercontextuality, and the issue of truth in German systematic theology (5.3) and, concluding, I will formulate in the form of theses what I consider to be the questioning of systematic theology from the intercultural perspective, in brief, why this perspective is necessary not only for a particular theological discipline, but also for the "essence" of theology and, in this respect, raises a demand for academic teaching and research (5.4).

5.1 Christianity on its way to the South

In his appreciated writings, historian Philip Jenkins spoke of "The Next Christendom".[5] According to the author, his fundamental thesis has been widely accepted: "Far from being an export from the capitalist West, a vestige of Euro-American imperialism, Christianity is now rooted in the Third World, and the religion's future lies in the global South" (JENKINS 2007a, xi). Consequently, the centre of gravity (JOHNSON and ROSS 2009) of Christianity is displaced southwards, where it finds itself in frank progress and has already numerically surpassed North Atlantic Christianity. The expression "South" or "Global South", that has become usual in circles of the United Nations (UN) and others, is, as a rule, equivalent to the countries of Africa, Asia, Latin America and Oceania, even when they are situated in the Northern Hemisphere, whereas the countries of Europe and North America are considered as the Global North. Australia, New Zealand and Japan, as well as parts of Eastern Europe (JOHNSON and ROSS 2009, 352),[6] are controversial cases. Previously, one talked economically and politically about the Third World or the developing countries in contrast with the industrialised countries of the First and Second Worlds, in the bipolar world system; today, the criterion is formulated primarily in economic terms and, more neutrally, in political terms.

The numbers are unarguable, but their significance is also limited. Numerically, the Christian part of the world population has remained

---

[5] JENKINS 2007a. This book is the first of a trilogy to which 2006 and 2007c also belong.
[6] The use of the pair of concepts "Global North" and "Global South", however, is not univocal – neither in the different studies on world Christianity nor in the 2009 Atlas itself – since, for instance, Australia, New Zealand and Japan are among the Global North countries, whereas Transuralian Russia is seen, economically, as part of the "South". In this view, India would also be counted among the South, although it is situated in the Northern hemisphere.

practically unchanged in the last one hundred years, i.e. it is around 35% (1910) and 33.2% (2010), respectively (JOHNSON and ROSS 2009, 8f.; SHENK, ed., 2002, xii). However, the religious map has changed considerably. In 1910 more than 80% of Christians lived in Europe and in North America; today these are only 40%. In Africa the proportion of Christians among the population has risen from 9.4% in 1910 to close to 50% today. Two-thirds of all Christians live in the South today. Today more Christians speak Chinese than German.[7] Brazil is the country with the greatest number of Catholics worldwide; at the same time, it is the one that has the greatest number of Pentecostals and, as a whole, the second largest number of Christians worldwide, after the USA (cf. JENKINS 2007a, 104). The largest Anglican Church in the world will soon be domiciled in Nigeria. This confers on it a special position within the Anglican communion, which uses it to affirm a specific position. Its Primate, Archbishop Peter J. Akinola, has become renowned worldwide as a leader of the front against the ordination of homosexuals (JENKINS 2007b, 16). "This is an attack on the Church of God – a Satanic attack on God's Church", said Akinola, when the self-confessed homosexual Jeffrey John was named bishop of Reading.[8] The installation of Gene Robinson as bishop of New Hampshire, in the USA, led the Anglican Church to the edge of a schism, in an internal conflict that is still ongoing. Akinola was the mouthpiece of an assembly of "Anglicans from the South" who, among other things, said the following:

> We reject the expectation that our lives in Christ should conform to the misguided theological, cultural and sociological norms associated with sections of the West [...] The unscriptural [!] innovations of North American and some western provinces on issues of human sexuality undermine the basic message of redemption and the power of the Cross to transform lives. These departures are a symptom of a deeper problem, which is the diminution of the authority of Holy Scripture (quoted in JENKINS 2007a, 238).

---

[7] According to JOHNSON and ROSS 2009, 225, the number of German-speaking Christians is 47,444,000, and of Christians who speak Chinese or Mandarin 88,673,000 (in 2010).

[8] JENKINS 2007a, 237, 236. In response to an urgent request by the Archbishop of Canterbury, John waived the appointment. Available at: http://www.timesonline.co.uk/tol/news/uk/article1148858.ece [accessed May 4, 2011].

This shows that there are quite a few churches of the South that are a stronghold of orthodoxy, which openly challenges the North and does so as it feels very close to the biblical message and the experience of the first congregations. Peter Berger likewise talked about two global religions with huge vitality: conservative Islam and conservative Protestantism (BEYER 1990; COLEMAN 2000, 3), which places both of them automatically in the surroundings of fundamentalism.[9] However, even if this is right as regards the general tendency, it is necessary to look accurately in order to see the considerable differences also among the conservative groups. Worldwide opinion and field polls already performed in the 1960s and 1970s found much greater differences than had been previously presumed: there is no vestige of fundamental unity, for instance, in the concept of church neither in the progressive nor in the conservative view (USTORF 2007, 38; 2010). With our increasing knowledge regarding actually experienced and believed-in Christianity in the different regions of the world, this perception of the huge disparity tends to grow even more.

Thus, this new visibility of the churches of the South in fact is an ambivalent process. On the one hand, it should be welcomed without any restrictions that the Christian mission has abandoned its North-Atlantic centre and that there is no longer a unilateral, paternalistic relationship between "mother-churches" and "daughter-churches". Christians in the Global South for a long time now have become independent in terms of their congregational life, their organisation, their mission, and also their finances. Brazil and South Korea, as well as Nigeria, send missionaries all over the world, thus showing the great vitality and spreading force of their churches, but also their great strategic and financial potentials. The migration churches come to Europe and North America and are partly

---

[9] Obviously, this depends on the definition of fundamentalism. If we define it more along the lines of the *Fundamentals* of 1910-1915, there will be considerable differences between fundamentalists and charismatics, because the former valued orthodoxy, the literal interpretation of the Bible and anti-Liberalism more highly than the direct experience of the Spirit; see COLEMAN 2000, 24f. On the other hand, there is another definition that includes the Pentecostals; thus RIESEBRODT 2001, 52ff., distinguishes a "legalist-literalist" type from a "charismatic" type of fundamentalism (both are characterised, according to RIESEBRODT, by a "mythical regress" and an "ethical-legalist strictness") which he distinguishes from "progressive" religious movements of revitalisation, including liberation theology in Latin America and South Africa and the "red Shi'ism" of Ali Shariati (ibid, 53).

even active in missionary work in these places.[10] Insofar as this is an agency from the so-called "younger churches", often falsely seen as passive or as primarily in need, it is beyond any doubt a positive development. Philip Jenkins rightly says: "If a single lesson emerges from all the recent scholarship on the rising churches, it is that they define themselves according to their own standards, despite all the eager efforts to shape them in the mold of the Old Christendom" (JENKINS 2007a, 25).

On the other hand, however, often the mission from the Global South is no more sensitive to local cultures than the North Atlantic missions proved to be in their time. Moreover, it also involves the attainment of political and economic power. Many people claim that nowadays the field of religion itself has become a disputed and highly competitive market – not only between different religions but also and precisely between movements and denominations of one and the same religion. Prophecies, visions, dreams, healing, and exorcisms are part of the everyday life of many of the new strongly growing churches, which arouses in many people (generally bad) memories of the Middle Ages.[11] It is not by chance that Jenkins' book was described as a "warning" (cf. USTORF 2007, 32).

In more neutral terms, the religious communities and, among them, also the Christian churches, are part of a worldwide community of communication of the kind described by Niklas Luhmann (1971) forty years ago as a world society determined decisively by simultaneous, global communication. Indeed, communication is writ large also in the self-export of churches such as the Neo-Pentecostal IURD: by using the electronic media available, as well as in a visible representation by building temples that can be seen far and wide, and more recently also the reconstruction of the "Temple of Solomon" in supposedly original size and shape (see above, Chapter 3, and below, Chapters 11 and 12). Considering the growing variety and the claims to power of many churches, at the end of his text, Jenkins (2007b, 32) asks: "For anyone accustomed to living in the environment of 'Western Christianity,' the critical question must be to determine what is the authentic religious content, and what is cultural baggage. What, in short, is Christianity, and

---

[10] In Europe their main purpose is to re-Christianise secularised societies, although not very successfully. Their sphere of action is essentially limited to the migration churches; about this, see WÄHRISCH-OBLAU 2009.

[11] "For better or worse, the dominant churches of the near-future could have much in common with those of medieval or early modern European times" (JENKINS 2007b, 19).

what is merely Western?" We might also add: "What is merely Southern?" As to this point, one hopes that the "authentic religious content" is peaceful and cooperative. However, a look at the Bible texts and at history easily shows that this is not self-evident. And the question concerning what is necessarily and universally part of Christianity, and what is not, has moved it since early times and always will, since there are more or less plausible arguments to consider, but with no conclusive answer.

Issues of identity of increasingly globalised religions are central not only to Christianity, although the latter is the focus of my reflections. When Islamic thinkers reflect on Islam in modernity, especially in Western modernity, they are concerned with analogous issues.[12] The known controversies around the need or not for Islamic women to cover their head or wear a burka, as well as around the construction of minarets in Western and Central Europe, are signs of discussions of this kind that are waged by both sides (TANNER, MÜLLER, MATHWIG and LIENEMANN, eds., 2009). Also, in Buddhism, there are controversies regarding identity and contextuality.[13] And religions that so far have had strong ethnic ties are beginning to become universal, such as the African-Brazilian religions, which, according to statistics, today have more white members than black, so that they also need to redefine some aspects (cf. HÖLLINGER 2007, esp. 181).

This is in no way a new question. Ever since the beginning of the history of mission there have been many encounters between cultures and religions, as well as reflections on the issue of identity that became necessary because of those encounters. Christian apologetics sought a dialogue with contemporary philosophy, intending to clarify its compatibility with Christianity, but also the latter's superiority. Similar examples can be found also in the Jewish Diaspora, such as those dealt with in the discussion about a "transpositional hermeneutics" (LANGE and PLEŠE 2014). These questions require theological reflection and

---

[12] See AHMED and DONNAN, eds., 2003; also the reflections in RENZ, GHARAIBEH, MIDDELBECK-VARWICK and UCAR, 2012. I am grateful to Prof. Reinhold Bernhardt (Basel) for the latter reference.
[13] See HEINE and PREBISH, eds., 2003. According to KOSCHORKE 2010, 204, in the 19th century there was a movement labelled "Protestant Buddhism" in Sri Lanka, which was a renewal movement that, for instance, also led to founding Buddhist *Young Men's Associations,* in an analogy to the YMCAs; the same also existed in Hinduism (YMHAs) and in Islam (YMMAs).

particularly systematic theological reflection. Accordingly, recent history is rich in proposals from all over the world aiming at communicating the gospel in a contextualised version. These attempts range from the "Theology of the Pain of God" of the Japanese Kazoh Kitamori (1972/2005), via Kosuke Koyama's (1974/1999) – a Japanese missionary who graduated from Princeton and, at the time, worked among farmers in Thailand – "Water Buffalo Theology" to the "Third Eye Theology" of Choan Seng Song from Taiwan, the "Theology of Liberation" of Gustavo Gutiérrez (1972/1988) and the "Coconut Theology" proposed by Sione Havea (1986). On a humorous note, today we can even find a "Theology out of the [Beer] Barrel" (*Theologie vom Fass*), which is, however, much more modest in its claim and apparently limited to Austria.[14] No matter how eccentric these titles may sound to ears that are not used to them, these were and are serious attempts at translating the gospel into local languages and ideas, in a creative interaction with the respective context. Although these initiatives arose from an assimilation of classical North Atlantic theology, they, at the same time, show a clear delimitation which, in those days, was certainly necessary regarding the theology the authors had learnt in Northern seminaries. What was initially in the foreground was a position that advocated the legitimacy of "local theologies" (ROBERT J. SCHREITER).[15] Once this legitimacy has been basically accepted through an intercultural approach, a constructive critical dialogue, or, as some people now call it, a *polylogue*, can be initiated. With this I reach the topic of the next section: intercultural theology.

---

[14] Available at: http://www.theologievomfass.at [accessed March 29, 2011].

[15] SCHREITER 1985. However, Schreiter precisely refers to a contribution of these theologies to the Christian (ecclesial) tradition, which he sees as "a series of local theologies closely wedded to and responding to different cultural conditions" (93). The understanding of "local" (mistranslated into German in the book as "regional") is based on the Roman Catholic view of the local church. "It takes the dynamic interaction of all three of these roots [sc. feeding the development and growth of a local theology] – Gospel, Church, culture –, with all they entail about identity and change, to have the makings of local theology" (21).

5.2   Intercultural   theology: The   perception   and interpretation of world Christianity

From its inception, missiology has dedicated itself to these processes and their implications. That is why one of its results, somewhat naturally, is an intercultural theology.[16] The section "Religious Studies and Missiology" of the German Scientific Society of Theology and the Administrative Board of the German Society of Missiology formulated a position on this issue in 2005; in 2008, the name of the traditional *Zeitschrift für Mission* [Journal for Mission] was changed to *Interkulturelle Theologie* [Intercultural Theology], although it kept the subtitle *Zeitschrift für Mission*. According to this position,

> [I]ntercultural theology/missiology must be described as a theological discipline that reflects on (1) the relationship between Christianity and non-Christian religions and worldviews and on (2) the relationship between Western Christianity and its non-Western cultural variants (FACHGRUPPE "RELIGIONSWISSENSCHAFT UND MISSIONS-WISSENSCHAFT" 2005, 3).

Additionally, in connection with religious studies, it is "fundamentally relevant for evangelical [*evangelische*] theology *as a whole* within the horizon of global challenges" (ibid, 4). In this way, if I see it correctly, the following points, among others, are made: (1) Christianity recognises itself as polycentric and its many forms of expression have basically the same rights, so that the centre is now occupied by the relationship between theologies in different cultures, and no longer by missionary work of a particular origin. (2) Missiology – qualified as intercultural theology – takes on tasks with a view to theology as a whole; in this way

---

[16] In Germany "intercultural theology" began to appear in the 1970s, explicitly from 1975 onwards, as an anti-hegemonic programme (as opposed to a systematisation) around Walter Hollenweger and Hans Jochen Margull, thus within the framework of a Western European academic missiology. At the University of Heidelberg, Theo Sundermeier wanted to found a Department of Intercultural Theology; for more about this see USTORF 2008; 2011. Furthermore, intensive research has been carried out on hermeneutic issues at Heidelberg, Kampen and Berlin (Sundermeier, Küster, Feldtkeller). Although hermeneutic issues belong to fundamental theology, intercultural theology is permeated by an antidogmatic trait and post-colonial criticism, among others, because systematic (European) theology is perceived as insufficiently sensitive to the phenomenon of World Christianity in its plurality.

it is displaced from its position as an "exotic" discipline to the centre of a scientifically responsible account of faith, a point where it encounters systematic theology. This controversial re-naming or change of emphasis of missiology does not simply represent a change of labels[17] or an improved, apparently more acceptable missionary tactics. It involves, rather, a more profound reflection on the contact between cultures and religions. For this reason, ecumenical theology, theology of religions, and more recent projects, such as comparative theology (see KÜSTER 2011, 131ff.; BERNHARDT and VON STOSCH, eds., 2009), are also part of this context. Intercultural theology claims to be, at least initially, a science of perception that should not be subordinated to normative judgements or tactical intentions, but to a process of understanding.[18] This science has to do mainly with the perception of the existence of autonomous theological approaches in the South. Because of the multiple forms of expression that are often not encoded in writing, this also involves particularly the exchange of experiences, narratives, as well as images and other works of art.[19]

Intercultural theology is thus mainly concerned with a nuanced perception of forms of faith and a reflection on them, of a type that is usually not found in the classical dogmatic textbooks[20] and cannot be seen from a unilaterally negative perspective of mission as associated with colonialism. There was no possibility of recognition due to the lack of a hermeneutics of the "stranger/other". In this situation, the only conceivable modalities of perception were the "noble savage" or the "monsters" which supposedly existed in the New World, a back and forth of the Conquista between the alternatives of paradisiacal exuberance and diabolical threat.[21] The voices of the indigenous peoples and, above all, of the Africans who were transported to South America as slaves, were practically not heard. In Western theology and philosophy, in the

---

[17] KÜSTER 2011, 30, 110, warns about a "label fraud".

[18] See DEHN 2011; KÜSTER 2011, 27ff.; WROGEMANN 2012, esp. 43-159.

[19] See KÜSTER, 1999; SUNDERMEIER 2007; 2010; WEBER 1982; 1984. DE GRUCHY 2008.

[20] Even in more recent introductions in German, the world dimension (including intra-European distinctions) of Christianity is widely ignored. See, for instance, DANZ 2010; first of all, the book refers almost exclusively to Luther and very little to Calvin and Zwingli; secondly, it cites likewise almost exclusively German theology; and, thirdly, it largely dispenses biblical references, central for most Christian theologies. Unfortunately, there is also lack of a programmatic introduction as well as of a conclusion of the same type.

[21] See GREENBLATT 1992; BITTERLI 1993; TODOROV 1999.

meantime, it was customary – with exceptions – to absolutise oneself. Thus, for instance, Hegel assumed that the "temperate climate zones, more precisely ... their northern part", were the "only true stage of world history" (HEGEL 1822/1970, 107). The New World, America, had shown itself to be "physically and spiritually impotent ... and still shows itself to be so" (ibid, 108). Georg Christoph Lichtenberg was also not free of such tendencies: in his satire on Chinese philosophy, he cited a mandarin who had said to his informant, a cultured English butler:

> The only use we make of reason [...] is as though we amalgamate it bit by bit to the body in the form of instinct and artistic leanings, and make of human beings superior animal species, endowed with instinctive arts that still look entirely like supreme reason, but have nothing proper to do with it any more. [...] Now one philosophizes as if one were applying enamel according to recipes. Or, as we have people who play music [*Musikanten*] and no longer have musicians, in the same way we have would-be philosophers [*Philosophanten*] and would-be physicists [*Physikanten*] and no longer genuine philosophers and physicists (LICHTENBERG 1796/1985, 113; cf. WIMMER 2004, 86f.)

Cuban intercultural philosopher Raúl Fornet-Betancourt underscores that the concern of an intercultural philosophy must be that peoples should be able to speak with their own voice.[22] Since the stranger, with whom apparently one had nothing in common, had historically been denied, intercultural dialogue – philosophical circles gathered around the Viennese Franz Martin Wimmer refer to a democratic polylogue[23] – has to involve a "conversion" process, namely, turning to the stranger and

---

[22] "Intercultural philosophy represents an attitude that not only tolerates other ways of thinking, but is also solidary with them. ... Intercultural philosophy considers cultural multiplicity as wealth and advocates the right of peoples to their own culture. Precisely this right is being threatened by globalization". This is found in the ten theses about interculturality as an alternative to globalisation cited by BECKA 2007, 82.

[23] The basic rule is: "Do not consider well-grounded a philosophical thesis which was elaborated only with the participation of people belonging to a single cultural tradition" (WIMMER 2004, 142). Universality is expressed as "tentative centrism" (in contrast with expanding, integrating and separative centrism, ibid., 15-17), i.e. it seeks to accomplish in common dialogue the task of reaching universal validity. Wimmer, however, considers that an inter-religious polylogue is impossible, because "religious arguments ... must be seen as procedures for persuasion and seduction" (WIMMER 2003, 89); cf. GMAINER-PRANZL 2010.

adopting a self-critical and self-transforming attitude.[24] Also, in the context of historical research, the pervasive Eurocentrism is being surpassed today by a new comprehension of "global history" (e.g. OSTERHAMMEL 2001; 2009). In church history the importance of extra-European Christianity is still small, but is being increasingly recognised (cf. KOSCHORKE 2009; 2010).

Therefore, interculturality is, first of all, a questioning of all certainties, the detection of diversities, resistances, and peculiarities.[25] Boaventura de Souza Santos talks of a "diatopical hermeneutics",[26] which tries to translate between the different cultural *topoi* in the multicultural contact zones, but the *topoi* must first be obtained through argumentation in dialogue. According to him, this involves "establishing cognitive justice based on epistemological imagination" (DE SOUZA SANTOS s.d.). Taking as his point of departure Leibniz's critique of a "lazy reason",[27] De Souza Santos demands that the experiences and expressions of groups so far ignored and silenced be included – e.g. indigenous groups and groups in a lower social position – on the way to a "cosmopolitan reason" that is capable of welcoming such experiences. This is, undeniably, the point of departure of any intercultural theology,

---

[24] Thus, for instance, FORNET-BETANCOURT 1997, 119, quoted by WIMMER 2004, 133f.; therefore, this involves a "conversion process" in order "to found a new dynamics of universal totalization with the other, based on mutual recognition, respect and solidarity".

[25] See also HOCK 2011, 108ff., who proposes, along this line, together with others, an approach based mainly on the hermeneutics of difference. However, on doing so, some catholic, uniting elements are underemphasised.

[26] This is also found in PANIKKAR 1979; 1998; see VON SINNER 2003, 256-258; 2016; NITSCHE 2008, 117-119. However, nowhere, not even in Panikkar, is the concept explained more precisely; it is rather explained indirectly through other concepts of Panikkar.

[27] LEIBNIZ 1996, 19, 21: "But when the good or the evil is remote and uncertain and the remedy painful or little to our taste, the lazy reason [*raison paresseuse*] seems to us to be valid [...] one will employ the lazy reason, derived from the idea of inevitable fate, to relieve oneself of the need to reason properly" [English version taken from http://www.gutenberg.org/files/17147/17147-h/17147-h.htm, accessed August 12, 2021]. DE SOUZA SANTOS (s.d.) further distinguishes the laziness of reason by referring to an "impotent" reason (surrendered to outer determination), "arrogant" reason (unconditionally free, without one being able to indicate what this freedom really is), "metonymic" reason (there is only one form of rationality to which the others at most mean raw material), and "pro-leptic" reason (the future is already known as progress of the present); this indolence either considers dialogue as superfluous or reason as already sufficiently (and unilaterally) defined.

and intercultural understanding necessarily presupposes "hermeneutical fairness".[28]

It is clear that, in this perception, aspects such as ambiguity, fluidity, hybridism, creolisation, syncretism, and everything that is designated by similar terms, take on an important role, because it aims at avoiding any form of hegemonisation.[29] However, what is often not clear is how to analytically use these – in heuristic terms, initially directly plausible – concepts in such a way that they can account for the resulting identities and also the influences preserved in them.[30] On a theological level, the intention is to ask about the coherence and identity of Christianity, without these having to be understood as a new *theologia perennis* or metatheology. The intention is, rather, taking as point of departure the multiple forms of manifestation of Christianity and their explicit or implicit theologies, to ask about the elements and criteria of what is Christian. Now, this is a genuine task of systematic theology, which I shall now discuss.

5.3 Intercultural theology and systematic theology

In 1987, the Swiss theologian Walter J. Hollenweger gave a lecture on intercultural theology as a visiting professor in Basel (during my first semester of studies). Pentecostal emotionality, Reformed theology, intercultural experience, and his challenging tone created a mixture that

---

[28] See HOLENSTEIN 1998, esp. 288-290, where he talks of *aequitas hermeneutica*, of hermeneutic equity or fairness; see also WIMMER 2004, 147-150.

[29] In my view, the emphasis precisely on those aspects that are now already familiar to German scientific debate creates a bridge to the current German Systematic Theology, which becomes visible, for instance, in the rehabilitation of liberal theology; see, e.g. KÜSTER 2011, 13, with his emphasis on the "spirit of liberty" and his profession of (radicalised) Enlightenment. See also HOCK 2011, 150, who likewise professes Enlightenment and the acknowledged scientific discourses, but at the same time warns against a "modernist hegemonic claim" of a "merely European modernity", a "positivistic reductionism" and "post-modern arbitrariness". USTORF 2010, 68, explicitly identifies the "inconclusiveness" and "provisionality" of each variant of Christianity and the credibility of faith only against the background of its respective "cultural topography" in an analogy between Christians of the South and the North and claims that the latter "dare to put one foot into the biblical world and the other into scientific culture".

[30] NEHRING 2010, esp. 184ff., is among those who undertake a problematisation of the identity discourse on this side of and beyond the traditional mission theology, as well as in post-colonialist discourses.

fascinated not only me, who in those days was a provincial inhabitant of Basel. Although in the three volumes of his *Intercultural Theology* there are several aspects of systematic theology, in itself it claims that it is not "an elaborated Systematic Theology", but a discussion of topics directly connected to the author's life experience.[31] According to Hollenweger, current theology can only be done as an intercultural theology which is anchored in a given culture, but is aimed at universality – thus without having an absolutisation in mind.

Four years later, in the context of the debates about the First Gulf War, theologian Friedrich Wilhelm Graf of Munich claimed, as a counterpoint, the "fundamental right to provinciality". According to Graf (1991, 172), regarding this aspect, "the most important achievement of intercultural theology is precisely to accept its own particularity and, on the solid ground of this self-delimitation, to enable for dialogue with others". In those days he still presupposed a broadly homogeneous German society, a perception that twenty years later must be surpassed. The more recent German Protestant theology has discussed the cultural anchoring of Christianity – let us say, its contextuality – with growing seriousness, casting more frequent looks at the "lived religion" and at the linguistic processes of interpretation.[32] For many German theologians, the understanding of the current Christian religion as a religion that takes experience as its point of reference has become a central point. In this respect it is generally seen as a religion of interiority, with an individual nature, which appeals to Schleiermacher and 19th century liberal theology. Such an understanding deliberately moves away from theology

---

[31] "For this reason, these three volumes of *Intercultural Theology* are not an elaborated systematic theology, but a theological work that discusses – certainly systematically but not completely – the topics about which I was able to gather some life experience"; HOLLENWEGER 1988, 18.

[32] See, for instance, LAUSTER 2005. Looking at the future, Lauster still refers to ecumenical and inter-religious hermeneutics (185); here recognition of "coherence and power of the other system of interpretation" does not occur as "hermeneutics of trust" because the latter is excessively subject to "good will moods"; it should occur as "cognitive obligation" (187). As can be assumed, the background of this thinking consists in anchoring such a hermeneutics exclusively in the academy, as well as a restriction to confessions and religions with explicit self-comprehension, recorded in writing, which is unlikely to be up to the worldwide pluralisation and transformation of Christianity described above (not to mention other religions).

and Karl Barth's negative concept of religion.[33] It is interesting that this "antitotalitarian" Schleiermacher renaissance, taking as reference freedom and the subject, coincides with a tendency to highlight freedom and subjectivity which is also present in other contexts. However, this position is quite often associated with a tendency towards the essentialisation of culture and context. In Hans-Peter Großhans' view, both are at risk of a "regressive acceptance of given traditions, cultures or contexts, insofar as from the reference without content to God as the total horizon of one's own reality of life it is no longer possible to derive truth claims that might challenge the given reality".[34]

Wilfried Härle characterises the "current life world as the context of dogmatics" and takes the "cultural sphere" – which in his case is the "Federal Republic of Germany within the ensemble of Central and Western European societies" – as his point of departure. He connects this to the respect for the fact that "other theologies arise under other contextual conditions and must subsist under these conditions", which, in fact, is self-relativising, but naturally also suggests that there are fundamental differences that do not concern the others.[35] However,

---

[33] In this case theological dogmatics is converted into a "theory of a religion that is tasked with spelling out religion by means of science". It describes in a reflective way "faith as the event in which human beings come to understand themselves as a finite beings" (DANZ 2010, 22f.). The radical change of position of the former Vienna systematic theologian Falk Wagner (1939-1998) – who went from a speculative theology on the lines of Hegel through an "empirical-historical turn" to a theory of Christianity guided by sociology of religion – can be seen as an exemplary case of this recontextualisation of German theology in modernity; see U. BARTH 2003, 173.

[34] GROßHANS 2011, 29. Großhans identifies a potential connection between Schleiermacher "and most of the current ecumenical and intercultural theologies" (29, footnote 55). For Großhans, however, the main problem consists of neglecting reason as a universal practice of communication over against the "multiple forms of estheticizing (re) dramatization of the Holy" (30), rather than, for instance, of the intersubjective identity formations with their religious and social dimensions. About these, see, from a sociological, but theologically well informed perspective, e.g. SCHÄFER 2005.

[35] HÄRLE 1995, 178. A similar argument can be found, to my surprise, also in HOCK 2011: in his view, the discourse on mission and dialogue can be "placed only [sic] within a given context". "In our case this can only be the Western one, possibly even only the (Central)-European, in any case that of late Modernity, with an academic orientation, that understands itself – sensitized and inspired by post-Colonialist debates – as one among many others. Only with this presupposition our theological reflection can prove to be intercultural (and ecumenical) since only thus does it become aware of its 'provinciality'" (98). The surprising fact in all of this is not contextualisation as such –

precisely this should be questioned in the light of the "one Gospel", but also of globalisation, migration, and cultural exchange. Fundamental questions asked of Christianity arise in other contexts too and should also be considered at the transcontextual level.[36]

At least some standard reference works acknowledge that the worldwide presence and multiplicity of theologies should not be neglected. The *Theologische Realenzyklopädie* (TRE) does not contain an entry about intercultural theology, but one about "missiology".[37] In the latter, intercultural problems gain expression, but in 1994 they were not yet discussed under this name. Within the entry on "theology", published eight years later, the TRE refers to "theology in the emerging world society", referring to feminist theology, Liberation Theology, inculturation theology and theology of religions (HEINE, BRANDT, BLASER and LIPNER 2002). The contribution on systematic theology, however, does not discuss this aspect (STOCK 2002). Christoph Schwöbel's entry on "Systematic Theology" in the 4th edition of *Die Religion in Geschichte und Gegenwart* (RGG) also deals only indirectly with the issue that is our focus here, by introducing among the criteria of the historical-hermeneutical aspect of forming a theological-systematic judgment their "adequacy to the respective situation", and he immediately also presupposes that "from its inception Christian faith [...] raises a claim to truth that applies to all periods, as well as in each context and, thus, also to the respective present moment", and that this "claim to the transcontextual truth of the Christian faith" constitutes precisely "the

---

which is completely unquestionable – but the "only", that is also capable of reinforcing provinciality.

[36] The issue of the contemporary mediation of the gospel is centrally important for JOEST. However, he only discusses intercultural problems peripherally: "Indeed, this issue [i.e. the identity and relevance of the word of God] concerns not only the temporal sequence of different periods, but also the fact that different cultural spheres exist side by side. Also here stepping into another sphere requires a 'translation' of the one message of Christ into a form that will touch the specific conditions of life and comprehension of this sphere. This is a problem that is now virulent for the Christian mission and in the relationship between 'young' churches and the European type of theological and ecclesial tradition"; JOEST 1989, 90.

[37] USTORF 1994. Thus, missiology seeks to accomplish a "universal theological task" insofar as it deals with the "movement and reception of the Christian message in the cultures of humankind". "Like theology in general, missiology is particularly an action connected to the Church, which responds based on faith and does not subject the truth, but rather the search for truth to scientific rules" (89).

foundation for its respective contextual relevance" (2004, [p.] 2016). He deals more extensively with this aspect in the entry on "theology", where he assumes all theology is contextual (2005, 297). According to Schwöbel (2005, 198), "'contextual' theologies [...] were conceived as theologies of local communities".

> However, in the wake of growing globalization it is also necessary to think critically about this concentration on the local community, because the communication of the Gospel at a local level also takes place within the horizon of a global mission (see Matthew 28:19f.) and the forms of mediation between locality and globality are especially important for the communication of the message of the Gospel. The contextually defined theological identity must prove itself in the local, regional, national and global context as regards the possibilities of communication and interaction inaugurated by it (ibid, 300).

As Hans Waldenfels also emphasises in his contextual fundamental theology, contextuality is not a particular form of theology, but a "fundamental task of theology" (2005, 21), and in this sense, also a principle of its (self) criticism and (self) restriction. The "question about a comprehensive communication, communicability and understanding" is always connected to it, and in it also a new raising of the question about truth (2005, 23).

As I understand it, systematic theology is a methodologically founded critical exposition and examination of the faith convictions of a given religion, its ethics, its myths, rites and practices in relation to its binding texts and the challenges of the present time.[38] This definition should, basically, be accessible also to other religions.[39] Additionally,

---

[38] Compare also the definition by LIENEMANN (2010, 15): "'Theology' to me is the systematic exposition and examination of the faith convictions that are determining for the adherents of a religion, as well as of their faith, its origins, contents and goals, the binding texts and doctrinal statements, the common rites and practices, as well as of the notions and obligations that guide the action of the respective community. This form of organized reflection, often scholastically professional, serves at the same time for the theoretical and practical formation and assurance of the religious identity of the respective community, as well as of its members".

[39] A formally neutral concept of theology of the type suggested by Lienemann appears to be compatible also with the self-comprehension of other religions. There is, for instance, a master's course on "Islamic Theology" at the University of Münster, in which, among other things, the following is recorded: "Islamic theology deals with the foundations of religion, on which also Islamic law is based. The purpose of this module is to convey to students the fundamental issues and viewpoints of Islamic theology, as

Christian theology is characterised by its relationship with ecclesial practices; in the context of a public theology it also addresses society. Its intention, in all of this, is to adequately express God in life. According to Schwöbel (2004, [p.] 2011), the "task of Systematic Theology is to spell out in an organized manner the understanding of reality of the Christian faith considering the certainty about truth contained in it and the guidance of action that closely linked to it". Indeed, there is access to this truth only in a fragmentary manner through experience and language, but these never stop asking about the truth that is believed in. In this sense, Christian theology remains *fides quaerens intellectum*.[40] Now, if one says, as Volker Küster does, that truth "can always only be experienced in context" (2001, 198; 2011, 85), this is correct, but not yet the end of the debate. Insofar as contextual theology is Christian theology, it is not limited to a given concrete context. "Contextual Christian theologies are linked to each other at least *intentionally* by faith in Christ, the revelation of the triune God" (VON SINNER 2003, 43). Through their origin and their claim, they participate in the catholicity of faith and give their contribution to the global discourse about their content. Particularly in the theology of liberation, it has always been clear that the demand for

---

they are handled in systematic theology (*kalam*), in philosophy (*hikma*), in Islamic gnosis (*irfan*) and in expressions of a fundamentalist nature (*salafiyya*). [...] The areas that constitute the core of Islamic theology (gnosiology, unity of God, justice of God and the problems of theodicy, the doctrine of God's judgment and the hereafter, prophetism and the doctrine of the imamate) are discussed, taking into account the opinions of all theological schools, philosophers, and gnostics. The foundations of the respective viewpoints are presented and analyzed. [...] The purpose is to learn how to understand and convey historical and modern theological positions and contents, to be able to take a critical position regarding current developments and also to participate actively in the dialogue of religions". Cited according to the information found on the website's homepage at http://www.uni-muenster.de/ArabistikIslam/Studieren/MA/it.html [accessed March 25, 2011].

[40] KARL BARTH (1931/1981, 25f.) always pointed out this circular structure clearly, as for instance in his book about Anselm: "The person who asks about Christian knowledge asks – based on the presupposition that at no time is questioned, namely, that it is as they believe it in Christian terms – to what extent this is so. Not in a different way, and not asking about anything else!" However, Barth did not deny that this presupposition may very well or repeatedly be questioned by human beings. The presupposition is not a human hypothesis, but God's faithfulness and constancy – completely unlikely from the human point of view – which are the foundation that enables the human question about God. – I owe this reference to Wolfgang Lienemann who contributed very stimulating reflections to this section.

"the liberation of theology" (SEGUNDO 1976) always refers to theology in general and not only to Uruguayan or Latin American theology. Correspondingly, it had a verifiably worldwide repercussion by exerting great influence on black theology in South Africa under the apartheid, on *Minjung* theology in South Korea during the military dictatorship, and on *Dalit* theology in India under the caste system, as well as on feminist theology and public theology in the North and the South.[41] However, at the same time, this theology must expose itself to the questions that come from other approaches, both in its own context and in other contexts by allowing its understanding both of the Bible and tradition as well as of the context to be tested. The look beyond its four walls occurs not only because of curiosity about what is exotic (although this too is in no way forbidden), but because the experience and formulation of the Christian faith by others can question, challenge, enrich, and also confirm one's own Christian existence and theology. All of this, however, is only possible when Christians are prepared to render accounts mutually of their positions and their foundations. From this, a constructive, i.e. intercultural critical dialogue, may and should emerge.

In this sense, I conclude by examining the initial issue of this contribution: intercultural theology as a challenge to systematic theology.

5.4 Intercultural theology as a challenge to systematic theology

The previous reflections have shown that theology, and particularly also systematic theology, must be done in an intensely contextualised manner and that, at the same time, the worldwide perspective cannot be renounced. This is corroborated, first of all, *in pragmatic terms* by the present interconnection in a worldwide, transnational network, also of the Christian churches and movements, by the migration of Christians from other quadrants of the globe to the Global North and the challenging of universal certainties by the growing religious pluralism both within and outside of Christianity. In this situation, an urgent need arises to show a profile of one's own[42] and even to promote a certain competition which, in ideal terms, occurs in dialogue with other traditions and one's own

---

[41] Cf. BRANDT 2002, 310f.: from "prophetic" to "planetary" theology.
[42] See about this, for instance, K. BARTH 2008, with a view to the world religions.

tradition and ends in a modest positioning of one's own with a disposition to learn, but to also provide information about oneself.

Ethically, this question involves interaction with other people who understand and experience the same faith in another way, or who have another or no faith, for which it is essential to have mutual trust, knowledge, comprehension, and understanding. Since the forms of faith most distant from the traditional churches of the North are experienced by migrants who are mostly in a worse social situation, this point is particularly important.[43] Furthermore, it also involves considering the possibility of formulating common positions about urgent ethical issues concerning human sexuality, family life, bioethics, social justice, etc.

Epistemologically, one's own theological views are challenged insofar as one's own identity is questioned or even brought to awareness precisely in the encounter with the other. This also brings about questions about one's own rationality and the other's rationality, about the character of scientific theology in its relationship with the academy as well as with society and the church, about the significance of individual and collective experience, the analysis of the respective life world each in its relationship with the explanation of the faith, etc.

Theologically, this question involves the catholicity of Christianity. Since its inception – as shown by the Pentecostal speaking in "other tongues" (Acts 2:4), so that "each heard them speak in their own language" (Acts 2:6), and by the so-called Council of Apostles in Jerusalem, as well as the subsequent dissemination of mission – the act of crossing borders has always been a central characteristic of catholicity. Hence, the need arose to translate the Christian story, its ethos, and its rite into various languages and cultures, just as the content of the faith also had to be repeatedly normatively defined in synodical resolutions and confessions. This led to episcopal and synodal structures and to the formation of the Biblical canon. Only in this way was it possible to continue to live out the identity in diversity and to make it publicly visible. It goes without saying that, due to the pluralisation and transformation of world Christianity, this definition of identity is always precarious; however, this does not make it superfluous.

Thus, the demand for interculturality in university teaching and research has mostly not yet been fulfilled in the sphere of theology in the

---

[43] See HOCK 2011, 121-124, about justice.

German language. I hope to have presented convincing arguments to show that this situation should change.

Chapter 6

Theology in Dialogue with the New Worlds[*]

Dietrich Ritschl, born in 1929 in Basel, Switzerland, to a family originally established in Bohemia and expelled from there, spent many of the years of his life and work in the New Worlds of North America, Australia and New Zealand, years that marked him as human being, thinker and teacher, but also as a political contemporary. From this emerged, among others, a beautiful little book with reports and analyses from America and Australasia under the title *Theology in the New Worlds*, with which he sought to advance "the understanding of theological work in English-speaking countries" on the continent (RITSCHL 1981, 7). Consultations, lectures, and varied contacts also took Ritschl (2017, 46) to other new worlds, such as Eastern Europe (former Czechoslovakia, the Soviet Union), South America (Brazil, Mexico), Africa (Cameroon), Asia (India, Sri Lanka, Taiwan, China, South Korea) and Oceania (Fiji). Some of these new worlds – in fact old and even very old, yet indeed new for the so-called discoverers of the beginning of the Modern Era, for Western Europe and for Ritschl himself – became very familiar to him, while others remained strange, despite all the interest. While the relationship between Jews and Christians became for him the ecumenical theme *par excellence*, the semiotic systems of other religions, especially from Asia, seemed so different from Christianity that, except in the context of personal contacts and in ethical matters, he saw few possibilities of approximation between them.[1] This, however, did not prevent him from admiring the fact and the way in which some of his students advanced, at this point, more than he could do himself.

---

[*] Originally presented at the academic celebration in honour of Dietrich Ritschl in the Old Auditorium of the University of Heidelberg on January 18, 2019. A publication of the German text is underway with Evangelische Verlagsanstalt Leipzig in the series *Beiheft zur Ökumenischen Rundschau,* edited by Martin Hailer and Friederike Nüssel. A Portuguese version, translated by Luís Marcos Sander, was published as "Teologia em Diálogo com os Novos Mundos: Contribuições ecumênicas de Dietrich Ritschl (1929-2018)", in *FACES* 2/2 (2021), 89-102. Translated from the Portuguese into English by Alexander Busch and revised by the author.
[1] "In the last analysis, Christians, along with Jews, live in an entirely different semiotic system" (RITSCHL 2003, 27).

The fate of many ecumenists is to be in many places at the same time, but not to be at home anywhere. In such a situation, one can easily end up being "on the fence". Dietrich Ritschl was able to understand breadth and migration not as a problem, but as enrichment. On his way into the New and Old Worlds, he created a huge network of contacts and friendships, many of which he maintained and cultivated over many decades. Nevertheless, he was constantly returning to his home in Reigoldswil, where proximity and distance came and went without a problem. His theology is not conceivable without this constant dialogue, which included not only an objective interest, but always and chiefly a personal interest in the dialogue partner. Even where he had reservations, he got involved in other positions and became, motivated by his interest in people in their concrete life circumstances, a true *pontifex*, a bridge builder between people, contexts, confessions or denominations, between new and old worlds.

Ritschl was able to connect people and integrate aspects that for many other people, perhaps for most, were irreconcilable. He was able to deal both with his feudal, military and honourable academic heritage and the centenary values of the Order of St. John[2], to which he belonged as a knight of justice, as well as to participate in a march on the streets for the civil rights of blacks in the USA; he treated people on the margins of society in the same way as notable people; he could learn from Barth without becoming a Barthian. He told the following about his childhood: "My family was full of university professors. When I was young, I thought that apart from the milkman and our neighbour [...], all the men in the world were university professors ..." At the same time, however, he learnt from his father Hans, who was a professor of economics in Basel, that educated people only pushed "things back and forth in a new way, organized them in another way and occasionally had original ideas". Also, in the academic field, "fairness and courage to make exceptions [...] [were] more important [...] than the paragraphs of the regulations" (RITSCHL 1998, 5). Indeed, he would later suffer from the fact that these paragraphs were able to prevent creative solutions in an ecumenical open attitude. Ritschl would have felt it to be almost like martyrdom if he had been assigned to implement the Bologna Process of reform in higher education – he managed to escape this danger by retiring at the right time.

---

[2] See https://www.johanniter.de/johanniterorden/ [accessed June 28, 2021].

Also on the side of his wife, Rosemarie Courvoisier (1926-2014), raised in Potsdam, there were university professors. With her, he shared more than 60 years of married life, but above all, love. In the last years of her life, after she suffered a stroke, he took care of "Billy", as he called her, in a moving way. He used to say that nursing was the last profession he was learning. Because of this responsibility, he gave up, to a large extent, writing theological texts. For Dietrich, life, love and people came before all erudite words and voluminous books. Already in his childhood he had a daily co-responsibility to take care of his younger brother, who had been born with a severe heart disease. Later, as a psychotherapist, he accompanied many people in their suffering and healing process. At the same time, all these engagements and experiences were fundamental for theological reflection, building up his thinking and shaping him as a person.

In the years he spent in the USA, he was mainly confronted with the Death of God Theology and Process Theology. In this context, the Anglican theologian Paul van Buren (1924-1998) became a lifelong dialogue partner, especially, to an increasing degree, in matters concerning Judeo-Christian ecumenism. In addition to the theological debate, the concrete involvement in the civil rights movement on behalf of black Americans in the USA, for which students and teachers, as well as pastors and rabbis, demonstrated on the streets, was an important attestation and, at the same time, a task for theology. Ritschl maintained a – genuinely critical – dialogue with Martin Luther King, Jr. (1929-1968) and wrote texts intended to explain to the European public what was at stake behind the demonstrations.[3] In 1969, he became professor at Union Theological Seminary in New York along with black liberation theologian James Cone. Like Ritschl, Cone also passed away in 2018; he too deserves an honourable remembrance.

In his contribution to the collection *How Karl Barth Changed My Mind*, he wrote, "In one of the last conversations I had with Karl Barth, I told him that my ambition was to be a good player in the orchestra of theologians. He quite strongly disagreed and smilingly admonished me to play a solo instrument. I think now, as I did then, that the time for this is over" (RITSCHL 1986b, 91). Theology is conversation, dialogue, and,

---

[3] RITSCHL 1986a, 316-33 (on Martin Luther King, Jr.); 1962. As RITSCHL (2017, 2) notes in his bibliography, it was only later that the word "negro" was used sarcastically, like "nigger".

moreover, as we shall see, also play. This play took place, for example, in the ecumenical dialogues of the Faith and Order Commission of the WCC – he had an important participation in the studies on the apostolicity of the faith and the church and on the *Filioque* – where he made music not only in the metaphorical sense, but also real with other people and thinkers very different from him, such as the Presbyterian liberation theologian Rubem Alves, his schoolmate and ecumenist Lukas Vischer of the Reformed Church, and the orthodox bishop Michael of Leningrad (as the city was known at that time).[4] I can imagine that, even with a common score, the different musicalities sounded clearly and did not prevent, but rather enriched the joint musical experience.

Ritschl was a *sui generis* personality in the academy, particularly in Germany. For me and many other people who knew him as a teacher – in my case, this happened in the early 1990s in Heidelberg – his way of approaching topics was like the first drops of rain falling on dry ground. Many of us were hungry for new worlds, new horizons, and new approaches that did not reject or neglect tradition, but managed to move beyond it. We longed for a convincing link between theory and practice. In those years, we asked, during a very controversial intensive seminar in Heidelberg, about God and the world, power and politics, the meaning of the 500 years of the so-called Columbus discoveries. Dietrich questioned some of our radicalities and was nowhere near convinced of everything; still, he supported us as a teacher, father-like friend, and dean. He always had great interest and immense respect for students, was attentive, had a sense of humour and was captivating. While teaching he was refreshingly sincere, admitting many peculiarities and absurdities of the academic environment and even criticising it, with a touching ability to self-irony. He was refreshingly accessible and, at the same time, inspired great respect for his comprehensive knowledge and his competence in leading discussions. He succeeded to draw on both experience and knowledge. Ritschl managed – and in what follows I will explore this a little deeper – to connect three dimensions whose connection is quite clear and, even so, anything but obvious. I describe the first dimension with the term *loyalty*: the insertion in the "megastory", as he called it, the trust in *Christus praesens*, the being rooted in the church, the primacy of doxology and prayer over rationality (6.1). But – and this is the second

---

[4] RITSCHL 2003, p. 11; the information about Rubem Alves was given to me by Dietrich Ritschl on a visit to Reigoldswil.

dimension – he would not give up rationality, but make it part of the play for critical analysis – guided by philosophy and rooted in the history of theology, of our theological discourse to unfold the logic of theology. In this context, then, theology could be a "theologia ludens", a playful theology. Therefore, I describe this dimension with the word *play* (6.2). Finally, I describe the third dimension with the term *verification* [*Bewährung*]: theology is verified in the ecumene of the world and in the practice of the church (6.3).

6.1 Loyalty

Dietrich Ritschl was always a teacher, but also a pastor in everything he did. In his self-presentation as a systematic theologian, he reports that, at the end of his study period, he had a clear desire: "I really wanted to become a pastor. In the pastorate my theology could be confirmed – or else it was worthless. I realized for the first time that the church was synonymous with the case of emergency, but that theology was a play, a beautiful and serious play" (RITSCHL 1998, 9). For him, as he writes in another of his publications, the church was "the great discovery", distinct as an assembled congregation, but also from the very beginning and specifically as an "ecumenical reality that encompasses the whole world" (RITSCHL 2003, 2). Thus, he was initially a candidate for the pastorate in the canton of Basel-countryside (*Baselland*), later a pastor among German migrants in Scotland, who, like himself, were forced to live in very precarious conditions. Among these people were German wives of Scottish soldiers – so-called "war brides" – nurses, students, and many former prisoners of war. There Ritschl built the church in both a metaphorical and literal sense: he built, with his own hands, the pulpit from of an old dance school turned into a church in Edinburgh. There, being the pastor, teaching theology and caring for the souls became indissolubly associated. He was a husband and father of four children, and in the evening hours he wrote his doctoral thesis in patristic theology, *The Concept of Union with Christ in the Early Catholic Church* (1957). He became increasingly interested in narratives or, as he preferred to say, *stories* – the *stories* of the Bible, but also, and especially, the *stories* of the people. The *stories* of people who believe are part of a current with innumerable others, not because they would swim uncritically with the current, but indeed because they do not remain outside, but stand in the middle of God's great *story* with Israel, Jesus, and the church.[5] For Ritschl, this always needs to be taken into consideration by theology, despite all the necessary criticism of the church – and Ritschl expressed this criticism constantly, but more in the form of a question than an accusation. In this sense, for Ritschl, the love for the church is – just like the church itself – always conceived and practiced ecumenically. Consequently, such ecumenical love manages, based on an anticipated trust, to lead to "curiosity and patience", which, as he writes in his introduction to ecumenical theology, "make it possible to take seriously also issues and questions that are important to other people, even if for the moment they do not yet seem relevant for me. [...] The old Latin maxim of ecumenical work convincingly expresses this: '*In necessariis unitas – in dubiis libertas – in omnibus caritas*'. 'In omnibus caritas' – this means, for Christian people in the tradition of the Reformation, to seriously consider typically Catholic or Orthodox theological concepts, including the sacramental, and the curiosity and deep desire to understand what the veneration of Mary and the saints means for other believers".[6] He also said that "with the keyword 'love for the church' I would like to refer [...] to the experience that the encounter with the stranger, with the other, does not consist only of empathy, of placing oneself within the conditions of the other, but, primarily, of *joint participation* in a *third* element, the Bible's message, faith, and also the church" (RITSCHL 1994, 51, italics in original). This is not about an update of ancient biblical texts for our time, but to allow God to contemplate and interpret our world, by considering and clarifying our current seeking of and discourse about God in the light of Scripture and tradition. To believe is to live in God's perspective (RITSCHL 2008, 11). He further writes that "God interprets history, and does not cause it" (ibid, 34). His interest, inspired mainly by the Torah and the Old Testament prophets, was precisely to investigate the basic features of God's "counter-project" for our world (ibid, 68-74).

After 20 years of meeting and discussing with Christian people from the New Worlds, especially in the so-called Global South, I can say that this way of thinking, and especially Ritschl's attitude, are of enormous importance. In many places, the basic attitude of the church

---

[5] See the Introduction in BERNHARDT, HAILER, VON KLOEDEN and LINK-WIECZOREK, eds., 1994, 17.

[6] RITSCHL 1994, 50. This maxim he has also placed at the beginning of a previous text: 1986c.

unfortunately is neither guided by mutual trust nor interest and cooperation, but intense competition. God is too easily co-opted for self-interest, also and precisely for political purposes – not even a shadow of a "counter-project" or prophetic criticism. Unfortunately, in Brazil, my homeland by choice, one can currently clearly see where opportunistic political alliances with religious overtones can take us.

I would like to include yet another recurring metaphor in Ritschl: "to inhabit" the *stories* of life and the Bible. The concept of *story* was elaborated by Ritschl in dialogue with exegetes, mainly from the Old Testament, such as James Barr (1924-2006), and also in dialogue with analytical psychotherapy. *Stories* are the raw material from which theology is conceived – but not simply in a cold and detached way (RITSCHL and JONES 1976). Thus, he states: "I intend to inhabit the *stories* of the Bible and use the semiotic systems, the linguistic buildings of the church, fashioned by its intellectuals and also by simple believers to guide my life by *stories* and, ultimately, by what they stand for. From this perspective, theology is also more like a play, a serious and beautiful play, which must be verified by its guiding power, while worship and soul healing, preaching and ethics are the case of emergency that needs this orientation" (RITSCHL 2003, 19). In addition to the intellectual element, the "complex system" in theology also includes "internal images, piety, solidarity, loyalty and [...] trust": "Sometimes I dream of an ecumenical theology and cooperation in which not only God and Jesus Christ are spoken about, but in which the work of God in the Spirit is considered possible and taken seriously" (ibid, 5). He dedicated several lectures, later turned into a book, to the theory and concretisation of ecumenical theology under the keyword "hermeneutics of trust". In this context, trust means, above all, trust in the presence of Christ, precisely in a confessional tradition or denomination that is not familiar to us. Since the 1960s Ritschl advocates the position, developed in detail in his book *Memory and Hope*, that the theological problem itself is not the tension between the historical Jesus and the Resurrected, the Christ of faith, but the tension between the historical-paschal Jesus and the *"Christus praesens"*, "as God who calls and the human being who answers in a vicarious role" (RITSCHL 1998, 14). For the lives of the faithful and the church, it is this latter who is decisive, in whom they can trust.

For Ritschl, prayer, the ascriptive talk *to* God, always precedes the descriptive speech *about* God. Theology is second order language, a subordinate linguistic form, albeit in no way without importance.

Theology has a "doxological border" always focused on the triune God. "Doxology has in itself the strength to verify the statements of faith upon which theology reflects analytically" (ibid, 14). Let's move on to the next section: *play.*

6.2 Play

If, therefore, trust in the *Christus praesens*, loyalty to him and finding oneself within the *stories* of life and the Bible are the starting point, one must now ask how one can talk about this in a comprehensible way. On this point Ritschl could be very clear: for him, one of the biggest problems was fundamentalism, which he many times encountered, not least in the New Worlds. Difficult and even unbearable for him was a theological language that starts from God's direct interventions, or even attributes to God's action – hatred, destruction, discrimination, murder, and other terrible things. In an interview, he expressed the following idea: "The very short proposition that God would have guided and done all this is, in my opinion, heretical" (quoted in MÜLLER 2001, 189). Theology must counter this absurdity through critical-constructive reflection. Theology searches for the truth, but is, at the same time, aware that access to the truth is precarious. For Ritschl, the truth lies behind language, but we encounter it in language. In this sense, language, including the language of the believers, is guided pre-linguistically by what he called "implicit axioms" (cf. RITSCHL 2008, 75-172). These axioms work implicitly, but they can be formulated, as has often happened in ecumenical councils. Ritschl considered the election of Israel and its expansion to the church, one of the most tremendous theological propositions, but also one of the most irritating that could be articulated (quoted in MÜLLER 2001, 187). Therefore, although implicit axioms can be formulated, they cannot become main premises stated once and for all, from which one could then make deductions in a rigorous and unequivocal manner. It is obvious that different traditions and confessional stands in the ecumenical universe come to very different conceptions, although they share the same premises. As an Orthodox bishop said in an ecumenical dialogue: "Christians are united around the Bible – as long as it remains closed". As soon as it is opened and read, disagreements become legion.

    For Ritschl, the logic of theology is established in such a way that, starting from the "momentarily urgent" of the situation given in each case, it calls for the "permanently important", the great and constant theological themes. The "permanently important" lies behind the biblical texts, but not in them, although in the Bible itself there are summarisations – e.g. the history of the exodus – and also derivations of these summarisations – e.g. the cross as indicator of redemption in Christ. Strictly speaking, God cannot be described by concepts, but by metaphors, whose use, in turn, are guided by the implicit axioms. Just as axioms guide the development and acquisition of speech in early childhood – Noam Chomsky's "deep structures" – just as they govern ethical and political beliefs and social behaviour, so do they also offer guidance in the lives of the faithful, which needs to be analysed theologically (RITSCHL 1986a, 42; 2008, 111-23). Thus, the central question that Ritschl has been concerned with all his life has been how the discourse about God functions in shaping faith, preaching, and theology. In this sense, for him, many science theorists and hermeneuts were too deductive, as were certain positions in political theology and Liberation Theology. The analytical philosophy of language, in turn, whose school he attended, "begins with the language of the believers, with the intention to analyse, examine and lead in an innovative way" (BERNHARDT et al., 1994, 24). In doing so, theology is only to some extent "scientific" – behind this comprehension stands Francis Bacon's distinction between *theologia inspirata* and *theologia naturalis*, as well as the very different conceptualisation of *science* in English and *Wissenschaft* in German (see RITSCHL 1981, 16-27). For Ritschl, this is basically so because theology, on the one hand, as he experienced in the New Worlds, is closely linked with the church and the faith, being, as stated above, initially ascriptive and not descriptive, and, on the other hand, because he wanted to understand theology more as wisdom than as science. Another question that Ritschl (2003, 27-42) was concerned with and which he answered with some reticence is whether in theology – including ecumenical theology – there could be in a strict sense research and, therefore, also development and new knowledge. For Ritschl, theology, in contrast, behaves more like art, which also contains a playful element. In his main work, *Zur Logik der Theologie* [The Logic of Theology], he wrote: "The freedom for serious playfulness and light humor in dealing with our own ability to think, that is, the perception that everything could also be different and that we need to start from the beginning again – these would not be bad gifts from theology to the university and the world of science" (RITSCHL 1984, 16). In his very first text published almost exactly 70 years ago in the newspaper *Basler*

Nachrichten under the title "Theology of Dance", which referred to a lecture by Gerardus van der Leeuw at the University of Basel, Ritschl writes: "To play [...] is simultaneously to be lighthearted and serious, it is to be authentically a child and, therefore, the true being of the human being. [...] Perhaps human beings will never find in their lives the seriousness they had when playing as a child".[7] Therefore, the theological play, the proper way of doing theology, happens between language and reality, the reality of God and the world. The question for Ritschl was not how we can include God in the play of our world, but in what way we can playfully imagine how our world should be viewed from God's perspective. Ritschl did not develop an explicit pneumatology, but it was clear to him that it should start from this point (RITSCHL 1998, 12). Here we would have a starting point for dialogue with Pentecostal churches, which continues to grow, especially in the Global South. In any case, this contemplation of the world from the perspective of God, however pretentious and fascinating it may be and can and should be carried out in the laboratory of academic theology, is not purely an end in itself, it is not simply "art for art's sake", but it needs to be verified in the world, in the concrete reality. Theology is not only ascriptive and descriptive, but also performative (cf. RITSCHL and HAILER 2010, 365-375). With that, I move on to the third dimension: *verification*, to which I focus attention, very selectively, from the perspective of new worlds.

6.3 Verification

Doing theology in the New Worlds, especially in North America, Australia, and New Zealand, requires a certain amount of pragmatism. This means that it is always necessary to ask about the concrete consequences of practice and teaching. This applies even more to the other new worlds that Ritschl took to heart with seriousness and interest, but towards which he remained quite critical and detached. He was very reticent about the "indigenous theology" discourse – which had been common for a while – and the criticism it contained of an apparently homogeneous "Western" theology. Still, he wanted to understand the important matters of the – at the time – so-called Third World, which would contribute to, in his words, "to perceive what God is doing now, what 'is going on with God now'" (RITSCHL 1986a, 197). Confronted

---

[7] Published on January 21, 1949, quoted by BERNHARDT 1994, 60.

with the current theological approaches of the New Worlds, this attitude and critique should be heard and, in turn, critically reflected and discussed. In any case, it soon became clear to Ritschl what only much later became obvious for much of European theology, namely, that "the influence of the church [...] [started to shift] from the European and North-American world to the Third World, especially to Africa" (RITSCHL 1984, 14). In this regard, but also in general terms, a purely historical theology and exegesis of the classics has always seemed insufficient to Ritschl. Scottish theology had taught him, in his own words, that "one cannot provide historical answers to authentically theological questions" (RITSCHL 1998, 10). In any case, this is the origin of the perception that ideologisations should be avoided. "There can be no doubt about the claim that the church must defend people who are sick, weak, poor, unjustly treated, discriminated against, imprisoned and persecuted. In this sense, the church must take sides. But if the church restricts itself, through its spokespersons, to this or that political ideology and displays the historical truth in a partisan way, as it is often doing today in the four corners of the world, the church contradicts its mission and is ethically unbearable" (RITSCHL 1984, 323). Ritschl could understand and recognise that partisanship could be at the service of the "momentarily urgent", but he protested against fads that lost sight of the "permanently important". However, we only have access to the "permanently important" through confrontation with the "momentarily urgent" and, therefore, with the present time and other human beings; yet, ultimately, we can only understand the "moment" from the perspective of the "permanent". It is only from the "permanently important" that the question about God and the legitimacy of the action can be raised (ibid, 121). Today, taking into consideration the current post-colonial and decolonial perceptions and approaches, we would probably have to ask whether access to the "permanently important" is not clearly more difficult than Ritschl thought. Furthermore, nowadays, considering the urgency of suffering of human beings and Christians in many places of the Old and New Worlds, one would need to ask what pertains to the "permanently important", since maybe new themes may not emerge – or perhaps they do? – but new accents that have their relevance not only temporarily or on a local level. In fact, Ritschl recognised and included among these themes, in the 1980s, "the concerns regarding peace, food security for the world's population, human rights and the scarcity of natural and energy resources" (ibid, 122). As shown above, the exchange of ideas with Martin Luther King, Jr., and the struggle for civil rights in the USA, taught Ritschl that justice had to be achieved on the streets as well. In this case, struggle was the best option. However, because of the collapse of the pacifist movement, the setbacks in the dialogue between Christians and Marxists in which he had participated through the peace conferences in Prague, as well as the deep disagreements in the wake of the 1968 movement, his interest shifted from political ethics to medical ethics. In this area, however, he intended to pay attention not only to the ethics of the doctor as an individual, but also and precisely to public health policy issues. And he did not entirely ignore political ethics; he highly valued ecumenical initiatives like the Decade for Overcoming Violence sponsored by the WCC, in which one of his students played a central role.

I conclude with a statement inspired by Rubem Alves, with whom Ritschl had discussions and, as mentioned, also made music – a statement with which Ritschl also would have agreed: "Theology is a play that is played when life is at stake" (REBLIN 2012, 5ff.). It is certainly a play on words, but there appears to be a genuine interest in the seriousness of concrete life and the depths of the Divine.

Chapter 7

Secularisation in a Global Perspective[*]

The debate over secularisation has not ended, as shown by the large numbers of recent publications. For a long time, it was almost uncontested that secularisation would be an inevitable, gradual process of the regression of religion until its total privatisation or disappearance. However, mainly since the 1990s, the counter-thesis started to gain ground, that is, religion has changed, but in no way disappeared or withdrawn to the private sphere. José Casanova spoke of "public religions" and "deprivatization" (1994), Peter Berger of "desecularization" (1999), and Friedrich Wilhelm Graf of the "return of the gods" (2004), to mention just a few prominent authors. On the theological side there has been an effort, for example, through a so-called public theology, to ensure the continuity of the communication of Christian values and theological positions in public discourse. This is a Christian-theological contribution in a narrower sense, that is, defined internally by the constituted churches and denominational theological faculties and externally communicated. This approach connects quite well with civil society and the juridical-constitutional discourses about the religions, as theology and the church are no longer seen as dominant bodies that dictate culture and politics, but are seen as important contributions for the common good. Another reaction, mostly coming from the theological academy, which has a more critical stand towards the church, consists in locating the religious dispositions in culture or in individual religiosity, where theology, taking up the thought of Schleiermacher, becomes a theory of the religious subject's self-understanding (e.g. U. BARTH and GRÄB, eds., 1993; U. BARTH 2003a, 2003b; GRÄB 2006). This, in turn, can be linked with postmodern and post-colonial approaches, driven by differences, although the common global dimension here and the critique of power asymmetries are hardly

[*] Originally published as "Säkularisierung in globaler Betrachtung, in *Verkündigung und Forschung* 61/2, 99-112 (2016), written during a research period as a CAPES / Humboldt senior research fellow at the Ludwig Maximilian University in Munich, and in Portuguese (translated by Luís Marcos Sander) in Iuri Andréas Reblin and Rudolf von Sinner, eds., *Reforma: Tradição e Transformação* pp. 157-178. São Leopoldo: Sinodal 2016. Translated from the Portuguese by Alexander Busch and revised by the author. Used with permission.

articulated. One also finds here the tendency to classify worldly concepts and phenomena as secularised forms of religious content, as Carl Schmitt (2006) has already done in his "political theology", according to which, for instance, the power of the worldly sovereign would be a secularised form of divine omnipotence. Among the most recent approaches in this direction, mention should be made, for instance, of France's former education minister, Luc Ferry (2002), for whom religion is diluted in human reason. In what follows, I will limit myself to recently published literature in Germany.

The different approaches to secularisation, of course, depend upon how this term is defined. In each case, there are mainly three points that must be clarified: (1) the processes of differentiation or de-differentiation between state, society and religion; (2) the nexus of secularisation and modernisation, which can then, on a global level, lead to the recognition of the existence of multiple "secularities" and "modernities"[1], among which there are only limited causal associations; moreover, one must then ask, whether such modern secularisation must necessarily lead to a suppression of religion; (3) the public and private reach of religion in its particular context and the interaction between religion and other spheres of society, which can lead to both reconfiguration of that reach and mutual influence.

If I see correctly, there are three factors involved in contributing to the new situation in this discussion. (1) Comprehensive empirical studies enable a better understanding of long-term trends and correct traditional preconceptions; (2) due to multiple criticisms against the Eurocentric perspective and conceptualisation – which, at most, still took into consideration the USA – research is currently being done and compared more and more on a global level; (3) theological contributions (not only Christian) are more often intentionally included, rather than pursuing a purely external approach. It has to be stated also that theologians are by no means necessarily opponents of secularisation, but they can, on the contrary, rightly emphasise the worldliness of the world, which, in this case, is not perceived as deficient or decadent, but, along with Dilthey, as "emancipated" in the sense of "adulthood" (a concept used by both Bonhoeffer and Gogarten in theology) and, precisely as such, as a field for religious and ecclesiastical presence, interaction, and

---

[1] See, the now classic essays and works of EISENSTADT 2000, ed., 2002; COSTA, DOMINGUES, KNÖBL, and DA SILVA, eds., 2006.

interpretation. Conversely, representatives of the secularisation thesis are by no means necessarily opponents of religion.

In recent years, empirical and theoretical approaches have been proposed mainly by the cluster of excellence "Religion and Politics in Pre-Modern and Modern Cultures" at the University of Münster. Detlef Pollack (2012), a sociologist of religion with a theological background in Münster, is one of the most articulate defenders of a theory of secularisation, albeit modified. He defines secularisation as "a process of decline of the social importance of religion, which in some, still to be more accurately specified way is associated with modernization processes" (ibid, 5). In this context, religion is defined from a combination of functional analyses and substantial arguments, in order to maintain the possibility of distinguishing religious from non-religious solutions to problems. He then draws/inscribes religion, in terms of ideal types, in a quadrant (ibid, 52) that shows functionally the consistency and the coping with contingency, and substantially the mutual relation between transcendence and immanence. For a vital religiosity to emerge, the religious question and the religious answer must come together, that is, the coping of contingency and transcendence must converge – otherwise, either the answer remains without a question (religious routine), or the question without an answer (religious search), or no religious question is asked at all (pragmatism). As a scholar and intellectual who widely operates in an empirical way and can support his work theoretically, he is able to question some of the theoretical approaches that have already become classics. He does this by using Germany as an example, but recently he has also taken into account other contexts (see 7.1 below).

A similar direction is taken by the collection of articles in *Religion und Säkularisierung: Ein interdisziplinäres Handbuch* ["Religion and secularization: an interdisciplinary manual"], edited by Schmidt and Pitschmann (2014), with explicit and positive reference to Pollack. Secularisation and religion are perceived as open and ambivalent concepts, whose meaning is influenced by social discourses, while simultaneously shaping these discourses. Accordingly, the interdisciplinary group of authors, mainly from Europe, especially Germany, were not initially given a conclusive definition. The first part, entitled "conceptions", exposes important historical and contemporary positions from Jean-Jacques Rousseau to Martin Riesebrodt (2007); the second part, "categories", covers central concepts such as fundamentalism, the public sphere, pluralism, and religiosity; the third section, "conflicts", deals with discourses such as, for instance, the relation between faith and knowledge, religion and the secular state, and secularisation and world society. A global and intercultural dimension comes forth especially in the contributions of the following chapters: "Multiple modernities" (Julien Winandy), "Religion and the secular rule of law" (Stefan Grotefeld), "Secularization and world society" (Michael Reder), and "Secularization and the world religions" (SCHMIDT 2014). In this context, reference is repeatedly made to José Casanova and Talal Asad, who propose a contextualised approach to secularisation and religion and their interaction. Also useful is the quadruple distinction of political scientist Alfred Stepan (ibid., 359ff.), who proposes a reciprocal tolerance (twin tolerations) between religion and politics in the respective context of "multiple secularisms". Thus, we have then (1) the separatist model (France, USA), in which, despite all the advantages, there is no basic link with democracy or a guarantee for religious freedom (China, for example). (2) The model of state religion, which may foster democracy and religious freedom (England, Denmark, Norway, Greece), although not necessarily (Saudi Arabia). (3) Furthermore, there is the state-sponsored "hospitality" model in multidenominational states (Holland, Belgium, Switzerland, Germany), which, however, entails a certain privilege for historically established and well-organised churches. Finally, (4) the model of "respect for all, active cooperation, principle-based distance" (India, Indonesia, Senegal), effective in countries with high religious heterogeneity and limited separation of the public and private sphere of religion, in which, however, the state can intervene against religious-motivated discrimination (e.g. the caste system). Thus, several contextual realities are considered. Taking into account the "post-colonial studies" that emerged in the 1970s (SAID 1979; SPIVAK 1988; BHABHA 2004), the terminology, precisely those referring to "religion", "secularity" and "modernity" – which are all terms derived from Western language and conceptualisation – must always be verified regarding their adequateness in other cultures and contexts. "The global expansion of the discourses and voices of other cultures refer to their respective concepts in their particularities and perspectives, to which the scientific terminology needs to respond appropriately" (SCHMIDT, 2014, 367). Furthermore, it must be taken into consideration that many religions are nowadays global players, with all the ambivalences associated with this;

this too calls for a "revision of a strong paradigm of secularization and a new attentiveness to religion in the contexts of world society" (ibid, 354).

In what follows, I will address specifically the contributions that bring different contexts in terms of the sociology of religion into conversation with one another and, on the other hand, those theological contributions confessionally rooted, yet ecumenically oriented – and that refer to, and focus on its original meaning, "the inhabited earth", the world and, therefore, the *saeculum* – which seek to develop theology in a juridically secular, religiously plural public sphere.

7.1 New approaches to religion and secularisation in German publications

Several volumes have undertaken extensive investigations, which here can only be exposed through examples, under the assumption that they have a special interest in global and comparative references. A slightly older collection, whose initiative came from Germany, but striving to bring a wider range of perspectives, was edited by Manuel Franzmann, Christel Gärtner and Nicole Köck (2006) under the title *Religiosität in der Säkularisierten Welt* ["Religiosity in the Secularized World"]. In addition to a discussion on current theories about secularisation by some of its main exponents, including Steve Bruce, Detlef Pollack and David Martin, and three texts on historical development, there are five case studies on secularisation in mostly Christian countries (Germany, Wales, Romania, Brazil, and Mexico) and six more contributions on secularisation in Islam. According to the introduction, secularisation is understood (and defended) in classical terms, taking up Max Weber's definition, namely, as a "value-free sociological concept in analytical terms", which implies the process of a comprehensive "disenchantment of the world", that is, "the worldliness or citeriorization (Verdiesseitigung) of worldviews and belief contents as part of the rationalization process underway in universal history" (ibid, 13). In this case, secularisation tends to be understood as a process of erosion of the social significance of religion, especially with reference to individualisation and pluralisation, but also to processes of change. Detlef Pollack (2006) critically discusses, with empirical data, the "rational choice" theory disseminated in the USA and whose exponents are Rodney Stark, Roger Finke, and Laurence Iannaccone. As is well known, this theory asserts that higher religious plurality and, thus, increased "supply" creates more "demand" and leads to greater religious vitality insofar as competition moves religion providers out of their comfort zone. According to Pollack, the existence of such a correlation with a religious market, especially in Europe, could not be demonstrated. But also in the USA, according to the editors of the collection, religious vitalisation should be viewed with caution, because the low numbers of "church membership" in the 18th century, given the migration of religious dissidents fleeing from a country with religious monopoly, can hardly serve as a point of comparison, and, moreover, the American denominations were constituted as sects – following Weber's concept – with a high level of personal involvement, thus presupposing already in their constitution a high religious vitality. Against Pollack, however, the editors warn of understanding Eastern European countries too hastily as secularised, because atheism, as well as scientism, nationalism, fascism, and other positions present in these countries, "still contain clearly religious traits" (ibid, 20), which means the transfer of religious elements into the secular sphere – this stand is actually controversial, as will become clearer in other publications I present below. In his contribution, David Martin (2006) proceeds in an explicitly comparative manner, namely between the (Protestant) "North" and the (Catholic) "South". In doing so, Martin emphasises the existing connection between religious and political forms. In the USA, this connection manifests itself as a "decentralized political-religious, voluntary and entrepreneurial culture" (ibid, 117), and in Scandinavia, as a monopolistic church amid a dominant social democracy. Martin also notices the existence of an analogy between the "Christendom" of medieval Spain and the current "Islamia", assuming a fusion between religion and nationalism. The anti-colonial reflexes make it difficult, in this context, for secularisation to develop as a liberal democracy. Secularism in Turkey (see Kaylzan Delibas, in ibid, 375-394) was a matter for the elites and it did not gain acceptance among the population – just as the French-inspired secularism (laicité) of the intellectual elites did not spread in Latin America. For Martin, the fast-growing Pentecostal movement in Latin America means the search for a connection with modernity – in this case, through a new form of religion, and not through secularisation. In relation to Italy, Roberto Cipriani (2006, 123-140) speaks of the existence of a "diffuse religion", which, unlike the "invisible religion" of Luckmann, is not opposed to ecclesial religiosity, but stands in diversified continuity with the Catholic Church. About 18% of Catholics belong to the "open radicals" (ibid, 138), who carry an ecclesial legacy, but show little connection with the official church, defend their own opinions, and have a positive view both towards modernity and towards secularisation and religious pluralism. The chapters on Islam in the collection take note of its strong connection with cultural identity, also – and precisely – in diaspora contexts, such as in Great Britain, where there are effectively multiple possibilities of living this connection, something which is generally not noticed by perspectives blurred by stereotypes (Talip Kucukcan, ibid, 333-356). In this sense, we are approaching, for instance, the variable intensity of the feeling of belonging and its combination with the content of faith and ritual practices. The thesis of "believing without belonging" of the British sociologist Grace Davie (1994) cannot be corroborated in this case. Writing about the largest Islamic nation in the world, Indonesia, Susanne Schröter (2006) describes the "politicization of religion and the sacralization of politics" and considers it "once again uncertain" (ibid, 372) whether the evolution of events will lead to a secular state with free practice of religion or to a growing fundamentalism. In the opinion of Ulrich Oevermann (2006), Islamic fundamentalism is the product of both its own streams of tradition ("the obedience of each individual to Islamic tradition and the inseparable unity of religious socialization and statehood, of religion and politics that mutually support one another" (ibid, 426), as well as the rejection of "Western" tendencies, which arose in the framework of the two other monotheistic, secularising and modernising religions, in relation to which Islam considers itself superior. This thus entails a "double blockade of modernization": the rejection of trends towards universalist rationalisation and the defence of a competing universalist religious principle, advocating it as genuinely true, to which obedience is owed. The Koran lacked, Oevermann argues, potential for autonomy and freedom, because, for example, the fall in sin is reduced to a simple scheme of disobedience worthy of punishment. In this case, agreeing or not with the author, it is important to highlight the existence of a confrontation with theological elements and their repercussions on social and political processes – an interaction that is certainly not unilinear, but important.

The volume *Umstrittene Säkularisierung* ["Controversial Secularization"], edited by Karl Gabriel, Christel Gärtner and Detlef Pollack (2014), combines sociological and historical analyses and deals mainly with the issue of differentiation between religion and politics, which is examined in four analytical steps beginning from fairly traditional moments in European history: initially in relation to the Investiture Controversy (1056-1122), followed by the confessional era (16th/17th centuries), the Enlightenment associated with the French and (North) American revolutions of the 18th century and the birth and universalisation of human rights, and, finally, in regard to the "long" 19th century. In each analytical step, a sociological contribution is followed by various historical analyses, which, by way of conclusion, are once more interpreted from a sociological point of view. In these texts, both defenders and critics as well as proponents of a moderate theory of differentiation bring forth their perspectives. However, they all agree that history does not follow a linear progression and argue for the exclusion of determinism and automatism – understood as the inevitability of a specific form of modernity and an equally particular form of secularisation that would follow on its heels. In his contribution, Hugh McLeod (2014) outlines a historical trajectory from the rather pragmatic separations of church and state (USA, 1791; France – for a brief interstice – 1795; Holland, 1796), via reflections upon religious and namely Protestant motivation for the liberation of the churches from state subjugation in Switzerland (Alexandre Vinet, 1842) and Great Britain (Edward Miall, 1844), up to the controversial and anticlerical separation in countries dominated by Catholicism. It is interesting to note that many Latin American countries have approved the legal separation of church and state before the Europeans: Mexico (1859), El Salvador (1871), Guatemala (1879) and Brazil (1891), all before France (1905), Portugal (1911) or Spain (1931). According to McLeod, there are four reasons why this was more an ideal than a reality: (1) the elites privileged the religion to which they belonged (e.g. in the USA); (2) parties with denominational ties were able to maintain a more advantageous position for their church (e.g. the Netherlands); (3) the state depended upon the social and educational services provided by the church (e.g. Germany); and (4) some states implemented systematic secularisation, to the point of even persecuting religious people (e.g. the communist countries). Therefore, the commonly assumed differentiation for secularisation is by no means simply given, as religion is still very present in the diverse contexts of society. One could, however, speak of the existence of a "decrease in the scope of ecclesiastical authority" (ibid, 479), particularly where the state has taken over several tasks which, traditionally, belonged to the churches. By comparison, Germany, with its subsidiarity principle, is the exception rather than the rule.

In the chapter on secularisation and de-churching, Antonius Liedhegener (2014) deals with long-term trends based on empirical data. For this author, secularisation means, as a partial constitutive process of European modernisation, "the growing autonomy of society and its partial systems vis-à-vis traditional Christian premises in terms of meaning and tradition", which would comprise a substantial concept of religion in a variant that applies specifically to Christianity (ibid, 492). Referring to José Casanova (1994), Liedhegener notes that this would have consequences at the level of society as a whole, of the church as an institution and of individuals, with the plausibility of Christianity decreasing on all three levels. At the same time, he maintains that Christianity, characteristically constituted as a "community of memory and life" (ibid, 496), cannot, therefore, be reduced to purely subjective or culturally anonymous forms of existence. According to available data, in the Protestant churches of the 19th and early 20th centuries there was already a de-churching (cf. HÖLSCHER 1990), whereas in the Roman Catholic Church it started only after 1945. As a minority religion, the latter was able and, indeed, needed to establish itself as an independent social body, providing it with a high degree of stability. In the 1980s, after the Roman Catholic population, for the first time in recent history, surpassed the Protestant residents, not least due to the migration increase, following the *Wende* in 1989 and the reunification of the country with the integration of new, formerly atheistic states to the federation, the pendulum clearly swung to the side of people without denominational affiliation. As to the Catholics, due to the sexual abuse cases that were gradually becoming known, from 2010 onwards the number of people who left the Catholic Church increased rapidly. Therefore, even though secularisation as de-churching is a clearly perceptible and demonstrable master trend, this in no way represents the disappearance of Christian church life or even religion in general. In his theoretical contribution on process concepts in the history of religion, Volkhard Krech (2014) stresses that, apparently, the semantics of religion and of secularisation are mutually conditioned: "It seems that, the more the factual and orthopractic embodiment of religion disappears (which appears to be in itself a product of the history of religion in the modern West), the greater the frequency of religion becoming an object of reflection and the more the question about the place of religion in modernity becomes, in itself, a figure of reflection" (ibid, 575). In the German and European context he investigates secularisation and immanent sacralisation – in which the "difference between transcendence and immanence is introduced again and *permanently* into the immanent element" (ibid, 579), for instance, through the sacralisation and, thus, religious exaltation of culture – the individualisation of the religious element as well as its pluralisation as concepts referring to processes, that is, as a "research program with an open outcome" (ibid, 566), thereby making comparisons possible, namely, to compare to what extent each of these processes takes effect. Following up on this, Hans Joas (2014) warns sociologists and historians not to derive from such concepts, respectively, a historical foundation or an orientation based on the social sciences. What is at stake in this case are issues of differentiation, rationalisation and modernisation that must not be understood along the lines of a unilateral, unilinear, and "western-centered" (ibid, 621) interpretation, as in Max Weber and Émile Durkheim. In scientific terms, it must be replaced by the analysis of processes with an open outcome, whose "scope, degree and direction", however, "would need to be themselves measured against the religious and secular ideals of lifestyle and shaping of the world" (ibid, 622), and whose own claim, therefore, should be taken seriously.

The volume *Religion in der Moderne: Ein internationaler Vergleich* ["Religion in the Modern Age: An International Comparison"], by Detlef Pollack and Gergely Rosta (2015), deserves special mention for two reasons. On the one hand, the book relies on empirical data and adopts a long-term and comparative perspective as the basis for discussion which, as one of the measuring factors of religion, continues to intentionally address the institutionalised forms of religion. On the other hand, it broadens the horizon beyond Western Europe and the USA and looks into Eastern Europe (Russia, Eastern Germany, and Poland), South Korea and, to a lesser extent, Brazil, which is important in terms of the rapidly growing Pentecostal-charismatic movement within Christianity in Latin America, a growth that is also occurring in Africa and Asia. The authors explicitly do not presuppose that modernisation automatically leads to secularisation and that secularisation necessarily has a negative effect upon the role of religion in society, nor that religion's role in society is influenced solely by modernisation. Even so, the correlation between modernity and religion is the focus of investigation and one conclusion that stands out is "the relatively high probability of the occurrence of negative consequences of modernization on religion" (ibid, 484). Although religion has gained more attention in public discourse, the decrease in its social importance, as verified from the available data, is empirically undeniable.

At first, modernity is defined by the following characteristics: (1) functional differentiation, which means that there can no longer be "a uniform interpretation of the world" (ibid, 41). Moreover, this differentiation (2) is not only given horizontally (in law, science, economics, politics, education), but also vertically (levels of constitution of society), thereby granting a special role to mediating instances between society and the individual, such as political parties, labour unions, companies, health clinics and volunteer organisations, including churches. (3) While some functional systems are more reactive and, potentially, perform an enabling function (family, education, religion), others perform an impelling function (economics, politics, science) and are in constant competition. Since modernity is reflexive, it can learn from its mistakes and, consequently, correct and restrict itself. "The civil spirit [*bürgerliche Geist*] has a world-shaping power which, despite all its own dynamics, manages to establish limits for itself and precisely in this way – and only in this way – is able to influence and change the world" (ibid, 47). As indicated above, religion is here defined both in functional and substantial terms, as standing in the tension between the revelation of contingency and facing it, or between transcendence and immanence. Thus, the religious phenomenon can be delimited in relation to others and can be named for communication purposes, while, at the same time, the definition remains open for empirical verification. In methodological terms, there are three dimensions of religiosity that are empirically apprehended: the dimension of belonging (membership, but also trust in and identification with a religious community), the dimension of practice (the frequency of church attendance, prayer, request for occasional services) and the dimension of experience and conviction (faith in God, destiny, life after death, reincarnation, astrology, and so on) (see the table in ibid, 84). Furthermore, it is necessary to ask about the relative value of religion in the individual's life; therefore, its importance in comparison to other spheres of life was examined. In these perspectives, the authors analysed a large amount of empirical data (e.g. World Value Surveys, Surveys on religiosity [*Religionsmonitor*] and social cohesion in Germany [*Eurobarometer*]) for secondary analysis.

In their book, Pollack and Rosta defend a number of theses with which they refute basic assumptions that are, in part, widely disseminated. (1) Contrary to the market theory of religion that is common in the USA (increased religious supply creates higher demand), a higher religious plurality does not lead to higher religious vitality, not even in the USA. On the contrary, there is a positive correlation between religious homogeneity and vitality. Moreover, a significant factor for the high religiosity in the USA – in addition to the proximity between profane history and history of salvation of the so-called "civil religion", that is, the high plausibility of religion in society – is the scale of social inequality. This last aspect also applies at the international level, so that a high importance attached to belief in God correlates with high Gini indexes (thus, with a high degree of unequal distribution of income and property). According to the authors, however, likewise and especially important are convictions regarding content, as particularly noticeable in the USA, such as, for instance, the belief in an intervening God who is directly concerned with the individual, or a dualistic worldview in which good and evil are in constant battle. (2) Religiosity not linked to a church is more dependent on the context (e.g. education, wealth, and religious pluralism) than the one connected to a church, and, precisely for this reason, is neither autonomous nor consolidated. A vigorous belief in God is correlated with an active church membership. Less surprising is the fact that (3) religious vitality increases where there are more points of contact between the state, society and religion, and where, therefore, religion is perceived not only in a narrow sense, but also in its social, moral and political contributions beyond the church subsystem. This brings forth a greater plausibility and, thus, also acceptance of religion, which, in turn, has a positive effect on the disposition for religious belonging. This, however, is associated with the danger that religion is defined by its usefulness and, therefore, may not only give up what is proper to it, but also places itself in competition with other providers of equivalent benefits. Nor is it surprising that (4) a religiosity influenced by the church has a preventive effect against a selfish and deceptive private morality – which is not exactly the case of extra-ecclesial religiosity – thus contributing to a "public morality" (ibid, 454).

From the wealth of data, information, and reflections on the different case studies, it is possible to point out here only some of the examples. In the case of South Korea, one finds that Pentecostal/charismatic Christianity is often connected with social ascension; however, insofar as social ascension takes place, church membership is no longer necessary. Similar trends can be observed in other contexts. These churches, therefore, in a way become victims of their own success. The growth of Pentecostals in Latin America is also correlated with the high acceptance of belief in spirits, demons and magic, which in Germany and Europe was greatly weakened by the Enlightenment; in this regard, it should be mentioned, moving beyond the aforementioned authors, that, especially in Brazil, there are reflections on a religious matrix, to which such ideas belong, but which then clearly differ from other matrices (see, for instance, the research of religion scholar Fritz Heinrich at the University of Göttingen). Furthermore, the widely held assumption that religious vitality in Russia has increased enormously is discredited. Although there is an increase in church attendance, it is more "an expression of political and national expectations projected onto Orthodoxy" (ibid, 313) than an expression of religious awakening, since the existence of a "deeper religiosity" in regard to practices or beliefs cannot be ascertained (ibid).

An explicitly global approach, particularly Latin, is adopted by the volume *Trends of Secularism in a Pluralistic World*, edited by Jaime Contreras and Rosa María Martínez de Codes (2013). According to the editors, the old categories and relations between religion and secularity are outdated; in a globalised society, it is up to the individual to find and interpret the best way to experience both their religion and its secularity. "Secularity and religions have developed to the point that confrontation is no longer possible, but there is a need to create [mutual] participating universes [...] from the point of view of development, [they should] advance a globalized society inspired by a global ethics" (ibid, 27). In his contribution on the global challenge of secularism to religious freedom, David Little (2013) distinguishes between (1) a very restrictive and even exclusivist secularity, and (2) a secularity that is more friendly towards religion. In regard to the former, only one of the five "belief rights" mentioned by Little – which he derives from human rights conventions, namely the International Covenant on Civil and Political Rights – would be considered worthy of protection, namely, the prohibition of hate speech against religions. The latter, however, which is preferred by the author, in principle would also protect the other "belief rights", namely, the right to the free exercise of religion, the protection against discrimination, protection of minorities, and the right of the parents to determine the religious education of their children. To this end, it presupposes the secularity of the state in order to guarantee equal freedom to all religions. In legal terms, it needs to show its validity based on individual cases, and therefore the boundaries between secularity and the practice of religion should not be drawn too sharply. In his essay on secularism, the secular, and secularisation, T. Jeremy Gunn (2013) in etymological and historical terms, deals in detail with the relevant concepts and theories, examining the different positions with regard to their implications. In doing so, he considers the three levels of the state, society, or social institutions in the public sphere, and of the people both as individuals and within collective bodies. He is particularly interested in the latter level, raising the question whether people are becoming more secular – a difficult question to answer. Gunn proposes that secularity and religion should be treated more as "fluid concepts", in constant interaction, than as clearly opposite poles. Similarly, for Joseph Ratzinger in his dialogue with Jürgen Habermas (2007) on the *Dialectics of Secularization*, the Christian faith and Western secular rationality don't need to be in opposition, but can become main partners in a global and intercultural discussion. For Gunn, the real enemy of religion is "possibly not the convicted secularist, guided by his own principles, but the person who lacks an authentic personal religiosity and uses religious language in the public sphere to acquire power and influence" (ibid, 105).

7.2 Perspectives

To conclude, I would like to return to the three aspects I mentioned in the beginning. (1) It seems that processes of differentiation or de-differentiation between state, society and religion co-exist. They are in constant negotiation, and, at the global level, there is a multiplicity of correlations. (2) There are, it seems, links between secularisation and modernisation, which, however, are neither coercive nor unilinear. There is, at a global level, a trend towards legal and political secularisation, but also opposite trends tending towards the establishment or perpetuation of authoritarian regimes based on religion or power pretensions of hegemonic and counter-hegemonic groups, as I will emphasise below. Religious beliefs and practices are receding in certain contexts, especially in Western and Central Europe, but this does not represent a worldwide and certainly not a homogenous movement. (3) The public and private reach of religion or religious communities is therefore in flux and subject to both power struggles and complex negotiation processes. In any case, one cannot speak of a general privatisation of religion.

Particularly the research by Pollack indicates, with abundant empirical evidence, that religiosity, even when expressed in anti-institutional and individualised form, depends on forms of communitarisation and maintenance of a religious memory. Where the religious community disappears, religiosity also disappears. For the religious community and the theology associated with it, this means that they cannot forego saying and practicing what is constitutive for them. The outlines for a public theology available in the anthology *Grundtexte Öffentliche Theologie* ["Basic Texts of Public Theology"], which was recently edited by Florian Höhne and Frederike van Oorschot (2015) and presents a global and contextual approach, are indicative of the effort to bring Christian theology to the current public sphere making use of the elements that are proper to it. Public theology is concerned, for instance, with "the public discourse of the church, the religious dimension of politics, the public role of religious orientations based on particular traditions, the responsibility of Christian people in the public sphere" (ibid, 7). To the authors of the essays in this volume, it is clear that the purpose is not an attempt for domination, much less the establishment of a theocracy, but that public theology, anchored in a particular religious community and its theology, has a specific contribution to a pluralistic – also and precisely in religious terms – secular and democratic society. However, there is a search for power and dominance, and not only in the Islamic world, in which one is immediately inclined to think of the terrible actions of groups such as ISIS (Islamic State) in the Near East, Boko Haram in Nigeria, or Al-Shabaab in East Africa, but also the authoritarian regimes such as in Iran and Saudi Arabia. The IURD, for example, which was founded in Rio de Janeiro in 1977 and is particularly influential in Brazil, but has long been active worldwide, discloses, at least in its country of origin, pretensions of power in an increasingly explicit way. To this end, it makes use of its great public visibility through its immense buildings such as the "Temple of Solomon" inaugurated in São Paulo in 2014 and ownership of the second largest television network in Brazil. The name of the church itself is already a project clearly directed against the Roman Catholic Church, which has been dominant since colonisation and, in turn, is in no way willing to give in without a fight. Both (and many other) churches, however, are also important, indeed indispensable, agents of diaconal work, who, through their almost

ubiquitous presence in all layers of society, as well as in the poorest areas
and places of daily violence, reach out to people to whom the state has no
access. In Brazil, religious diversity is increasing with each passing day;
in the 1990s, a new church was founded in Rio de Janeiro every weekday.
Some are and remain small communities that meet in a simple garage,
while others, such as the IURD, have become multinational corporations.
Twenty-five percent of the population declared that they have already
changed their church or religious community affiliation at least once.
This poses enormous challenges, just to mention two examples, for
religious education in public schools and for religious service in
hospitals, prisons, and the armed forces. Brazil is also a secular state, that
is, neutral in religious terms, which, analogous to the First Amendment
of the US Constitution, prohibits both the establishment of a state religion
or the favouring of a religion, as well as the obstruction of the (also
public) practice of religion. In political and technological terms, Brazil is
undoubtedly a modern country, and legally, religion and politics are
differentiated from each other. On the other hand, it must also be said that
92% of the population claims to belong to a religious community – the
majority, Christians. Therefore, people and, through them, society,
cannot be considered secularised. Even science, in many areas under
strong French influence and shaped by a non-religious or even anti-
religious secularism, cannot escape the impact of religion. As already
indicated, religion also has a strong public presence – but not only in
regard to pretensions of power, as it also contributes, in a courageous,
discreet and cooperative manner, to citizenship (cf. VON SINNER 2012a).
In Germany, religious pluralism is far less pronounced, and churches and
other religious or (even atheistic) worldview-bound communities – a
unique phenomenon of legally recognised entities – mainly Protestant
and Catholic churches, continue to have a prominent position in the
public sphere. In this sense, they are clearly perceived by politicians, as
well as the media and the population in general in their public
pronouncements, as influential leading personalities, and are widely
recognised in their church-led and state-sponsored diaconal and
educational work – which is also a unique phenomenon worldwide. At
the same time, however, society is increasingly de-churched, especially
in the states that were part of the former German Democratic Republic,
where not only church membership is declining, but also the intensity of
religiosity in general.

A major trend reversal is not in sight. But the more the church needs to strive for its plausibility and social visibility, the more it is challenged – and encouraged! – to recommit to the message of the gospel which has been entrusted to the church, and to give verbal expression to it in a changing public sphere. Obviously, the language of the gospel must be presented, especially in the academic and political fields, in a broadly intelligible way, and therefore interdisciplinary information and orientation are required. But this cannot mean a denial or dilution of its own language and theological content in such a way that they become unrecognisable or simply replicate the discourses of others. Considering the plurality – also within the church – and the advancement of the priesthood of all believers, churches and theologians cannot and should not simply pretend that they are proposing a uniform discourse. They can and should, however, help to ensure that the constitutive elements of the church and theology are expressed in an appropriate contemporary language, guided by the gospel and the theological tradition in a way that is relevant to the daily lives of the people.

Chapter 8

The City and Religion – Cacophony and Resonance[*]

> *"Humanity is not a theme among others,*
> *in Theology, but it is the central theme."*
> José Comblin (1987, 13)

> *"Religion [...] becomes a relationship [...]*
> *promising to guarantee,*
> *in the categories of love and meaning,*
> *that the original and basic form of existence is*
> *a relationship of resonance and not of alienation."*
> Hartmut Rosa (2016, 435)

Religion and the city have a close but ambiguous relationship and history. In the Bible, the paradise of the garden of Eden of the beginning is relocating to the heavenly city of Jerusalem of the final revelation. Augustine (413-26/1886, 649) contrasts the cities of Babylon and Jerusalem: "two cities have been formed by two loves: the earthly by the love of self, even to the contempt of God; the heavenly by the love of God, even to the contempt of self". The city of God (*civitas Dei*) gives identity and guidance, but being an attitude rather than a worldly reality, it does not govern the earthly city alone. It is not a theocracy, but it is precisely as citizens of heaven that Christian people act as citizens of earth and collaborate with other people towards building the common good. And, while justice and salvation are present in the world through the city of God, at the same time, sin is also present through the city of the devil. Inspired by Aristotle and his perception of the *polis,* as well as the Roman architect Vitruvius, Thomas Aquinas, in his work *De Regimine Principum*, writes about the art of building cities, which had a lasting impact on the foundation and development of cities in America

[*] Originally published in Elias Wolff, Antônio Ernesto Palafox and Benjamin Bravo Perez, eds., *A teologia e a pastoral na cidade; desafios e possibilidades atuais,* pp. 251-278 (São Paulo: Paulus 2021). Translated by Alexander Busch and revised by the author. Used with permission.

during the Spanish conquest.[1] Likewise, he addresses the human autonomy to build cities governed by human laws that are oriented towards the common good and inspired by divine law.[2]

In colonial Brazil, religious buildings were traditionally erected in the centre of the cities and/or on high ground overlooking the urban space, often next to other public buildings such as the government house, the parliament, and the court house. The growth of the cities, along with their concomitant diversification of religious presence, brought a new use of space, becoming a place of dispute and competition instead of traditional monopoly. The old parish churches are still standing, but what used to be the centre of the city is no longer in the centre, or has just become one of the many centres in a polycentric city. In this new situation, it is necessary to be creative to conquer and dominate space, to gain influence and visibility.

The Neo-Pentecostal Universal Church of the Kingdom of God (*Igreja Universal do Reino de Deus – IURD*), founded in the 1970s, systematically implemented a new way of being present and accessible: it bought commercial stores and movie theatres, easily accessible from the street and with open doors for most of the day, unlike traditional churches. One enters the church building from the sidewalk, just like any other store (CAMPOS 1999). Thus, the IURD transformed profane space into sacred space and gained visibility amidst the commercial activities. Since 1996, however, in the so-called "cathedral age", the IURD has been building temples, in neoclassical style, easily recognisable as religious buildings, that occupy highly visible and well demarcated spaces, distant from the street with their own parking area, some even include a helipad. With the construction of its main cathedral in São Paulo, the so-called Temple of Solomon – the Third temple, which does not exist in Israel and was built with stones imported from that country – the IURD achieved historical visibility, thus claiming to be a legitimate universal church in clear opposition to the Roman Catholic Church (cf. AMIGO 2014). This huge cathedral placed *evangélico* churches in the Brazilian cultural heritage itinerary – traditionally their religious buildings were not included – creating, in the words of Henri Lefebvre (1991, 220), a "monumental space". In 2008, in Rio de Janeiro, in a location with high

---

[1] COMBLIN 1991, 7. This book is an abbreviated and simplified version, without scientific apparatus, of the full-bodied *Theólogie de la ville* (1968).
[2] AQUINAS 1265-74/1997, I-II, q 100, a 5; cf. PASSOS 2012, 265.

mobility, thus, easy access, an entire city, idealised by the Bishop of the IURD Marcelo Crivella, was built – a scaled-down replica of Jerusalem in biblical times, a sign of the presence of the sacred, even if through a miniature model and the creation of a cultural monument, expressing Judeophilia, a common attitude among certain *evangélico* groups.[3]

Therefore, gone is the traditional attitude of Brazilian Protestantism standing against the world, of a church that denies the world, symbolised as it was by the city as the icon of temptation. The common picture that used to come to mind was that of the two paths: the wide road of damnation (represented by the city, its pleasures and sophistication) and the narrow road of salvation (represented by the rural world of simplicity and hard work; cf. CUNHA 2006, 103f.). Now, if, on the one hand, there is a massive and visible religious presence of Neo-Pentecostal churches in the city, on the other hand, there is also a discreet but no less important religious presence of *terreiros*, sacred spaces of African Brazilian religions, generally found in private homes with little visibility, but known and sought after by interested people who know their location. Mapping the religious presence in the city, as I have done several times with students of ecumenism at Faculdades EST in São Leopoldo/RS, brings to light this diversity, which, for many students, is unexpected (cf. FOLLMANN 2001).

If the built space conveys messages and pretensions of power and can be a matter of dispute, the city airspace likewise carries potential for conflict. Sound can stand out and be inviting – while at the same time it can annoy the neighbours, from the traditional ringing of the church bells, or the sound coming from the amplifiers of the pastor preaching or the church worship band. A true cacophony can be heard in the cities (cf. DE THEIJE 2012, position 2169.2238). Not to mention that, historically, there has been a persecution against the *batuque* – drums of African origin; its sounds were chased after by vigilant police officers (cf. MONTERO 2006; 2011). Today, to avoid the accusation of persecution against evangelical groups, there is a bill in process that will establish new federal guidelines for noise pollution in order to explicitly protect churches from abusive fines and the restraining of "the exercise of religious freedom" of thousands of people; a similar project has already been approved by the

---

[3] Available at: <http://centroculturaljerusalem.com.br> [accessed May 08, 2020]; cf. COLEMAN 2012, position 1019f.; WACHHOLZ and REINKE, 2020.

corresponding committee of the Chamber of Deputies.[4] Such approach is the common defence argument of who wants to perpetuate a practice that is already underway, generally with little regard for the interests of other people. As demonstrated by Oosterbaan (2009), in a favela in Rio de Janeiro evangelical music bands compete with funk balls in a battle for sound supremacy – a clear expression of the dispute between the church and the drug trade. On the other hand, the government and the occupying police force also made use of evangelical music as a strategy for pacification in the Alemão favela complex, to prevent the devil from occupying people's minds, following the traditional motto: "an empty mind is the workshop of the devil" (MACHADO 2013, 15). Also noteworthy is that, in this particular favela, the legitimate mediator for the gospel music show was the NGO AfroReggae, which, because of its ties with African culture, is regarded as demonic by *evangélico* people in the community. And, on the other hand, the main entertainer of the show, the *evangélica* singer Ana Paula Valadão, wore an army uniform. "Thus, the religious element which, in modern cities, may seem residual and encapsulated, emerges in the social life of these locations in close and often conflicting dialogue with political, economic and cultural actors" (VITAL and MENEZES 2017, 9).

Also on the ground, there is no lack of potential for conflict. The practice of African-based religions in placing offerings at street intersections and sacrificing animals is still controversial; in regard to the latter, the Federal Supreme Court recently determined its legitimacy.[5] The presence of other religious communities is annoying to many – be it due to disagreements in doctrine, of principles, or because of sounds, smells, objects, or practices that become the object of dispute – a conflict of religious nature that moves to the secular realm, that is regarded as a

---

[4] Available at: <https://www.camara.leg.br/proposicoesWeb/prop_mostrarintegra; jsessionid=94FDDA9057279A8694AAC9494ECBCDB1.proposicoesWebExterno2?c odteor=1304807&filename=PL+524/2015> [accessed February 26, 2020].

[5] On this see, Verdict, on March 29, 2019, of the Extraordinary Appeal (EA) 494601, deciding, by unanimous vote, the constitutionality of the Rio Grande do Sul state law (12.131 / 2004) that allows the sacrifice of animals in religious rites. Available at: <http://www.stf.jus.br/portal/cms/verNoticiaDetalhe.asp?idConteudo=407159> [accessed May 02, 2020]; see also, Ezequiel HANKE. *Do que são feitos os sapatos do estado laico?* Liberdade religiosa versus direitos dos animais. Doctoral Dissertation. Faculdades EST: Programa de Pós-Graduação em Teologia, São Leopoldo, 2020.

common instead of a specifically religious crime, such as noise pollution, protection of animal rights, and maintenance of public health and order.

At the same time, it is urgent to consider the positive elements of the presence of all this religious diversity, because the capillarity of religious communities in the diverse urban spaces – from ecumenical chapels in shopping malls to the "consumption" of spiritual benefits in a "cathedral", from an Umbanda *terreiro* in a private house to a church meeting in a garage in the favela – offer enormous potential for spiritual and material support for the surrounding community. Since the local problems extend beyond the religious boundaries and their solution is of common interest, we may come to the conclusion that what is at stake is the human, its relationships and coexistence – both in the city as such, and in the religious communities. During the COVID-19 crisis, the demands for cooperation and mutual care and protection have become especially visible.

It is thus important to highlight that the religious presence in the city is by no means limited to architectural works, especially of its temples, although they continue to have great visibility and, as we have seen above, they are built in the contemporaneity to stand out as monumental structures, even in the favelas, where *evangélico* drug dealers change religious references according to their own new preferences (VITAL DA CUNHA 2015). Its presence is also not restricted to apparently religious spaces, such as temples, cemeteries, shrines, sign boards, statues, or other religious symbols in the public square.[6] The religious presence in the city consists, not least, of the qualification of relationships and interactions that constitute a social space. Within it, according to sociologist José de Souza Martins, "religions occupy an increasing space in social reality [...] In Brazil, the main political clash [...] is religious. [...] A religion of power is emerging here and through it the power of religion is established. [There is a need for] a return to an insurgent Christianity standing against the temple sellers and the dehumanization of human beings" (MARTINS 2020, n.p.). Furthermore, a more attentive look perceives the religious in unusual, ephemeral, and

---

[6] The tour to visit sacred places is limited to temples, terreiros, and places of worship. Available at: <https://www.curitiba.pr.gov.br/noticias/pais-e-filhos-podem-explorar-lugares-sagrados-de-diferentes-religioes/44609>. On the outdated restriction of the Geography of Religion for the aforementioned spaces, see GIL FILHO 2013, 279; nowadays, a "second more comprehensive hermeneutics is being sought in explaining the meaning of the world of religion", within, of course, spatial categories (ibid, 284).

marginal places – as, for instance, in the motto for the Corpus Christi Feast in Sao Paulo in 1996, "the homeless Body of Christ in the city"[7], of the Roman Catholic Church, which, at the time, was under the guidance of Cardinal and Archbishop Paulo Evaristo Arns, Ordo Fratrum Minorum (OFM) (1921-2016), herald of a liberating and people-oriented theology. Theologically, the question is about the presence of God in time and space. This presence, perceptible through human actions, is not necessarily symphonic or harmonious, as it takes place amid the conflicts and precariousness of the city. But it is a presence that provides resonance. In what follows, I will deal with the Christian tradition, to which I belong, and which is still predominant in Brazil, although in increasingly different forms. First, I will introduce the ambiguity of the city in the Bible and in the theological tradition (8.1). Then, various forms of public presence of the church in the city will be addressed (8.2). Finally, I will present the theory of resonance according to Hartmut Rosa as a promoter of communal coexistence and a significant religious presence in the city, with the aim to contribute to a truly and deeply human city (8.3).

8.1 The ambiguity of the city in the Bible

The city has a bad start in the biblical story – in the first fratricidal murder, Cain kills his brother Abel because God accepts the sacrifice of the nomadic shepherd, but not of the settled farmer (Gen 4:5). Soon afterwards, Cain builds the first city (Gen 4:17). And not long thereafter, human beings build "a city and a tower" to reach the heavens and make "a name for ourselves" (Gen 11:4). God reacts to the endeavour by creating linguistic confusion. Babel, a reference to Babylon, is a recurrent biblical image for everything negative in human behaviour and that can serve as a name to represent, in a veiled but recognisable form, any imperial and dominating power – e.g. the Roman Empire in the Book of Revelation. In Babel, diversity seems like a punishment that dismantles and disempowers. Thus, one city is born out of murder, the other out of

---

[7] Seen in Sao Paulo, while living there to do some research work. In 2018, in Rio de Janeiro, a sculpture was opened, showing Christ, wrapped in a blanket, sleeping on a bench in a public square, in front of the metropolitan cathedral. Available at: <https://oglobo.globo.com/rio/escultura-jesus-sem-teto-inaugurada-em-frente-catedral-metropoli tana-23243347> [accessed March 06, 2020].

megalomania. At Pentecost, in Jerusalem, the Holy Spirit allows everyone present to understand, in their own language, what the disciples are saying. In this case, diversity is neither negative nor uniform, but the Babylonian confusion is overcome by mutual understanding and interaction.

Throughout the biblical narratives, the city has an ambiguous status. On the one hand, it is the place of witness to the divine blessing on human endeavour. At the same time, there is the criticism of the prophets against the injustice committed in the city. They demand respect for the rights of the widows, orphans, foreigners, and the poor. The main city, Jerusalem, the site of the sanctuary, the temple, is not spared from criticism. Jesus weeps over Jerusalem (Lk 19:41), just as he laments the iniquities of other cities (Chorazin, Bethsaida, and Capernaum, Mt 11:20-25). He conducts "the cleansing" of the temple by turning over the tables of the money changers and saying: "Is it not written, 'My house shall be called a house of prayer for all the nations'? But you have made it a den of robbers" (Mk 11:17). Even so, the temple remains as a symbol of the presence of God, therefore, affirming God's presence amid the ambiguities of life, including religious life. Interestingly, the heavenly Jerusalem, the utopia of the city in the kingdom of God, has no separate sacred space: there is no temple in the new Jerusalem (Rev 21:22), for Godself will be the sanctuary. In the eschaton, profane and sacred space are confused. The garden of the origins (Gen 2:8) becomes the city of the end time.

For Paul, the real *polis* is in heaven: "For our country [*politeuma*] is in heaven, and it is from there that we are expecting a Saviour, the Lord Jesus Christ" (Phil 3:20). In the Letter to the Hebrews, the author points out, in a pun in Greek, that "for here we have no lasting city [*menousan polin*], but we are looking for the city that is to come [*mellousan*]" (Heb 13:14). The First Letter of Peter is addressed to "the foreigners in the dispersion", the purpose of the writing being "to interpret this foreignness as a mark of the essence of being a Christian" (FELDMEIER 2008, 1).

In times of rejection and persecution, it is understandable that there is an idea of being a foreigner in this world, a perception that is both realistic and hopeful. Here, the world is perceived as a place of danger and temptation, from which one must protect oneself. The situation of living in exile in a strange land is also prominent in the Hebrew Bible, with people in exile being instructed to pray for the good of the city:

"Seek the peace of the city where I have sent you into exile, and pray to the LORD on its behalf, for in its peace you will have peace" (Jer 29:7).

Historically, since its inception and increasingly thereafter, Christianity has been an urban phenomenon. In the Old Testament, God is initially perceived as a nomad deity accompanying a group of believers through the desert and later becomes an urban deity, seated in the temple in Jerusalem. Jesus is portrayed as being familiar with the rural setting – his parables deal with themes from the countryside, he talks about the shepherd, the sheep, the plough, his disciples are from the hinterland, many of whom were fishermen. The gospels reflect a predominantly rural context, and, indeed, even cities like Nazareth and Capernaum were in fact villages at the time. Most cities, which depended upon the rural surroundings for supply, had no more than 15,000 inhabitants and were comprised in total of 5% to 10% of the population (VOIGT 2014, 31; STEGEMANN and STEGEMANN 2001). However, already then, cities were considered more attractive because of better possibilities for work and income, better access to supplies, more security, and more cultural offerings.

The countryside (Galilee) is contrasted with the city (Jerusalem). In the city, the disciples face rejection and violence – they are recognised by their Galilean accent (Lk 22:59), they are despised by the Jewish elite, who want to get rid of Jesus. The Gospel of Luke centres its narrative on the sayings and deeds of Jesus mostly on his way to Jerusalem, moving, therefore, from the rural to an urban setting, from the margins to the centre of power (Lk 9:51-19:27), even while going through different cities. In Jerusalem, Jesus is arrested and crucified on the edge of the city ("outside the [city] gate", as highlighted by Heb 13:12), in a public place reserved for the execution of those who were not Roman citizens. As emphasised by Vítor Westhelle (2012, 79), Golgotha is the "the place [topos] on the outskirts (*chora*) of the holy city of Jerusalem in which God is abandoned, dead, and absent (*apousia*) and yet, *sub contraria specie,* present (*parousia*) and revealed".

Christian mission, on the other hand, not before long, travels through the cities, where it finds hospitality among newly converted people, an audience to evangelise and possibilities for further missionary work. Paul is active in the cities, as they offer a public space conducive for mission, hospitality among converts, and the possibility of self-sustenance through work. His letters are addressed to communities located in cities (MEEKS 2003). Initially centred around Judaism, the

Christian faith did not gain much attention, but then, it was severely persecuted to eventually emerge as a new (THEISSEN 1999) and, later, even official religion of the Roman Empire. It is possible that urban Christians were not all poor, but some belonged to a middle class.[8] In religious terms, the ancient city, with its great diversity, resembled a public market, and, in this sense, was much like a modern city (FITSCHEN 2001b, 102).

In the city of Antiquity, the church flourished, built temples, established episcopates, practiced charity and hospitality (MÜLLER 2010). Later, during the industrialisation period, in an extremely precarious urbanisation process, new Christian initiatives emerged such as the *Hell's Kitchen* of Walter Rauschenbusch in New York (1886-1897) and, a little earlier, in Great Britain, the *Salvation Army* of William and Catherine Booth, which, under the motto "Soap, soup and salvation" was active in city quarters of precarious conditions (BAKER and GRAHAM 2017). Service and hospitality are intrinsic to the Christian faith, and essential to its self-definition – the church is constituted by *kerygma* (proclamation), *leitourgia* (worship), *martyria* (witness), *diakonia* (service), and *koinonia* (fellowship). Without all these elements, the church is not the church. Also, other religions, such as Spiritism or those of African origin, for example, practice charity by extending social services and assistance to needy people.[9]

With the rise of Latin American Liberation Theology, a new impetus was given to the analysis and critique of poverty, claiming not only for social services or emergency help, but also for the transformation of society. The CEBs of the rural areas, but also strongly present in the periphery of the cities, took over with the support of the church hierarchy, especially during the military regime, the struggle for the improvement of life in the city – in terms of education, health services, sanitation, employment opportunities, and so on – based on and inspired by their popular reading of the Bible. How can, in the present day, such public and diaconal presence be recovered (cf. VON SINNER 2020)?

---

[8] FITSCHEN 2001a, using Meeks and Theissen as a reference.
[9] In the public perception in Brazil, it is precisely charity that made these religions socially acceptable; according to MONTERO 2006; 2011.

8.2 Public presence of the church in the city

On the Roman Catholic side, the theologian and priest of Belgian origin, José Comblin (1923-2011) was the first to deal explicitly and consistently throughout his life and work on a theology of the city. With constant attention to the centrality of anthropology, and God's call for human beings to become more and more human, he has been insisting that a church, structured around a rural, territorial, or parochial reality, cannot survive in the urban context, as it loses connection with the urban human being, especially the poor. Comblin himself followed the rapid and disorderly urbanisation of the continent since he had come to live there, in 1957. In the face of this geographical, but also cultural change, that brings about a new way of ordering human life, he is convinced that the church needs to reinvent itself (SOUZA 2014, 571). An important dimension, however, should remain present, that is, the communitarian dimension, constituted by the collective memory and the meeting places: "in the city what is essential are the human relationships" (COMBLIN 1996, 46), offering thus another model of city than the functional model – a city divided into separate sectors – or the model of city as centre of power. "In Christianity, what makes cities sacred is human activity itself. For human beings renewed by the Spirit and acting out of a creative and unifying love are the temple of God" (COMBLIN 1996, 29). The city is constituted not only of buildings, but also of values, so it is not up for the church to simply deplore its decay, such as the dissolution of the family. Although community life in the city is different from the rural setting and there is, in fact, greater isolation among people, the great gain is freedom and privacy. According to Comblin (2014, 581), the constitutive project must be guided by the principles of freedom, equality, and fraternity. "The Kingdom of God is embodied in the placement of bodies in a fabric of relationships. The Kingdom of God occupies a space and a time. Such space and time constitute cities. [...] The Bible describes the Kingdom of God in the form of a city. It is as a transfigured Jerusalem that the last prophets announced the advent of the Kingdom of God" (COMBLIN 1996, 28).

On the Protestant side, even a few years before Comblin's *Théologie de la ville*, the book *The Secular City* by Baptist theologian Harvey Cox (1969/2013) had a great impact. For Cox, secularisation is the natural outcome of faith, which, with God's approval, manifests itself by human beings building the city with autonomy and responsibility.

Faith focuses on the discernment of practices, not on the city and its construction. In this view, the city is devoid of religious meaning – disenchanted, to use Max Weber's term, and rationalised in the sense of a radically ethical religion. These are the last consequences of the entry of religion into the *saeculum*, arising from Christianity itself, especially Protestant Christianity and its high regard for the individual, his/her work, and his/her conscience. An important reference for Cox was Dietrich Bonhoeffer and his search for a non-religious Christianity in a world come of age, and the responsibility of the Christian person, in seeking to follow Christ and to do the will of God. Thirty years later, Cox (1995) relativised his radical position to see new forms of religion manifesting itself in urban spaces. Especially in cities south of the American continent, he did not observe the loss of enchantment, but its displacement. "Today it is secularity, not spirituality, that may be headed for extinction" (ibid, xv).

In Brazil, Magali Cunha (2006) has written a systematisation of the various positions of the churches and Christian people towards the city, by adapting the distinctions of the classic *Christ and the Culture* of H. Richard Niebuhr (1894-1962). In the early stages, Protestantism, especially the Presbyterian church, had successful conversions on the so-called coffee trail in rural areas, even while it had a strong presence in the city because of the confessional private schools it had founded. Protestantism was characterised as being "communitarian, rural, sectarian and anti-Catholic" (ibid, 102). Thus, Cunha identifies 1) the isolationist model or Church *versus* the City, shaped by a dualistic perspective (church-world), a Puritan moralism and an indifference towards the urban culture and its social demands (therefore, enforcing values of the rural world); 2) the interventionist model or Church *for* the City, which provides social services to people in need; 3) the adapting model or Church *of* the City, followed especially by (Neo-) Pentecostal churches and Charismatic Renewal groups of the Roman Catholic Church, which manage to better follow the pace and mobility of the city, but, because of their non-critical stand towards neo-liberalism and little emphasis on solidarity, are limited to offering individual help; 4) the responsible model or Church *in* the City – the ecumenical and prophetic movement of Christian social responsibility that has arisen especially in the 1960s, initially unable to act openly because of the military regime, but always present and now operating and contributing with more freedom (ibid, 105ff.). This model favours the importance of the church in providing spaces for community and solidarity, even if in small groups, where people can meet one another, and take care of the ecology of the urban space.[10]

It was the Methodist Clovis Pinto de Castro, in his doctoral thesis (2000), who began to reflect more explicitly on a particular public presence of the church in society in order to sustain a "citizen faith". In a seminar on Urban Ministry held at the Methodist University of São Paulo in 2005, with contributions from Cunha, mentioned above, this theme was further developed with the intention to expand the reflection upon "the public presence of the church in urban areas", thus expressing a form of public theology, although it was not called by this name (DE CASTRO, CUNHA, and LOPES, eds., 2006). One particular issue, among others, is the constant dilemma between having a visible and significant presence without favouring corporate or private interests of one specific community or church while occupying the space. This challenge is even more present when facing the growing religious and secular pluralism of the city.

I cherish and reinforce central elements from previous approaches, the importance to focus on human beings and their communal life, a culture shaped by common values, the benefit of people meeting one another and the sensitivity toward the most vulnerable urban populations. I propose in this last section a theology that fosters resonance in the cacophony of the urban environment.

8.3 Fostering resonance in the cacophony of the urban environment

Cities are places for the rationalising of coexistence, but also for migration and mobility. Their growth and expansion, often in a disorderly manner, make possible unusual encounters and mixtures. Cities undoubtedly benefit from well-developed urban planning, for example, in relation to public and private mobility, supply, sanitation, telecommunications, energy distribution, and other services. At the same time, their habitability highly depends on whether the built space favours

---

[10] On this see also OLIVEIRA 2014. The collection of articles on "urban scenarios" (*cenários urbanos*) in which this text was published, edited by missiologist Roberto Zwetsch, is from a post-diploma specialisation course in urban mission, sponsored by Faculdades EST from 2008 to 2010.

encounter, diversity, and spontaneity, or prevents them from happening by being too functional or unilateral, like, for instance, Brasília, the federal capital city of Brazil, which, by favouring automobiles, does not provide adequate space for pedestrians to circulate. Transitory mobility – a non-place, according to Augé (2009) – designates both metaphorically and concretely today's urban space, although there are also attempts to establish symbols of stability, such as the monumental structures mentioned above, including religious temples, and the apartment buildings and gated communities that have their own world, apart and hermetically separated from the external urban mobility by gates and locks. They are symbols of exclusivity and exclusion, of strictly controlled entry and, as is often the case, of social isolation of its residents.

In general, it is not surprising that, in the city, there is also extensive religious mobility, and people often choose their church for convenience of accessibility, proximity, adequate activities regarding format and schedule, and where they "feel good" (see VON SINNER et al., 2012). In this context, the reception and hospitality of the church are very important – are people welcomed? Are they immediately able to relate with members of the community and with the religious minister? Is their presence acknowledged, does someone take note of their names and personal contacts to send messages and invitations, without being too intrusive? How is hospitality practiced or is the underlining message that this is a closed group with no desire to welcome new members? Is the church building open or closed during the day? Does the church organise open neighbourhood parties that are inviting to anyone who passes by and are public and visible to the whole community? Does the church interact and is it integrated with other neighbourhood organisations, such as the local school, the local public market, neighbourhood associations, other religious communities, or community organisations? Religious communities have a great power to mobilise, and when the focus of the gatherings is not so much to concentrate – such as huge church gatherings in football stadiums – but to extend – for instance, street parties or gatherings at the public square – they can contribute to creating open spaces for encounter, interaction and mutual recognition, where neighbours who have perhaps never spoken to each other can now greet and get to know one another. The gratuity of hospitality and the disposition to welcome new people without commercial intent makes a huge difference.

To use another terminology: churches can be spaces of resonance, where people can test their self-efficacy and receive positive feedback. According to the German sociologist Hartmut Rosa (2016), resonance creates relationships between people, as well as with objects and with God, as made visible in the Eucharist or in the blessing through its "resonance axes": vertical (towards God), horizontal (towards the community), and diagonal (related to the elements, bread and wine, and the sign of the cross done in the blessing). From this perspective, God "is the representation of a responsive world", while religion is a relationship governed by the categories of love and meaning, "promising to guarantee that the original and basic form of existence is a relationship of resonance and not of alienation".[11] For Rosa, culture, nature, and religion are part of the vertical axis of resonance. Unlike momentary resonance experiences, these axes are relatively stable. Besides, a disposition for a sensitive attitude toward resonance is needed that enables a real relationship with the other. In situations of fear, stress and time pressure, as is the case in many jobs, but also in everyday life amid violence, there is no possibility of resonance.

Resonance is not a mere echo, a reflection of sounds, but, rather, someone's authentic response to the vibrations that someone else is emitting. Deriving from acoustics, one observes that open or porous bodies do not have acoustic resonance, while fully closed bodies also cannot enter in resonance. "Resonance occurs [...] when the vibration of one body stimulates the *proper frequency* of the other" (ibid, 282, italics in original). This happens in a space that allows such resonance to occur, but not in a forcible manner. Nor does it mean consonance or harmony, but response, i.e. a responsive event. As such, it is a free event that recognises its limitation not to seek to possess the other whose identity remains unreachable.

For Rosa, resonance is an *emotional, neurological, and bodily reality*, a basic element of social and cultural existence. It becomes the main criterion for a successful life (*gelingendes Leben*) – in a broad sense, not only from an economic, professional, or consumer standpoint – which cannot be measured merely by access to wealth, options, or material

---

[11] Rosa 2016, 435. He refers to William James and Friedrich Schleiermacher as precursors of this definition that focuses precisely on the relationship with the world (*Weltbeziehung*), which is the heart of the book's argument. He also mentions Martin Buber's dialogical principle.

resources, but is measured especially by the quality of the relationship with the world. This relationship may be one of resonance, but also of indifference or aversion. The opposite of resonance is alienation. As stated on the back cover of the book, "Resonance remains the promise of modernity, alienation, however, is its reality" (ROSA 2017, 35). When resonance is denied, people get sick and may even die. According to Axel Honneth (1996), resonance is also understood as a modification and expansion of the concept of recognition. For Rosa, indeed, resonance is a more dynamic and processual event than recognition, especially legal recognition, which can be fixed and accumulated – resonance does not function this way. On the other hand, because resonance is an event between two people, it cannot be unilateral. While one can, and often must fight for recognition, it does not make sense to fight for resonance.

Religion, then, can provide spaces and possibilities for meetings that foster resonance experiences, overcoming the formality of work and business relations as well as the denials of resonance in relationships shaped by prejudice and rejection, due to social, religious, cultural, gender, or other reasons. Care and attention towards other people, emotional, spiritual and material support, as well as mutual collaboration and political articulation to struggle for housing and public services, are means to create resonance amid the cacophony and ambiguity of the city. Such meeting moments must be adapted to the time and space available to the invited guests, according to the dynamics of the city. In turn, however, they contribute towards the creation of more habitable cities.

Chapter 9

Populism, "People" and Public Theology: Precarious Realities, Precarious Concepts [*]

"A Spectre is haunting the world – populism". Social scientists Ghiţa Ionescu and Ernest Gellner (eds., 1969, 1) noted this over fifty years ago when trying to define the phenomenon during an interdisciplinary conference at the London School of Economics. Not surprisingly, they did not arrive – in fact, they did not intend to do so – at a consensus in relation to its conceptual and theoretical definition; the phenomenon was described as an ideology, movement, or way of communication in the "variety of its incarnations" (ibid, 5).

In recent times, the phenomenon has been detected in many contexts, as in the USA under Donald Trump and in Victor Orbán's Hungary, but also in considerable tendencies in Germany and France, to cite just a few examples. It is predominantly situated on the right side of the political spectrum, often with conservative religious connotations. Also in Brazil, sociologist Fernando Perlatto (2016, 92) depicted populism as a "kind of spectre that will be haunting, for good or bad, Brazilian politics for the next few decades".[1] The affirmation was made in 2016, that is, before the 2018 elections that brought Jair Messias Bolsonaro to the presidency, but served as a kind of prophetic announcement. What, precisely, are we speaking about when we say "populism", and what reality do we wish to denote by it?

Populism has been observed by French linguist Patrick Charadeau (2014) as a phenomenon in which the politician usually applies a discourse that denounces all that does damage to the people, pointing at culprits and emphasising values seen as necessary for the re-establishment of well-being and order. These values are, directly or indirectly, seen as present in a person or government: the politician himself as trustee of the discourse. For the author, what happens in the background is the "return effect". This is, then, a postulate capable of

---

[*] This version largely coincides with the one co-authored with Celso Gabatz which is being published in the *International Journal of Public Theology* 15/3 (2021). Used with permission.
[1] This one and all translations, unless otherwise stated, are the author's.

being constructed under the following order: "the state of victimization", "the satanization of the culprits", "the exaltation of [moral] values". Indeed, charismatic leadership is usually connotated with populism, which can be seen as an "exploitation of people's political passions", as Brazilian-German political scientist Paula Diehl formulates referring to Marc Lits, which the latter distinguishes from "popular" as the self-articulation of the people (DIEHL 2019, 129; LITS 2009, 9-27). In any case, the relationship between a populist leader and his followers is ambivalent or even contradictory; this is what Diehl calls the "twist" in democratic representation, which can lead to unexpected change as well as to distortion. According to Diehl's (2011) balanced conceptualisation, populism is a "thin ideology" (CAS MUDDE), rather a kind of "political doing", a phenomenon observable in different degrees rather than a clear category. Its core features are the (democratic) belief that political power belongs to the people, their (populist) idealisation as a homogenous unity, resentments against an elite seen as corrupt, incompetent, and disconnected from the everyday life of ordinary people, an intimate relationship between the people and their leader and the rejection of institutions as mediators.

Outrightly negative in his assessment of populism, German political scientist Jan-Werner Müller of Princeton University admits that populism can, "sometimes, bring positive effects to democracy", but, as such, "it is not democratic, and its tendency is, without doubt, antidemocratic".[2] In contrast, Ernesto Laclau (2005, 117) defends populism not as a content or specific political movement, but as a discursive strategy, a political logic in which a "global political subject" constitutes itself ever anew, "bringing together a plurality of social demands" in a construction of hegemony. For Laclau, populism is not a dangerous deviation from democracy or a threat to it, but, rather and precisely, its necessary form of being. Considering such divergences, but

---

[2] MÜLLER 2017, 14. I translate from the German version, because the English version is not identical (*What is Populism?* East Rutherford: Penguin, 2017, Kindle Edition), given the very different context and, precisely, the different understandings of populism: "The notion of populism as somehow 'progressive' and 'grassroots' is largely an American (North, Central, and South) phenomenon. In Europe, one finds a different historically conditioned preconception of populism. There populism is connected, primarily by liberal commentators, with irresponsible policies or various forms of political pandering ('demagoguery' and 'populism' are often used interchangeably)" (11-12 of the English version).

also a perspective of constant reconfiguration, it is evident that "the people" are a precarious category.

Kaltwasser, Taggart, Espejo and Ostiguy (eds., 2020) distinguish an *ideational* (MUDDE 2020), a pragmatic-strategic (WEYLAND 2020) and a social-relational approach (OSTIGUY 2020), while the important contributions by Laclau are taken up by others, but did not gain a proper chapter. Dutch political scientist Cas Mudde (2004, 543) defines populism as "an ideology that considers society to be ultimately separated into two homogeneous and antagonistic groups, 'the pure people' versus 'the corrupt elite', and which argues that politics should be an expression of the volonté générale (general will) of the people". Such a definition does not restrict populism either to the left or the right of the political spectrum; however, on the left side, according to Mudde, it is more likely to be compatible with liberality and pluralism.

In Brazil, the political class, against whom there is an already traditional distrust, is generically seen as corrupt and parasitic. A strong resentment against the long permanence of leftist governments (2003-2016) and the desire for a minimal state in economic terms among considerable sectors of the middle and upper classes, aligned to widespread conservative values as to family and sexuality, as well as the longing for a strong hand in the treatment of crime appeared to prepare the way for a hitherto improbable presidential candidate to be elected. He precisely promised to implement a combination of neo-liberal promises with a diffuse conservatism, promoting a militancy against what is understood as "socialism" and "gender ideology", unilaterally spotted on the opposite side of the political spectrum. The nation, represented by the national flag and the official motto of the "loved fatherland" – evoking the 1964-1985 military regime with its 'love it or leave it' – is unilaterally claimed by this position. Whoever takes a divergent position is seen as opposed to the national project and, thus, as not being part of "the people" (CASARA 2017, 179-210). Even with a disastrous record in view of the COVID-19 pandemic, which brought Brazil to the second (now third) rank in cases and deaths, second only to the USA, around 30% of the population used to firmly and consistently defend the Bolsonaro government.[3] Once the parliamentary investigation commission of the Senate exposed cases of corruption in the purchase or negotiation of vaccines, with the probable involvement of the president, the numbers

---

[3] See the data on <https://coronavirus.jhu.edu/map.html> [accessed July 23, 2021].

diminished.[4] Still, 24% judge the government to be "good" or "very good", which indicates the existence of a populist configuration in which the ruler – even if hardly charismatic in any traditional sense[5] – and the ruled form an affective unity against the political establishment, with a conservative agenda combatting liberal elements.

In my analysis, Brazil is still functional as a democracy, with the traditional media being critical, the Supreme Court being restrictive, and Congress continuing to be a plurality of voices in competition. While the president rehearses indications of authoritarianism and the critique of democracy, so far he has not been able to prevail with such positions. While social movements and left parties also invoke "the people" they claim to represent, in a social (*plebs, ochlos*) and political (*demos*) acceptation of "people", for Bolsonaro "the people" are national, *ethnos* rather than *demos*.

If, then, the issue of representativity is one crucial while precarious element in politics, this question also arises when the issue is religion. The religious communities as organisations of great capillarity in Brazil, present as they are in even the most distant and precarious locations, can point to their ample presence among the population, as well as amplify their rhetoric and strategic incidence on people's lives. The religion of "the people" has been, traditionally, Catholicism, within the understanding that whoever was Brazilian was, by definition, Catholic. It is important, however, to recall that even this religious matrix has rightly been distinguished into a more official version, aligned with doctrine and practices according to the corresponding manuals, and another, more popular version, visible in pilgrimages and devotions. Protestantism, increasingly present since 1824, was seen as of foreign origin, alien to the national spirit infused by colonisation – which is, of course, just as well relatively young and foreign (see Chapters 4 above and 12 below). On its part, especially Protestantism introduced by missionary work from the USA by default adopted, in many aspects, a behaviour that differed from common Brazilian culture. While in the 19th century, this could include to participate, together with liberal Catholics, Positivists and Freemasons, in the strive for modernisation consolidated by the Republic (created in

---

[4] While 24% still find the government is performing "well" or "very well", rejection ("poorly" or "very poorly") has now surpassed 50%. Available at: <https://www1.folha.uol.com.br/poder/2021/ 07/datafolha-rejeicao-a-bolsonaro-sobe-a-51-novo-recorde-do-presidente.shtml> [accessed July 23, 2021].

[5] On the overestimation of charism in populism, see PRIESTER 2012, 72-91.

1889), in the 20th century, the tendency was to align with established power, not least during the military regime, and to adopt more conservative positions. Pentecostalism, by extension, was understood as a foreign implantation despite its increasingly Brazilian leadership. It is important to underline the multiplication of denominations that developed on national soil, some of which have been exporting themselves to other countries. And, while initially alien to politics, it has developed considerable political power and interest since the 1980s.

It is precisely in the economically more vulnerable strata of society, the plebs so to speak, among whom Pentecostal and Neo-Pentecostal churches have had their major success and experienced quite expressive growth. The formation of a "Pentecostal people" happened, as Brazilian political scientist Joanildo Burity (2020) argues, after decades of being discarded as an insignificant, alien and dangerous minority, promoted a type of "minoritization", i.e. seeking to level "asymmetries between an emerging difference and established majority arrangements, which implies demanding equal treatment under the law between majority and minority(ies)", thus making the majority one "minority" among others (ibid, 86, note 5). Especially since the Constituent Assembly (1986-87), the *evangélico* minority has been seeking legitimacy and political integration, claiming to be part of "the people" (BURITY 2016). It is a minority in continuous numerical growth, reaching around 31% of the population according to a recent survey.[6] Such minority, which to a great extent had been supporting the Lula and the initial Dilma Rousseff leftist governments, gradually left this boat and joined a wave of a mix of anti-leftist, neo-liberal and conservative flags, re-inscribing, as Burity (2020, 90) says, "their demands and alliances into a new hegemonic formation". Rather than claiming a merely equal status in relation to the hitherto hegemonic Catholic majority, such numerical minorities now claim to represent the majority. In fact, this has been a recurrent argument in Bolsonaro's mouth: the state is secular, but the nation is Christian, thus claiming to stand both for (conservative) *evangélicos* and Catholics, now forming a mixed "Christian" majority with values to be defended against "communists" and a "corrupt" elite.

---

[6] DataFolha Research of December, 2019. It is noteworthy that among the *evangélico* churches, mainly Pentecostal and Neo-Pentecostal, there is a proportionally higher representation of black and brown people as well as women and youth. Available at: <https://www1.folha.uol.com.br/poder/2020/01/cara-tipica-do-evangelico-brasileiro-e-feminina-e-negra-aponta-datafolha.shtml> [accessed May 6, 2021].

Bolsonaro himself represents both strands: a Catholic by birth and upbringing, he is married in his third marriage to an *evangélico* and was (re-)baptised in the river Jordan by an *evangélico* pastor; however, he never renounced his being Catholic nor self-declared to be *evangélico*. The religious reference is then a diffuse kind of "ecumenical Christendom" as the nation's backbone.[7]

Religious freedom as the conquest of religious diversification in modernity, an important factor of the emergence of human rights, is an aspect of constant demand by Pentecostal and Neo-Pentecostal churches, usually for themselves and not necessarily to be extended to other religions. It is particularly these churches that, with their considerable public influence, helped to elect Bolsonaro to the presidency. He gathered two thirds (21.5 million) of the *evangélico* electorate, but also a bit over half of the Catholic electorate.[8] His motto "Brazil above everything, God above anyone", which originates from the military context – Bolsonaro was a parachute captain before becoming a politician – recalls historical nationalist formulations. It seeks to define "the people" mainly by alignment to this project which is, according to this view, the only true patriotic position. Hence, the government's official slogan is "beloved homeland Brazil" (*patria amada Brasil*), the last verse of the national anthem.[9] Bolsonaro supporters during their rallies generally wear yellow, green, and blue coloured clothes from the Brazilian national flag and wave these very flags, which makes it impossible for the opposition to connect to the national symbols and reinforces the idea that only those with Bolsonaro are truly Brazilians.[10]

Thus, "the people" is a highly precarious concept which refers to an only precariously describable reality. Attempts to create unambiguousness invoking race, ethnicity, nation and/or religion cannot stand in view of the necessary differentiations and questioning of its biological, cultural, historical, religious, and other presuppositions. The

---

[7] On – *mutatis mutandis* – similar aspects in the South African context at the time of Jacob Zuma's presidency, see FORSTER 2020.

[8] See the table based on a DataFolha research carried out on 25 October 2018, quoted by DE ALMEIDA 2019, 206.

[9] See, for instance, <https://noticias.uol.com.br/politica/ultimas-noticias/2019/01/04/bolsonaro-slogan-patria-amada-brasil.htm> [accessed July 25, 2021].

[10] See, for instance, <https://brazilian.report/society/2019/09/07/right-wing-seized-brazil-national-symbols/> [accessed July 25, 2021].

result of a totalitarian concept of "people" became visible in all its destructivity in the Third Reich – but, *mutatis mutandis,* also in South Africa under apartheid (HÖHNE and MEIREIS, eds., 2020; VOSLOO 2020).

This prevents, on the one hand, any unilateral definition, and, on the other, defends the recognition of the people as a dynamic collective of subjects in their concrete anxieties and desires, while it also calls for a critical observation. To this end, I shall first analyse the concept of populism and "the people" (9.1). I shall then deepen the discussion of the concept of populism in dialogue with Ernesto Laclau and Chantal Mouffe, in a conceptualisation that differs from the common acceptation and in our view allows for a fruitful theological discussion, although they do not develop such discussion themselves (9.2). Finally, by means of a theological reflection in the perspective of a public theology, I delineate possibilities for witness in society through the presence and persistence of the people's participation (9.3).

9.1 Populism and "the people"

As indicated above, there are many and diverging definitions of populism. One understanding is to be a "particular moralistic imagination of politics, a way of perceiving the political world that sets a morally pure and fully unified – but [...] ultimately fictional – people against elites who are deemed corrupt or in some other way morally inferior" (MÜLLER 2017, 19). In Europe, populism – with exceptions, like *Podemos* in Spain and *Syriza* in Greece – is usually associated with movements or governments on the right wing of the political spectrum, with a strong exclusivist agenda as to migrants and, especially, Muslims. In Latin America – with the recent exception of Bolsonaro's government – it has tended to be associated with left wing governments, like Lula in Brazil, Evo Morales in Bolivia, Rafael Correa in Ecuador, and Hugo Chavez and Nicolás Maduro in Venezuela. The historical paradigms for populism on the continent – with a strong social element, even if authoritarian and restricting political and civil rights – are Juan and Eva Perón in Argentina and Getúlio Vargas in Brazil. While such distinction of "left" and "right" has come to be questioned, it points to an important difference: populism in Latin America tends to arise from a vertical unease (the socially defined *plebs* against the elite). In Europe, for its part, it has a strong horizontal dimension (the nationally defined "people" against foreign intruders). While "left" and "right" are certainly not the only distinction that can be made, I believe it is still meaningful in terms of an at least intentionally inclusive or exclusive way of being populist (see also MOUFFE 2018).

If the concept of populism can be meaningfully applied to such diverse phenomena, it is then rather a "style" of doing politics than a specific substance. In Latin America, the traditional narrative tells us that the country's evils stem from an unequal relationship, destitute of any reciprocity and conversation: to a civil society incapable of self-organisation, "jelly-like" according to some interpretations, and a "weak" working class dominated by a state "which is capable of manipulating, co-opting and corrupting" (FERREIRA 2017, 62). For Perlatto (2016, 71), in the perspective of its critics, populism implies the

> Presence [...] of charismatic and personalistic leaders, the excessive control of the market by a hypertrophic State and an orientation towards the execution of social policies that are considered assistentialist or clientelist, and that would serve, solely and exclusively, to co-opt the popular sectors [...], [being seen as] masses for manipulation.

In this formulation, one can detect a latent disregard for the people ("masses for manipulation") that needs to be problematised.[11] Indeed, Brazilian historian José Murilo de Carvalho (1989, 10f.) affirms that there is a tendency to "bestialize" the people, considering them as a "powerless victim in view of the manipulations by the State or dominant groups". However, as all evil is not coming from the state, so all good is not coming from the people – and vice versa. The people are acting subjects and must not be seen as mere objects of other's manipulation which, obviously, implies the possibility to be destructive and even violent in the ambiguity proper to human life.

In the 2018 elections, it was the poor north-eastern population who benefitted from the social programmes of the PT governments that

---

[11] See for instance PRIESTER, 2012, 17: "The people [*das Volk*] do not have a good image. [...] The people are again the 'great slob' (*der große Lümmel*), ugly in their obesity, tasteless in their jogging suits, rampant in their craving for alcohol and cigarettes, politically volatile and prone to consent with authoritarian solutions like in criminal law"; also ROSANVALLON 2020, 9: populism "is, in the end, a doubtful notion – indeed it often serves only to stigmatize adversaries or legitimize under a new word the old claim to superiority of the powerful and educated over the popular classes that are judged to always be inclined to turn into a plebs ruled by ominous passions".

most resisted Bolsonaro's election. The affluent classes, in turn, in the more 'developed' states in the south and southeast of the country – and thus, contra-intuitively, not the deprived 'people' – tended to vote for Bolsonaro as well as politicians aligned with him, in a strong anti-PT attitude. In view of the theoretical definitions presented so far, we could ask, after all, on which side are "the true people"?

In the history of democracy, the transferral of the legitimacy of power to the "sovereign people" is significant and visible in the famous opening phrase of the Constitution of the USA: "We, the people..." The philosophical basis was provided by the social contract theories, an always hypothetical construction that shows, again, the precariousness of the concept "the people". Partly, in history, it counted on the importance of God, at least for moral discipline as maintained by Rousseau, for whom for a "civil religion" the idea of a God that punished the evil and rewarded the good was necessary.[12] Also for Kant (2015), it is here that God entered reason, practical and not pure, as a postulate that guarantees the interpellation of the ethical human being from the call of duty. This need of recurring to God as a guarantee for morality became more and more substitutable. However, the importance of a moral reference that would protect the various tendencies among "the people" against mutual destruction remained.

Democracy is constituted by the people's majority vote, but, I contend, equally by the protection of minorities – and, thus, the maintenance of pluralism – whose right to exist, to participate and to construct majorities is tantamount. It is from this comprehensive and structural proposition that the democratic, constitutional state emerges, based on the fundamental human rights it is to guarantee. Authoritarianism installs itself where such rights, even in the name of "the people", no longer serve as reference. In this direction, Carl Schmitt's (2006) comprehension of political theology, in analogy to God's omnipotence, identifies as sovereign the one who decides on the state of exception and, therefore, the suspension of the law that would normally restrict the government. For Schmitt, this role belonged

---

[12] ROUSSEAU 2019, Book IV, chapter 8, "on civil religion". While, for Rousseau, the religion of mankind is important and makes people brothers and sisters it tends to hold believers occupied with the heavenly fatherland rather than with the earthly, and tends to be exclusive and intolerant. The religion of the citizen, in contrast, promotes good citizenship in the earthly life. On a discussion of Rousseau in political terms see URBINATI, 2020.

necessarily to one person and not the collective of the people. In German Nazism, for example, which Schmitt supported, "the people" was not constituted empirically, but presupposed a concept constructed and controlled from above, in strict relation with the *Führer*, and became a nationalist category, extremely exclusive, in a totalitarian system that destroyed, systematically, whoever was conceived to be an enemy. Schmitt provided a meaning for what he saw as "empty rationality" of the Weimar Constitution which, however, could neither be filled with legal positivism nor with Christian values in a secularised world. He therefore connected, as German former judge and present theologian Karola Radler (2013, 276) argues, the idea of "the political" as a friend-enemy dichotomy to myth and meaning that would "entice human beings to willingly sacrifice their lives in conflicts that endanger the preservation of their own form of existence and the survival of a people (*Volk*)". Thus, in a religion-like political system, the ruler embodies oneness (under the idea of "sameness", rather than "equality", and ruling out diversity and pluralism) between the ruler and the ruled. Rejecting Schmitt's view and its presupposition that the state could and should create (rather than sustain) human life and community, Bonhoeffer's brother-in-law Gerhard Leibholz and Bonhoeffer himself expanded such monolithic notion to a twoness, and eventually three-dimensionality, respectively.

Although referring to Schmitt's view of "the political" as a field of conflict, Ernesto Laclau and Chantal Mouffe, as we shall see, perceive populism not as an authoritarian creation from above, but as a construction from below. Rather than objects, people are subjects and agents in the struggle for hegemony and the articulation of a diversity of demands that can bring them to power. Laclau (2005, 117) defends the pertinence of "populism" not as a content or specific political movement, but as a discursive strategy, a political logic in which a "global political subject" constitutes itself ever anew, "bringing together a plurality of social demands" in a construction of hegemony. For Laclau, populism, in this understanding, is not a dangerous deviation from democracy or a threat to it, but, rather and precisely, its necessary form of being. Considering such divergences, but also a perspective of constant reconfiguration, it is evident that "the people" are a precarious category.

In theological terms, also "the people of God" are a precarious category, not being clear (anyway for the human perception, i.e. Mt 13:24-30) from the outset who belongs to it. God's covenant with the people is not broken from God's side, but often enough from the – even if God's – people's side, which brings about frequent and harsh prophetic critique. Jesus was inclusive especially of people on the margins, while he spoke out in strong critique against the elites, namely the religious elites, sounding highly exclusive. Throughout the churches' history, there are visions of a more exclusive character and, others, more inclusive. One can recall here the notion of *corpus permixtum* of the Reformation, according to which believers and non-believers can be found both inside and outside the visible church even in a time and context of Christendom – there are true and false Christians in this view, although in the end only God sees the heart. Furthermore, a life of faith and a deep relationship with God are not necessarily constant, something Luther captured well in his *simul iustus et peccator*. I here suggest to take into account specifically the people as *ochlos*, the faceless and often poor multitude (the *turba*), and not only as *demos* (people in the political sense) or even as *laos* (the common term for people in the religious sense), and for this understanding of "ragtag" and "mob" we have a tradition in the liberation theologies of Latin America and elsewhere.

If, then, also theologically "the people" of God are a precarious category, marked by ambiguity, necessarily in a constant process of construction and reconstruction, there is the possibility that churches could be, rather than places of absolute truths and of corporative interests in the public sphere, places of searching, of dialogue, and the formation of horizons of meaning oriented towards the common good. Such precariousness and need for constant (re-)construction is what makes Ernesto Laclau and Chantal Mouffe pertinent discussion partners for theology.

9.2 Populism as the essence of "the political": a contribution by Ernesto Laclau and Chantal Mouffe

Laclau, an Argentinian political philosopher, had lived since the 1970s in England, where he taught at the University of Essex. He is known, together with his life partner, Belgian political scientist Chantal Mouffe, as a post-Marxist, post-foundational defender of what they call "radical democracy". Both are especially interested in the discursive and militant articulation of popular movements. Their theoretical contribution served as an inspiration for the popular Spanish political movement *Podemos* and the Greek *Syriza* movement. Although there are different nuances between them, both Laclau and Mouffe defend a post-foundational view, seeking to avoid both pre-figured and eschatologically pre-set foundations. They are informed by Antonio Gramsci's theory of hegemony, Lacan's psychanalytic theory of the subject and post-structural semiotic theory, among other resources (LACLAU and MOUFFE 2014). They also strongly resist the traditional way of despising the people as mere masses prone to manipulation.

For Laclau, this means to move from the universalism of the absolute to the universalism of the particular. He takes up the Gramscian distinction between *plebs* as particularity and *populus* as an abstract universality hegemonically constituted. At the same time, there is *populus* only as incarnated in the *plebs*, so it is not a pre-established given. The people and social order are not created by preconceived concepts, institutions or even a charismatic leader, but emerge performatively through discourse in difference and constant struggle. They dispense a non-discursive reference as foundation.

Such position comes in opposition to what Laclau sees as a liberal, formal, technocratic, and pragmatic occupation of politics and democracy, valuing excessively "politics" over "the political" as a space of articulation and hegemony of the people. Rather than any pre-political fundament on which to build, there is, for Laclau, an "empty signifier" which allows for a plurality of demands to be represented while a hegemonic position is constructed.[13] For him,

---

[13] Interestingly, LACLAU (2004, 280) can compare such emptiness, by contesting its supposedly merely formal character, to what he calls the "mystical intuition: God, as far as he is radically ineffable, is an absolutely empty fullness as far as conceptual determinations are concerned". And yet, God is neither subjected to formal rule nor abstract. He is again fairly analogical to theology when he speaks of the lack of normativity for which he was criticised: "the root of the ethical is the experience of the fullness of being as that which is essentially lacking. It is, if you want, the experience of the presence of an absence" (ibid, 286). The ethical principle deriving from the gap between what is and what ought to be (the "essential lack"), without being able to recur to previously defined ethical concepts like "justice", he calls *radical investment*. However, the ethical subject is embedded in a normative order as it looks for fullness and attempts to "name the unnameable" (ibid, 287) and can never question all of it at the same time. There is, therefore, a constant negotiation between such normative order (with is ideas on fullness) that produces investment and the essential emptiness of the goal that makes it radical. While he can agree with Lévinas' priority of the ethical over the ontological, he differs from Lévinas inasmuch as the latter bases his ethics on a demand rather than a lack.

The emergence of the 'people' depends on three variables [...]: equivalent relations hegemonically represented through empty signifiers; displacement of the internal frontiers through the production of floating signifiers; and a constitutive heterogeneity which makes dialectical retrievals impossible and gives its true centrality to political articulation (LACLAU 2005, 156).

For Laclau, "the people" are a "contingent entity", as are its forms of organisation. One can see the 2013 protests in Brazil as an example of an emerging populist process, especially because non-traditional manifestation publics took to the street. Rather than, as usually the case, being organised and led by parties and well-organised movements, the crowd even complained of the traditional pressure groups' presence and tried to keep them away. An outbreak of the popular, certainly, and a very diverse and amorphous one at that – triggered by the rise of bus tariffs, but then agglutinating a host of different and divergent demands. While there was, however, debate and discourse, there was little articulation and no strategic planning, and so the movement had no sustainability as such. At the same time, according to de Almeida (2019), it is this very amorphous movement that created the basis for the articulation of an opposition to the PT government, on the one hand, and conservative tendencies, on the other, which until then were usually not prone to take to the streets. There were follow-ups from both sides: one of political protest and articulation for social justice, defending Lula not only as a politician or person, but as an "idea", and one that presented itself as nationalist, against corruption and in favour of Lula's imprisonment, with Lula as the "idea" of corruption rather than social transformation. As such, popular mobilisation taking to the streets is a positive factor for democracy, with various groups claiming their demands and fighting for hegemony. However, there is, generally, no dialogue or articulation between the two groups, no debate with at least a common goal, just a destructive rhetoric of friend or foe, of "us" and "them", which in my view precisely precludes the emergence of a "people".

It is important to emphasise that this form of articulation tends to strengthen the climate of polarisation that can be observed to the point of bringing about a discourse of hate. Religious communities, as the cases of intolerance and even violence show, usually verbal, but sometimes also physical, are not exempt of this dynamic. The fierce reaction of conservative Catholics to this year's Ecumenical Fraternity Campaign in

Brazil (LIMA 2021) is, in part, a reaction to the request for an impeachment of president Bolsonaro due to his disastrous handling of the COVID-19 pandemic. Religious conservatism and adherence to Bolsonaro are not necessarily intertwined, but have been finding mutual resonance.

With the networks of communication and, recently, social media, the demonstrations of hate, intolerance, disrespect, and extremism had their reach amplified. Because of the difficulties in identifying authorship and the rare verification of news, some groups deliberately created, without scruples, fake news and brought to the fore what has come to be called "post-truth" (see KARNAL 2017). There are attacks, insinuations, defamations, lies, manifestations of xenophobia, homophobia, machismo, racism, exacerbating political and ideological divergences. These are only a few of the ingredients in this soup of bad taste and high peril in which Brazil is immersed today (cf. VON SINNER and WESTPHAL 2018).

Echoing the issues dealt with by Laclau in his *On Populist Reason,* it is tantamount to emphasise his theory of populism in which he sees it not as a pathology or dangerous deviance from democracy, but as its normality. As a performatively effective discourse, however, this appears to be, at least in principle, for all kinds of hegemonies. In our view, Mouffe goes further in her "agonistic" theory of democracy: rather than creating an opposition between insiders and outsiders, friends and enemies, the case is for struggling in a pluralistic democracy that has as its goals freedom and equality.[14] Rather than a division between friend or foe as Carl Schmitt would have it, we have here legitimate adversaries. A culture of conflict – not of violence, to be sure, but also not of false harmony – is certainly something that should be part of human conviviality and the construction of a just society. For Mouffe (2003),

---

[14] MOUFFE 2018, pos. 79-87.560: "The central argument of this book is that to intervene in the hegemonic crisis, it is necessary to establish a political frontier and that left populism, understood as a discursive strategy of construction of the political frontier between 'the people' and 'the oligarchy', constitutes, in the present conjuncture, the type of politics needed to recover and deepen democracy. [...] The strategy of left populism seeks the establishment of a new hegemonic order within the constitutional liberal-democratic framework and it does not aim at a radical break with pluralist liberal democracy and the foundation of a totally new political order. Its objective is the construction of a collective will, a 'people' apt to bring about a new hegemonic formation that will reestablish the articulation between liberalism and democracy that has been disavowed by neoliberalism, putting democratic values in the leading role".

different subjects can, at any moment, by the unity of their diverse demands, seek a privileged place in the construction of politics.

The originality of Laclau's concept of populism as a political logic lies in overcoming the organisational and simplifying need of a unified historical subject identified with a class, on the one hand, and in signalling the heterogeneity of the antagonistic field that constitutes "the people", on the other hand. The historical subject capable of carrying out the struggle is a priori not any specific class, but "the people" by means of the articulation of their demands: "as all historical experience shows, it is impossible to determine a priori who the hegemonic actors in this struggle will be. All we know is that they will be the outsiders of the systems, the underdogs – those we have called heterogeneous – who are decisive in the establishment of an antagonistic frontier" (LACLAU 2005, 150).

The formation of political subjects is, then, freed of any *a priori* essentialism. Any identity is configured under a relational perspective. This is about something not intrinsic to the subject, but always dependent on established relations in a system of historical differences composed of discursive and antagonistic structures that impede any closure. The concept of hegemony is retrieved and grows acquiring relevance in the formation and transformation of political communities. "Hegemony", Laclau and Mouffe (2014, 1) affirm, "will allude to an absent totality [...]. The contexts in which the concept appear [sic] will be those of a *fault* [...], of a fissure that had to be filled up, of a contingency that had to be overcome. 'Hegemony' will be not the majestic unfolding of an identity but the response to a crisis".

On taking on a reconstructive aspect, populism, as any other model, presupposes a certain instability. The "populist prerogative" is not to be located only on the level of rationality. Rather, it appears in the sphere of the will and, as Mouffe (2005) insists, of affection in the sense of passion and motivation. By stating a strong link between the factual dimension and the institutions, a sense of ethics and value, a renewed strive for legitimacy, what happens is that the delimitation of a perspective that is linked to the whole judicial and political order, in view of a reconfiguration of a new base of ethics and morality. It is because of such attribute that populism emerges as an important element in the counterhegemonic struggle in the structures of power that produce the oppression of the popular classes.

It is important to observe that, while the theologies and philosophies of liberation in Latin America tend to emphasise, even more so in a post- and decolonial mode, the overcoming of universalistic, essentialist and prefigured rationalities, modernities, democracies and religiosities, authors like Enrique Dussel make a more robust connection to normative and externally established elements, like, for instance, the preferential option for the poor or, more widely speaking, for the victims. For Dussel (2003), in the line of Lévinas, the messianic irruption of the other becomes determining. Following Dussel's logic, we suggest that, beyond the emergence of a popular impulse from below as in Laclau's theory, we need an ethical interpellation and references for a just proceeding and a reasonable definition of what is to be democracy, precisely in order to hear the voices of the excluded and marginalised and not succumb to the pure rhetoric or other power of a group that comes to dominate the other in an abusive form. What is, then, the opportunity and task presenting itself for a public theology that seeks to analyse the acting of religious communities in the public sphere, and what is its pertinence? We now come to the third and last part of this chapter.

9.3 The centrality of the people – tasks for a public theology

As we have seen, populism is a polysemic, ambiguous and often vague concept. In Latin America, sociologically and also theologically speaking, the majority of "the people" are the oppressed, the downtrodden, the excluded, and the marginalised as Liberation Theology has taught us. The Bolsonaro government – which by many would be called a right-wing populist regime, that, however, was unable as yet to imprint all its militarising, moralistic and authoritarian agenda – did not change such oppression, exclusion, and marginalisation. Instead, it deepened the rich/poor divide through a disastrous "handling" of the COVID-19 pandemic and a not viable neo-liberal economic agenda. Furthermore, it consistently ostracised those who were working towards inclusion of the excluded, combatting their "political correctness" as evil and "ideological" and calling them, among other terms, "communists". The Brazilian people, in their factual majority, are *plebs,* whether they see themselves as such or not (see e.g. DE SOUZA 2019).

Hugo Assmann, one of the most radical liberation theologians in the 1970s and 1980s, later questioned many of his own presuppositions and came to see the people not as only being in need of something they lack, but as bearers of desires. Their subjectivity and embodiment came into focus. At the same time, Assmann and Sung (2010) stated the need for an education that pre-eminently included the development of solidary competence and sensitivity. He also stressed the need of continuing Liberation Theology as a "theology of solidarity and citizenship" (ASSMANN 1994, 13-36).

Citizenship (*cidadania*) as both the existence and effective access to rights has been a conquest of the people that empowers them to effectively participate. It starts with the conscience of being a legal subject and legitimate bearer of dignity, contemplates the situation in is respective social, economic, educational and health dimensions, and infuses the perception of being capable of making a real difference not only by voting, but also through participation in movements and groups with power of articulation. The emergence and self-perception as a legitimate minority, to be "people", can have the effect of feeling, maybe for the first time, of being heard. The ambiguity, however, remains: what is seen as a conquest of one's own and own group, may easily turn into disdain and rejection of other groups when the minority feels to have power once it becomes part of the majority, as the one that elected the present Brazilian government.

Laclau, as we have seen, inverts the meaning of populism from a manipulation of the masses by a leader to a way of performative, discursive and pluralistic articulation of subjectivities that on acquiring hegemony emerge as "people", the *plebs* constituting itself as the *populus.* Theologically, this is relevant because populism, in this sense, is a call to be looking to the people, to the 'priesthood of all believers' in theological language, to the laity as the *laos theou.* For Latin American Liberation Theology, the freeing from bondage in Egypt led to the political and social liberation and a new configuration of the oppressed people of God (see Chapter 10 below; FIELD 2018). The interest for the people remains important and is intrinsically linked to the option for the poor, seeking their emancipation both in society and in the church (cf. GUTIÉRREZ 2004).

Within the urgency of situations in which the people found themselves massively oppressed, the notion of the "crucified people" was introduced, a kind of historical soteriology that links up the concrete suffering of the people to Jesus Christ's salvific work (ELLACURÍA 1993b). "The people" or "people of God" generally refer to the Greek *laos [theou]*, which in the Vulgate is rendered as *plebs* or *populus*.[15] The church, interestingly, uses for itself the term *ekklesia*, which originated in the political realm and designated the Athenian assembly of the (highly restrictive) *demos*. In a further radicalisation of Korean Minjung theology, i.e. "people's theology", the term "people" can also echo the Greek *ochlos*, the common people, a term used by Philo and Josephus and many others in a derogatory way, but portrayed positively in 'a close relationship to Jesus', especially in the Gospel of Mark.[16]

Theologically, one becomes part of God's people through baptism, which in the Second Vatican Council resulted in a quite revolutionary redefinition of the church from the hierarchically structured *societas perfecta* to the totality of the "people of God", ordained to be part of this *character indelebilis* by baptism, within which the hierarchy is situated (CALIMAN 2011). While baptism as ritual is a one-time event, an initiation, its consequences are lifelong as the baptised comes to better understand and adopt such condition on a daily and continuous learning basis. As Luther insisted in his Large Catechism: it is necessary to drown the "old Adam" daily, and, thus, live one's baptism throughout one's life. Baptism is a given, a moment, but also a process. To be a Christian is, then, something constantly in the making within the constant horizon of the scandal of the cross and resurrection of Christ. Similarly, a "people" is not a given, but in continuous becoming. From the amorphous mass emerges the people, the *populus* from the *plebs*, the people of God from the human species, the city of God within the earthly city.

"The people" in general and the "people of God" in particular are, then, not a given, but a process, an "event" rather than an institution, as underlined in their particular ways in Leonardo Boff's "ecclesiogenesis" (1987) and Vitor Westhelle's on "The Church Event" (2010b).[17] "The People" are, therefore, not simply a representation of a reality but a programmatic concept. The "people of God" as embodied subjects have

---

[15] See the call for a *laocracy* from both a theological and democratic-theoretical point of view, and, thus, not only focused on the church, but on society in RIEGER, SUNG and MÍGUEZ, 2009.

[16] KÜSTER, 1996, 59.

[17] BOFF, 'Was bedeutet theologisch "Volk Gottes" und "Kirche des Volkes"', in 1987, 64. He calls the masses "Non-People", with reference to Hosea 1:6-9 and 1 Peter 2:10. See also WESTHELLE 2010b.

as their dynamic, not predefined and yet constant horizon the incarnation, the embodiment of God in Jesus Christ. Such embodiment shows God assuming vulnerability, a vulnerability typical of the reality of most people in most contexts.

Also in Jesus' practice, the people he was sent to were not simply a given, but modified and reconstructed by his presence, words, and deeds. In and through Jesus the best and worst of humanity became visible – the generosity of the 'sinful woman' that anointed Jesus (Lk 7:36-50), as well as the brutality of those who condemned and crucified him. As Luther insisted, believers are simultaneously justified and sinners, justified *in spe*, in hope, and sinners *in re*, in fact. To live with such uncomfortable, but realistic ambiguity is not easy, but necessary to be able to constructively contribute to the church's edification and the construction of a just society.

A close look to who and where the people are, is then needed. In Brazil and Latin America, it has become common to state that 'while Liberation Theology opted for the poor, the poor opted for the Pentecostals', a statement I first heard from José Comblin, an eminent Belgian-Brazilian liberation theologian. Thus, the people can be found in settings where they theoretically might not be, because they lack the correct discourse. Indeed, there is little explicit conscience of citizenship and much less discourse on citizenship, social justice, and transformation in most Pentecostal churches (cf. VON SINNER 2012b). And yet, many of those churches are the most efficient in giving people a sense of being people, and articulating community. Liberation Theology, on its part, has continuously amplified and complexified its notion of "people" by looking at "new" subjects – not in fact new, but newly seen and becoming explicit subjects of church and theology – like indigenous peoples, people of African descent, women, LGBTQIA+ persons, and other mostly, but not necessarily economically poor people that are marginalised and in need of liberation.

This has to be taken into account by theology and, not least, a public theology, as a contribution to the emergence and construction of a "people" with visible dignity and effective citizenship. This becomes a task for public theology as, in the first place, a listening theology. It has to be a learning theology, and from there, an articulating, networking, conflictive, agonistic theology. With concrete bodies, concrete subjects thus being heard and perceived in the public sphere, their voice and contribution will emerge. That does not mean that it is automatically always edifying. One cannot escape ambiguity even within the church, and the church is part of the world's ambiguities.

Ideally, churches can provide a space where the concrete anxieties, needs and desires can be uttered and articulated, sustained by a theology that clearly situates them in the public sphere of each specific context and helping them to be "God's people" in the midst of the emerging citizen "people". This is what is needed today more than ever in Brazil and in many other contexts.

9.4 Concluding remarks

As we have seen, Brazil has been living, since tendencies of the 2013 protests, but more specifically since the election campaign that brought Jair Messias Bolsonaro into the presidency of the Republic, a phase of right-wing populism, in which "the people" are invoked in a nationalistic sense, combining conservative moral values with a neo-liberal political economy, reducing social programmes and inciting rather than reducing violence. This configuration, which can count on expressive support from religious groups, has a highly exclusive political, moral, and social potential. By naming such situation, often with disdain, as "populism", however, does not resolve the important issue of the necessary effective involvement and participation of the empirical people – the citizenry, especially the deprived *plebs* – in the struggles for their survival and in the configuration of the public sphere. From an analytical point of view, as an articulating logic, Laclau's concept of populism is helpful in avoiding any petrified or imposed definition of "the people", but to see the dynamics of a constant becoming in the plurality of forces and goals.

The churches, as an expressive part of contemporary civil society, are not exempt of the existing ambiguities and polarisations in today's Brazilian society. Rather, not too rarely, they take part in them. I have argued that both socially and theologically, conceptually as well as empirically, the category of "people" is precarious and needs constant (re-)construction. A public theology can and indeed should contemplate such discussion under the title of promoting citizenship and human rights that serve as an indispensable reference in orienting a vision that has, as its primary focus, the victims of society and vulnerable populations. At the same time, it sees the churches as active participants in the public sphere that have the right to the acknowledgment of their legitimacy, to be part of the people, while they need to see such participation as a contribution and not an imposition. The discussion as to the pertinence of such presence in the public sphere in articulation with the plurality of demands and normative convictions is an important task for a public theology.

Chapter 10

People's Church and Church of the People: Insights from Liberation Theology[*]

Liberation Theology, which was developed primarily in Latin America but then disseminated also to other continents, draws a line leading from the liberation of God's people in Egypt to the necessary political and social liberation of the oppressed people of God. The focus on the "people" is closely connected with the option for the poor and searches their emancipation both in the church and society (see GUTIÉRREZ 1979/2004). Thus, in the Latin American context, the term "people" in the phrase "people's church" or even "church of the people" (*igreja do povo, igreja popular*), refers, first and foremost, to a social group, namely the underprivileged majority of the people over against the affluent and powerful minority.[1] The term "people" can also refer to a political, territorially and culturally defined unit (such as "the Brazilian people"[2]), but it has practically no ethnic or national connotations. "As a rule, 'people' refers to those majority groups of the population that have always come off badly because of marginalization and exclusion. Thus, the term *pueblo/povo* refers to the people who are simple, small, impoverished, ill-treated, humiliated … ('ordinary people,' 'poor people')", as defined by Horst Goldstein (1991, 229) in his *Short Dictionary of Liberation Theology*.

---

[*] Originally published as "Volkskirche und Kirche des Volkes: Einsichten der Befreiungstheologie", in David Plüss, Matthias D. Wüthrich, and Matthias Zeindler, eds., *Ekklesiologie der Volkskirche. Theologische Zugänge in reformierter Perspektive,* pp. 372-383 (Zürich: TVZ, 2016). Used with permission. Translated by Luís Marcos Sander and revised by the author.

[1] This is also one of the senses of the word "Volk" in the Duden dictionary of German: "3. Die [mittlere und] untere Schicht der Bevölkerung [The (middle and) lower stratum of society]". Available at: <http://www.duden.de/rechtschreibung/Volk#Bedeutung3> [accessed July 30, 2021]; as a phrase, "dem Volk aufs Maul schauen [literally: looking at the mouth of the people]" is cited with reference to Martin Luther's "Open Letter on Translating" (Ein Sendbrief vom Dolmetschen 1530, WA 30/II, 637, 19-22), where he mentions "the mother in the household, children in the alley, the common man in the Market".

[2] RIBEIRO 1984; the original title is *Viva o povo brasileiro* [literally: "Hail the Brazilian People"].

This terminology has been used less frequently in recent years, and not only in Brazil. Various reasons can be adduced to explain this. On the one hand, the term is quite imprecise; there has been an attempt to look closer at whom or what is meant by "the" people or "the" poor. In addition to that, the strong and fast upward mobility in recent years has watered down the simple contrast between "people" and "elite". On the other hand, the great expectation of a revolutionary transformation of the Roman Catholic Church has been clearly frustrated by the policy of Pope John Paul II. This disillusionment is reflected in many groups and institutions that had been created with the prospect of a "church from below" and had to reorient themselves, if they had not already been dissolved. Furthermore, the high religious mobility and the significant loss of members mainly in the Catholic Church have prompted a new, defensive, identity-related and inward turned attitude and practice as well as, at the same time, a search for new ways of attracting people, which has reinforced a rather hierarchical image of the church.

All this, however, does not mean that what was meant by the term "people" and "church of the people" has become irrelevant or is not relevant anymore. Moreover, the fact that particularly in the Catholic milieu and in the German-speaking countries groups continue to gather around this terminology or its content is shown by still existing networks such as "Kirche von unten" [Church from below][3] or even relatively new movements such as "Wir sind Kirche" [We are church].[4] Both groups show clearly that Latin American Liberation Theology is one of their sources of inspiration. In Switzerland one can refer, in this context, to the

---

[3] This ecumenical network that resulted from the *Katholikentag von unten* (1980) understands "church from below" as "the community of people liberated and sanctified through baptism. We want to 'proclaim the God of the little people' who stands on the side of the weak, mute and excluded. Thus, we see things from below, from the perspective of the grassroots". It is unclear, however, whom exactly this refers to. Available at: <http://www.ikvu.de/profil.html> [accessed February 2, 2015].

[4] This "KirchenVolksBewegung [Movement of the Church's People]" was founded in 1995 in Austria in connection with de Referendum of the Church's People and, according to its own information, presently exists in more than 20 countries. It demands more participation of the laity in a "brotherly/sisterly church", full equal rights for women, including consecration to the priesthood, a voluntary celibacy of priests, a positive view on sexuality and "Frohbotschaft statt Drohbotschaft [good news instead of bad news]" for divorced persons who remarried, for instance. Available at: <http://www.wir-sind-kirche.de/?id=117> [accessed February 2, 2015]. On the issue, see one of its most prominent cosignatories: KÜNG 2011.

"Theological Movement for Solidarity and Liberation", which was created in 1982 and, although not using the term "people", also understands itself as standing within the "tradition of liberation theology".[5] The Croatian Miroslav Volf (1997) put, from the point of view of a free church tradition, the call "We are church!" on a trinitarian foundation. Can these positions be explored for the standpoint and programme of a Swiss Reformed *Volkskirche* (literally, people's church) (PLÜSS et al., 2016)? This question which was posed to me for the original publication of this chapter constitutes the background of my reflection. It later contributed to my reflections on populism (see Chapter 9 above).

In the following sections I focus first on what can be described more precisely as the church of the people in the Latin American, particularly Brazilian context, in order to be able to situate the concept of church of the people developed in that context in the reality of the Catholic National Church and to have a point of comparison for the Swiss context (10.1). In the second step I present the view on the church as God's people in Liberation Theology by making reference to Reformed theology (10.2). Then I approach some practical consequences (10.3). In the conclusion I sketch the potential relevance of these insights to a (re)definition of a people's church in the Swiss and Reformed context today from the perspective of a distant observer on his own origins (10.4).

10.1 People's church in the Brazilian and Latin American context

A significant difference from the terminology formed and used in German-speaking countries is the fact that in Latin America the "church of the people" emerged in the Catholic, rather than in the Protestant milieu, although its formulation has been accused of being "Protestant" (cf. VON SINNER 2007). In spite of the above-mentioned enormous religious transformations that have thoroughly eroded the equation

---

[5] It emerged 1982 in the context of the (Catholic) Theological Faculty in Lucerne but soon adopted an ecumenically open position. According to information on its website, the number of its members stabilized at around 400 in the 1990s. and today stands at 270. The movement intends "to sensitize and encourage to turn the concerns of people who are excluded due to economic exploitation, racism, sexism or other forms of injustice into the criterion of one's own or communitarian action and theological reflection". Available at: <https://www.thebe.ch/portrait/schwerpunkte> [accessed July 29, 2021].

according to which "to be Latin American (Brazilian, for instance) is to be Catholic", a progressive Catholic milieu continues to be the starting point and point of reference of a church of the people. With a few exceptions, the term "people's church" is absent from the Protestant and especially Pentecostal discourse, last but not least because of its connotations of belonging to Liberation Theology, and people in this context are usually critical of or even hostile to it.[6] However, looking at it from a distance, the emancipatory character of a church of the people represents a challenge not only for the Catholic Church, but also for the *evangélico* churches. The latter have, despite their democratic roots, created an authoritarian and clerical apparatus, which in the meantime has become manifest in actual hereditary dynasties, so that there are good reasons to speak of certain "pathologies".[7]

Precisely because the Catholic Church, as a church of the colonial power, had a *de facto* privileged monopoly status until late in the 20th century – which is presently more limited, but still clearly noticeable – what has been considered as *Volkskirche* since Schleiermacher can be applied to Latin America: a church to which one belongs neither on the basis of a state ordinance nor of a purely voluntary and subjective decision (SCHLEIERMACHER 1843/1999).[8] It is interesting that the Catholic Church in Brazil has increased its presence among the people since the system of patronage was abolished in 1890 and it was *de iure* separated from the state. Only this freedom from state control and the efforts of the Catholic Action to gather laypeople gave it the ability to autonomously organise itself in local churches and to actually reach its members, which in the first half of the 20th century included even trends toward a new Christendom and an anti-Protestant and partially antimodern integralism. In this case it is appropriate to say that there is a "people's church-related positivism" (HUBER 2003): for a long time –

---

[6] Exceptions are associations such as *Pastoral Popular Luterana* (literally, Popular Lutheran Pastoral Work) in the realm of the Evangelical Church of the Lutheran Confession in Brazil (see Chapter 4 above).

[7] On these pathologies in Roman Catholicism, see BOFF 2011, 65-88. In this context, "popular Catholicism" is designated "Christian experience that is being lived by the People of God" (ibid, 88).

[8] VOLZ 2001, 1709f. suggests a view that comes close to what is meant in this chapter by church of the people: "The concept of people's church serves, in this [sociological, critical] context, also as a critique of the middle-class church that is criticized as being bourgeois and as having 'forgotten' or insufficiently considered the lower classes or the workers".

meanwhile only 64% of the population say they are Catholic (census of 2010) – being Catholic was simply presupposed; all the same, today belonging to *one* Christian church is the normal case for 90% of the population.[9]

On the side of Protestantism, there is a similar phenomenon only in the Lutheran church formed through immigration, which also exhibits characteristics of a people's church in its ethnically quite homogeneous surroundings but came under pressure due to the growing integration into the Brazilian context. For this reason, it is certainly not by chance that in 1933 this same church – or, more precisely the then *Sínodo Riograndense* – submitted a motion to the constitutional convention designed to obtain for the churches (in the plural!) a status regulated by public law rather than merely by private law similar to the one provided in the Republic of Weimar's Constitution (*Weimarer Reichsverfassung*). But the call remained unheard, although it gathered as much as 53,000 signatures.[10] The other churches, particularly the strongly growing Pentecostal churches, are purely based on voluntary adherence both in terms of membership and financial contributions. There is no church tax system, not even for the Catholic Church for that matter. We have to wait and see whether in the long run a structure similar to that of a people's church can be maintained on this basis and in this situation. On the side of Catholicism, the fact that popular religiosity is strongly entrenched

---

[9] According to a recently published study by an organisation called *Latinobarómetro*, the number of Catholics decreased by 13% on average in 18 Latin American countries, viz. from 80% to 67% of the population (1995-2013). This applies particularly to Central America (from 77% to 44% in Nicaragua) and Brazil, whereas in Mexico Catholicism grew by 2%. A considerable secularisation in terms of leaving the church is found only in two countries, viz. Uruguay and Chile, whereas in the other countries there is primarily a religious mobility or transformation. On this topic it is, however, to be noted – an aspect not taken into account by the above-mentioned study – that in Brazil, for instance, those without a denomination are not necessarily unbelievers, but people who are not (or no longer) connected to an organised religion; see VON SINNER et al., 2012. In four countries less than 50% of the people declare themselves non-Catholics, viz. Guatemala, Honduras, Nicaragua and Uruguay. In two countries the difference between Protestants and Catholics is of less than 10%, viz. Honduras (6%) and Guatemala (7%); LATINOBARÓMETRO 2014., Las religiones en tiempos del Papa Francisco, document of April 16, 2014. Available at: <http://www.latinobarometro.org/latNewsShop.jsp> [accessed July 30, 2021].

[10] The then church President Hermann Dohms stated laconically that "the situation of the evangelical church in the First Republic (1889-1930) was briefly this: the state did not take notice of it" (quoted by PRIEN 1977).

among the population, mainly in particular regions of the northeast, is certainly relevant and was able to prevent an even greater exodus to other churches and religions (cf. SÜSS 1978; HÖLLINGER 2007).

After this brief contextualisation, I now address the theological and ecclesiological contents (see also VON SINNER 2012a, 149-165 and 198-215).

10.2 Church as people of God

The Second Vatican Council rediscovered the view of the church as the people of God (Lumen Gentium, chapter II: "De populo Dei") in continuity with the view of the people of the covenant (Israel) as a historical communion instituted as such by God: "As God's people, the church understands itself as the fellowship of believers called by the intangible [*unverfügbar*] freedom of God's love out of the entanglements of sin and to the service of reconciliation of humankind" (WIEDENHOFER 1992, 94). This is also and specifically related to the emphasis on the universal priesthood of those consecrated through baptism (see Lumen Gentium 10), which is very close to the Reformation's view.[11] Precisely in this way the Council enabled Liberation Theology's demand of an "ecclesiogenesis", the emergence of a new church close to the people, that is democratic, starting from the laypeople, particularly the base communities. This grassroots-based democratic understanding of the church coincides with Reformed theology, according to which "the primordial form [must be seen] in the concretely assembled congregation" (BUSCH 2007, 151).

Furthermore, from the point of view of Liberation Theology, with Jesus "the royal dominion of God over God's people [begins] to become effective: the oppressive chains are broken, liberation is announced to the poor, the powerful and rich are accused, the arrival of the Lord's day is proclaimed (Luke 2:47-55; 4:17-21). [...] The exodus serves as an

---

[11] See H.-M. BARTH, 1990; on the base communities and Boff's ecclesiogenesis, 134-140. Barth is right in noting that Boff speaks – in a broad sense – of "universal" or "general" priesthood, whereas Lumen Gentium refers to the "common" priesthood; in Boff's view, the community or congregation as a whole is directly (!) priestly (ibid, 148). From a Reformation point of view, Barth values Boff's emphasis on the emergence of the community from the proclamation of God's word, its emancipatory force and inspiration to take on responsibility as well as the universal priesthood based on baptism as being priests to each other (ibid, 157-160).

explanatory model for Christian ecclesiogenesis, the coming of Jesus, in turn, serves as the key to reinterpret messianic promises and the idea of the Messiah in order to strip it from nationalistic and political connotations, [i.e.] the longing for greatness and power" (ESTRADA 1996, 811). A new people is to be created, a people of equals, in which "authority is service, the richest is the one who gives up the most, the greatest is the one who humiliates him- or herself, the first one is the one who assumes to be last" (ibid). Because of the urgency of the situation, in which the people felt extremely oppressed, talk about the "crucified people" emerged in terms of a "historical soteriology" that continues Jesus' redemptive work in discipleship (ELLACURÍA 1993b; cf. WEBER 1999). Usually "people" [of God] refers here to the Greek word λαός [θεοῦ]. In a further radicalisation of the Korean "theology of the common people (Minjung)", informed by Liberation Theology, the term "people" also refers to *ochlos,* "the mob" (the plebs in Philo and Josephus), which plays a salient role mainly in the Gospel of Mark, where it "is in a close relationship with Jesus" (KÜSTER 1996, 59). The centrality of Jesus Christ both with regard to his life and testimony and with regard to his salvific work in death and resurrection as well as their effects on the community constituted in this way are also important to Reformed theology. In this sense, the rediscovery of the liberating moments contained in the Bible, including those with political implications, offer a significant challenge (cf. DE GRUCHY 1991).

Now, the status of belonging to the people of God is given through baptism, but the latter must also be understood and practiced as such. This is associated to the notion that the people in general is initially something *given*, but, from the point of view of Liberation Theology and pedagogy (Paulo Freire), must also *become* the people in a genuine sense by becoming subjects.[12] Thus, *the people* and *the people of God* are not a fact (*fato*) but an "event" *(feito)*, as emphasised by Leonardo Boff.[13] This event is also promoted by "popular education" (*educação popular*) and the "popular Bible reading" (*leitura popular da Bíblia*), in which the life world of the readers or listeners is connected to the people of God's life world in the Bible (cf. MESTERS 1983). The meaning of Scripture as a

---

[12] In this sense a distinction is made not only between people and elite but also between people and mass, and the distinction was defined, along the lines of Gramscian Marxism, through a "historical project"; see DE OLIVEIRA 1984, 506.

[13] L. BOFF 1991, 52. Accordingly, he also calls the mass "non-people" (*não-povo*), with reference to Hosea 1:6.9 and 1 Peter 2:10.

witness to God's Word, in turn, is in agreement with Reformed theology, which, in turn, is challenged by the contextual and popular aspect that is not alien to it, but is sometimes not given enough emphasis.

In Boff's view, the church is, moreover, the sacrament of a relationally understood Trinity, from which he derives demands for a democratic church model:

> Such a church, inspired by the communion of the Trinity, would be characterized by a more equitable sharing of sacred power, by dialogue, by openness to all the charisms granted to the members of the community, by the disappearance of all types of discrimination, especially those originating in patriarchalism and *machismo*, by its permanent search for a consensus to be built up through the organized participation of all its members. (L. BOFF 1988, 22f.)

In this sense, Boff could draw inspiration from the ecclesiology of texts of the Second Vatican Council that explicitly evokes the trinity: "Thus, the Church has been seen as 'a people made one with the unity of the Father, the Son and the Holy Spirit'" (Lumen Gentium 4). The Decree on Ecumenism is even clearer in this regard: "This is the sacred mystery of the unity of the Church, in Christ and through Christ, the Holy Spirit energizing its various functions. It is a mystery that finds its highest exemplar and source in the unity of the Persons of the Trinity: the Father and the Son in the Holy Spirit, one God" (Unitatis Redintegratio 2; cf. MOLTMANN 1993a).

Now, how is this underlying view on the church grasped more precisely in practice? The next section deals with this question.

10.3 Church of the people – church with the people

The terminology of "the people" was formed in a time of revolutionary projects, socialist utopias, and resistance against military dictatorships. Hermann Brandt rightly reminded that initially "people" was a pejorative term: "The reference to the 'ignorant people' several times mentioned by Mesters, i.e., the unknowing, dumb people, reveals that this reference was originally expression of the feeling of superiority of the ruling elite vis-à-vis the anonymous masses of the poor, suffering and uneducated people in the 'cellars of humankind' was and is. From this perspective from above, 'people' is a downgrading, thus an expression of *denied* identification" (BRANDT 1982, 11f.). By reversing this asymmetry and turning it into a positive identification it then became a self-confident self-denomination.

For this reason, "people" is not just a depiction of reality but a programmatic concept fostering transformation. The volume titled "The Oppressed People – Lord of History", edited by Hugo Assmann (1972), is a clear expression of that and of the certainly exaggerated expectation of a self-liberation of the people in the process of becoming subjects. Later Assmann himself asked about the real poor and not only about their needs, but also their desires and longings (cf. VON SINNER 2012a, 100-120). In his view, then, solidarity is no longer something naturally proper to the people, but must be elicited and nurtured through education.

According to Leonardo Boff (1987a, 65f.), the church becomes the people of God when the "constitutive features of a people are given", i.e. "conscience, community and praxis that corresponds to the achieved state of conscience and the concrete opportunities for participation, participation in decision-making and communion. A people only becomes the people of God when it allows for being evangelized, congregates around God's word, forms Christian communities and begins a praxis that is inspired by the gospel and the living tradition of the church".

In Boff's (1987a, 16) view, ecclesiogenesis is "a process resulting from God's power and human response from which – immersed in the conditions of the human way of life – the church emerges". The church is understood as a "network of many communities [...], in which all fully participate and together form a true people of God" (ibid, 67). Such a network of communities was seen and aimed at in the base communities, which from 1975 onwards got together in so-called "interecclesial gatherings" at the national level. According to the slogan of the 5th interecclesial gathering in Canindé/Ceará in 1983, the base communities were considered "seeds of a new society". According to Boff, they create "not only the new Christian who self-perceives as a citizen of the celestial Jerusalem that begins already in the city of just and solidary humans, but also the [earthly] citizen that engages for his brothers and sisters and has the courage to give his or her blood and life for a great cause" (ibid, 115). In his view, these communities are characterised by a great participation of laypeople, a strong rootedness in the base, little hierarchisation, a diversity of ministries in a democratic structure as well as a strong presence in the broader human community.

The demands and expectations that liberation theologians directed to the base communities and their members were very high and even at that time could only be partially fulfilled. This included the communion of goods required according to Acts 2:44 and 4:32-34, which implied that "both poverty and wealth [must be] extinct" (ibid, 69). And Boff (2011b, 12f.) adds that "The church seems more like its humble beginnings in the times of the apostles: It is poor, close to the people, in issues of justice and human dignity, prophetic and, in some regions, a church of martyrs". Community in this sense becomes, in Boff's (1988, 107) view, "a figure and analogy of the Trinity, making it palpable to humankind". The 6th interecclesial gathering, which took place in Trindade [= Trinity], in the state of Goiás, in 1986 wrote this literally on a banner: "The Holy Trinity is the best community" (ibid, 123).

In this sense not only the church or its leadership are taken up on their duties, but also the poor. As the sociologist Pedro Ribeiro de Oliveira (1984, 510) puts it, "It must not only be mentioned that the church takes a preferential decision for the poor, but there is also the opposite decision: of the poor for the church. Although it is true that the poor in Latin America always belonged to the church, but they were present in the church only in an anonymous and passive way". They were, in his words, "clients" of the church. Thus, while possibilities of participation are promoted, at the same time an actual participation is required. This was extended to society, particularly in democratic times: "Together with a project for society that emanating from the people in the direction of a participative democracy, which has the people as its basis and is pluralistically open for religion, one began to design a project for the church that emanates from the people – a new church for a new society" (BOFF 1987a, 273).

This high expectation and this moral burden could not be fulfilled and implemented at the level of the communities, ultimately to the benefit of a rather emotional religiosity and moral unburdening, as in Brazil ill-faring is often attributed to "evil forces" (cf. BURDICK 1993). It is not by chance that many leading persons of the ecclesial base communities ended up migrating to social movements and NGOs, where they could live out their militancy. In the context of a concept of people's church in Middle Europe, this way of being the church based on a high commitment would be closer to the free churches.

What insights result from the above discussion and reflection and to what extent are they relevant for the (re)definition of people's church in the Swiss and Reformed context? I'll sketch an answer in the concluding section.

10.4 People's church and church of the people

In section 10.2 I hinted at important points of contact or commonality between Liberation Theology and Reformed theology regarding the understanding of *people's church* or *church of the people*. Here I take up those aspects and set them forth in the form of brief theses. I hope this is a relevant contribution to this intercultural discussion. It is submitted on the basis of my – by now – geographically distant perception of the Reformed church in Switzerland.

1. A concept of church that is sharpened by its contact with the reality of the life world and establishes an intensive dialogue of lived religiosity with scholarly theology is nothing new for Reformed theology. But it is my contention that there is a danger that the Reformation view of the *subject* as standing directly before God will be reduced to a subject perceived from an individualistic and bourgeois perspective. The discursivity of the public sphere developed with an emancipatory and democratic intention by Jürgen Habermas, for example, might, just as Liberation Theology's concept of community, lead to a new way of looking at the intersubjective and communal references. And yet the claims or demands cannot be as high as they used to be in the base communities. But in a society that continues to be exposed to strong trends fostering individualisation and loneliness the provision of adequate, open, and inclusive spaces for communal experiences may be a beneficial and ecclesiologically adequate outreach initiative.

2. In these communal outreach programmes, the lower strata of society that have *for a long time been distant* from the church should then consistently be considered – blue collar workers and employees, but also migrants, i.e. the "common people", as they are also called in Switzerland. The insights of Liberation Theology might help to sharpen this focus. To do so, an openness for the perhaps unusual contributions and needs of these people must be presupposed. In this case the worship services and congregational activities would have to try to find forms to address and involve not only the intellect but also the senses. In the same way,

congregations would have to ask again how they might be really welcoming and helping to meet people's needs.

3. The *participatory Bible reading* developed in the milieu of Liberation Theology might lead to a fresh appreciation of the close and distant congregation members and their diverse interests and perspectives as well as their participation in theological reflection. Competent introductions into the Bible and a broad discussion about its texts might evoke resonances – which should always be hermeneutically reflected on – reawaken and intensify interest in its texts and the importance of its tradition. This may also lead to fruitful exchange in ecumenical or even inter-religious discussion groups.

4. Access to potentially all strata of society, especially in connection with occasional services, is a strength of the *Volkskirche*. For this reason, particularly its ministers have the opportunity as well as task of familiarising themselves with the life situation of the people and bringing it up in the public sphere with a view to *necessary societal transformations*. The latter is advocated by a public theology, for instance, which should not be understood as an antithesis to, but as a more constructive expression of a Liberation Theology within a democratic context (BEDFORD-STROHM 2015; SCHLAG 2012). In this context, reflections on the specific contribution of Reformed territorial churches in the Swiss public sphere and even beyond it are undoubtedly relevant. It must be at least questioned, however, whether the current loudly voiced call for a Reformed bishop does not aim at a personalisation of that contribution which runs contrary to the traditionally participatory leadership style of Swiss Reformed churches (KUNDERT 2014).

Chapter 11

"Struggling with Africa": Theology of Prosperity in and from Brazil. A Critical Perspective[*]

Brazil has been calling attention when the issue is religion. A continuously expressive, but ever more diverse religious practice and belonging makes it, at the same time, the most Catholic and the most Pentecostal country in the world. The *evangélicos,* including historical Protestants, Pentecostals, Neo-Pentecostals and so-called "undefined" *evangélicos* – a rather undefined category – have grown 540% since 1980 and sum over 42 million (22.2% of the population) persons according to the 2010 census (MARIZ and GRACINO 2013, 161). It is a field with an enormous mobility: 23% of the population affirmed to have changed their religious affiliation at least once in their life (cf. VON SINNER et al., 2012).

Beyond this situation of self-declared belonging, forms of syncretism and multiple belonging – declared or undeclared – are part of this religious field. For the anthropologist Gilberto Velho (2003, 53f.), "[T]rance, possession and mediumship (*mediunidade*) are recurrent phenomena in Brazilian society". Roughly half of the Brazilian population, he says, "participates directly in religious systems in which the belief in spirits and their periodical manifestation through individuals is a fundamental feature". African heritage is one of the notable ingredients of what many call a "Brazilian religious matrix".[1] Umbanda is seen by many as "the Brazilian religion *par excellence*" that "unites the white colonizer's Catholicism, religious traditions of the blacks and symbols, rites and spirits of indigenous inspiration, contemplating the three basic sources of Brazilian culture" (PRANDI 2013, 208) – and, one should add, Kardecist spiritualism imported from France, and today re-exported to Europe in a strongly missionary move (see LEWGOY 2012). However, such "Brazilian religion", according to the census, is losing

---

[*] Republished with permission of Peter Lang GmbH, Internationaler Verlag der Wissenschaften, from Andreas Heuser, ed., *Pastures of Plenty: Tracing Religio-Scapes of Prosperity Theologies in Africa - and Beyond,* pp. 117-130 (Frankfurt u.a.: Peter Lang, 2015); permission conveyed through Copyright Clearance Center, Inc.
[1] A good overview is to be found in HÖLLINGER 2007; also BOBSIN 2003; BITTENCOURT 2003; BOBSIN, LINK, DE LA PAZ and REBLIN, eds., 2008.

ground, both in absolute numbers and relative to the population and to the more explicitly African Brazilian religions, subsumed under "Candomblé". The total of African Brazilian religions declined, mainly due to losses of Umbanda. Candomblé, on the other hand, has grown nearly 70% between 1991 and 2000. However, African descendants, self-declared "black" and those of "mixed race" (*pardo,* literally "grey"), are to be found predominantly among Pentecostals and Catholics, even though their percentage is highest in Candomblé (68.5%), but much lower in Umbanda (45% – cf. PRANDI 2013; 2010). With a considerable number of white members, however, even Candomblé is no longer an ethnic religion, but has become universalised. Its declared members hold the second highest standard in education and income, second only to the (predominantly white) Spiritualists. This move is underlined by the fact that the percentage of belonging to African Brazilian religions is highest in Rio Grande do Sul state – heir to predominantly European immigration! – mainly due to Umbanda (89% of that religious segment) (cf. LEWGOY 2012). One of the factors of a strengthening of Candomblé is, probably, its proximity to social movements that affirm African ancestry and identity, as well as a by now vast academic production – initially from outsiders, now also from insiders – on African Brazilian religions which contributes to its legitimacy, further fostered by the highlighting of its works of charity (DUCCINI and RABELO 2013, 232f.). "In its transformation into a universal religion", Reginaldo Prandi (2013, 217; cf. 2001) contends, "Candomblé has known the movement of Africanization which presupposes reforms of intellectual orientation, like relearning African languages that have been forgotten throughout a century, the retrieval of the mythology of the *orixás*, partly also lost in those Brazilian years, and the restoration of African ceremonies".

Within this Brazilian religious panorama, there can be no doubt that the "health and wealth gospel" is on the rise. Even if, statistically speaking, numbers of Neo-Pentecostal churches based on a theology of prosperity are relatively modest in relation to classical Pentecostalism, their public visibility is very high, especially through a strong presence in public media, including some owned by them, and in monumental buildings. On July 31, 2014, a replica of "Solomon's temple" was inaugurated in São Paulo by the Universal Church of the Kingdom of God *(Igreja Universal do Reino de Deus* – IURD), in the presence of the then president of the Republic, Dilma Rousseff, and other political authorities.[2] According to Bishop Macedo, the founder and supreme leader of the IURD, "this is not a denominational project, much less a personal one, but something so glorious, from a spiritual point of view, that it transcends reason itself. Certainly, it will awaken the sleeping faith of the cold or lukewarm in faith and throw them into a national and, then, global awakening".[3] A clear pretension, with not least political implications (cf. FRESTON 2001a, 11-60).

Traces of the prosperity gospel are today to be found in most of the denominations, and particularly in Neo-Pentecostal churches like *Renascer em Cristo, Nova Vida, Sara nossa Terra, Igreja Internacional da Graça,* and *Igreja Mundial do Poder de Deus*, some of which have been exported to Africa. I shall focus here on the IURD, because it is the most publically visible and internationally present. This includes Africa, namely southern Africa, as stated by Paul Freston (2005, 33; cf. BLEDSOE 2010): "The Universal Church of the Kingdom of God [...], with its more than 400 congregations in southern Africa, is the first major example in the region of a new phenomenon: a successful church which is of neither First World nor African origin, but is part of the growing transnationalization of Third World evangelical religion". He continues affirming that "it is possible that no Christian denomination founded in the Third World has ever been exported so successfully and rapidly", in a "model of direct ecclesiastical transplant" (ibid, 33 and 36). In what follows, I shall present the (missionary) "struggle for Africa" promoted by the IURD (11.1); then, the "fight against Africa" seen as the root of

---

[2]   The inauguration ceremony can be viewed at <https://www.youtube.com/watch?v=eYprcb5Jg3U> [last accessed July 30, 2021]. Among other aspects, what catches the observer's attention is the constant references to Israel (the temple itself, of course, including its stones imported from Israel and ever-present *menora*, but also the presence of the Consul-General of Israel, the playing of the Israeli national anthem and the singing of Israeli songs, and not least the use of *tallit* and *kippa* by Edir Macedo and other protagonists in the act) and also to Africa, with the very notable presence of a choir from South Africa singing in English and Zulu. In the long greeting list, there were politicians, businessmen, judges, police and other authorities, and of course guests from Israel, but no representatives of other Christian churches, in a clear affirmation of the sought hegemony – the in Brazil hegemonic Roman Church only appears, in a "historical" success story from Abraham to Solomon and then Zerubbabel, Jesus Christ and Martin Luther (who rediscovered the Bible and the true faith) to its climax in Edir Macedo, as an "apostate church", "1200 years [i.e. from Constantine to Luther] of a church that spread darkness rather than light".
[3] Available at: <http://www.otemplodesalomao.com/#/otemplo> [accessed November 14, 2014].

all evils (11.2). Focusing on the theology of prosperity in the struggle for power and wealth (11.3) I finally present a theological critique under the heading of a "fight against grace" (11.4). I use quotation marks here – but not in the subtitles – to indicate that these are metaphorical expressions. Before I go on, let me state at this place a researcher's caveat. As I have not carried out any empirical research on Neo-Pentecostalism myself, either in Brazil or in Africa, I naturally rely on the works of other researchers through published texts that are available to me. Thus, I adopt the hypotheses that seem to make the most sense to me from my perception of Neo-Pentecostalism and the whole religious field as I live, listen, read, and teach in Brazil. This means that I cannot enter more deeply into the hypotheses themselves, their empirical data and pertinence. I still hope that the picture I draw is precise and correct enough to allow for the theological discussion I am proposing.

11.1 The struggle for Africa

As stated, the IURD has been especially successful in southern Africa. As is to be expected, it started in two Portuguese speaking countries, Angola and Mozambique. In 1993, in the wake of the end of *apartheid,* the IURD arrived in South Africa and installed itself especially in Johannesburg and surrounding areas, starting in Soweto. Today, this country holds the second strongest IURD flock in the world, second only to Brazil itself. "As with everything the Universal Church does, its transnational expansion is centrally planned. [...] an article in a UCKG [i.e. IURD] magazine (*Plenitude*, 75, 2001) tells us that the church sends abroad about one hundred Brazilian pastors per year", says Freston (2005, 38). While the church seeks to show itself, through its statement of faith on a South African website[4], as orthodox, Protestant, evangelical and Pentecostal, in fact its emphasis is on prosperity theology. This includes reiterated appeals to tithe as a "sacrifice" which is to be rewarded by God. At the same time, believers are exhorted and instructed to become self-

---

[4] "[T]he church comes solidly within orthodox Christianity (the Trinity), within Protestantism ('two ordinances, baptism in water and the Lord's Supper'), within evangelicalism ('the Scriptures as fully inspired and the supreme and final authority for faith and life'; 'the substitutionary sacrifice of Jesus') and within Pentecostalism ('baptism of the Holy Spirit'; 'divine healing is an integral part of the Gospel')" Available at: <http://www.uckg.org.za/about/about-us/> [accessed November 5, 2014]; FRESTON 2005, 41.

employed entrepreneurs. The IURD also attends to fears of evil spirits and witchcraft, and longings for fertility, good health, and a stable marriage. Leaflets in the IURD's Cape Town Cathedral claim that "above all, people without a name, without honour, without self-confidence and self-esteem (have become) dignities, honourable heads of families, skilled workers and motivated youth" (quoted by FRESTON 2005, 43). Such message fits well into an emerging country that is still held back by appalling poverty and inequality as well as racial discrimination – even if no longer as a political system – and widespread violence. In many of these regards, there are similarities to the Brazilian context that may facilitate the church's implantation in South Africa. André Corten (2003, 144) contends that "the follower of the Universal is the one that was able to free himself of the infernal cycle of misery", and sees an association in this with the African renaissance movement promoted by the African National Council (ANC), emphasising universality and social mobility.

The multi-racial setup of the IURD seems to be an item of attraction; according to Freston, there are very few white people congregating in South African temples. Pastors and bishops are either Brazilians or black South Africans, but not white South Africans. Freston (2005, 62) goes on to say that

> Globally speaking, the Universal Church of the Kingdom of God is almost exclusively a phenomenon of Christian poverty. Where Christians are not poor, or the poor are not Christian, it fares badly. In this sense, its expansion reflects the new global face of Christianity as more and more a religion of the poor from the global 'South' (and of 'southern' immigrants in the global 'North'). (…) It makes rich use of symbolic objects but is totally opposed to ancestor rituals and polygyny; it only promotes American prosperity preachers by selling some of their books, but never by any personal contact; its founders are not very well educated, but they do promote individualized urban lifestyles. It is thus an unusual mix in the African field of Pentecostal-like religion, and not only because of its 'exotic' geographical origin.

Finally, in Freston's evaluation, "Brazilian evangelical religion could have an important role in the global future of Christianity, since in ethnic, cultural and economic terms it is a bridge between the First and Third Worlds" (ibid, 63). Indeed, the IURD uses its communities in the Global South to enter the North (Freston 2001b, 214).

11.2 The fight against Africa

While there are, thus, notable connections between Africa and Brazil, these are not only missionary and social, but also clearly reflect the "spiritual battle" common in Neo-Pentecostalism. African Brazilian divinities (*orixás*) are being directly targeted by Neo-Pentecostal exorcisms (e.g. MACEDO 2004). To begin with, the "current of liberation" is held on Fridays, an important day for African Brazilian religions. Then, during exorcisms, the demons are forced to tell their name – they are of African origin. And, of course, people are to get rid of such "demons" because these are said to be the reason for all their misfortune, such as in their family or job. Such exorcisms are broadcast on television, or some material is posted on YouTube. Recently, the Federal Public Prosecutor of Rio de Janeiro adopted a case against *Google Brasil Internet Limitada*, asking for the deletion of such videos that show exorcisms of African Brazilian divinities, stating they were intolerant and discriminatory on religious grounds, unduly associating such religions to the "devil" – a figure which is not part of the African Brazilian religious universe, as the original plaintiff, the National Association of African (Brazilian) Media explained.[5] The videos are considered to fit into the *hate speech* category. The judge of the 17th Regional Federal Chamber of Rio de Janeiro rejected the plea for immediate exclusion of the videos from YouTube, saying that "African Brazilian cults did not configure religion", given they did not show the necessary traces of a religion, i.e. "a text fundament (Qur'an, Bible, etc.), a hierarchical structure and a God to be revered". This is, of course, a highly questionable and unilateral, but not uncommon definition, clearly oriented by the model of the Roman Catholic Church. The issue remains open – and must be thoroughly discussed in law, religious studies, and theology – as to what criteria can be applied to judge at what point freedom of religion and opinion becomes offensive to other religions to the stage that it configures, indeed, *hate speech.* A good number of the posted videos as described in the Prosecutor's argument are conversion testimonies that commonly tend to demonise the past and glorify the post-conversion situation (for Africa, cf. OMENYO 2012). Unquestionably, however, affirmations like the following are generalising in a discriminatory way: "I speak in two African dialects,

---

[5] This and the following details can be found in process number 0004747-33.2014.4.02.5101: MINISTÉRIO PÚBLICO FEDERAL/RJ.

Ketu and Angola; [...] it is impossible that someone is of witchcraft or black magic, or was, and does not speak in (an) African (language)", or that "every year the *baianas* that wash the stairs of [the] *Nosso Senhor do Bonfim* [church] carry on their head the name of the persons they killed throughout the year in black magic".[6]

While African Brazilian divinities (*orixás*) are being combatted directly by Neo-Pentecostal exorcisms, their existence is being recognised in a kind of "inverted syncretism".[7] Edir Macedo, himself a member of Umbanda before becoming Pentecostal, claims that, in his church, "we have hundreds of former (African Brazilian) priests (*pais-de-santo*) and priestesses (*mães-de-santo*) who were deceived by the evil spirits during so many years". They "were impressed", Macedo continues, "to hear the *orixás* and *caboclos* themselves confess before the mass that they are nothing more than demons, whose mission is to deceive, to bring to the ground and to destroy their 'horses'".[8]

In fact, the origin of all evil is seen as localised in Africa, and this message, brought to Africa by Brazilian missionaries, creates a movement of "deculturation"[9] with modernising tendencies. Linda van de Kamp affirms, based on her field research in Mozambique:

> According to Brazilian Pentecostal pastors, the root of all evil is in Africa, because the religions of African slaves that were sent to Brazil in the past form the basis of all kinds of African Brazilian cults [...] It is this evil which travelled with the slaves that they came to combat in Africa. [...]

---

[6] MINISTÉRIO PÚBLICO FEDERAL/RJ 2014, 15. *Baianas* are, literally, women from Bahia state. The term usually refers to women initiated in an African Brazilian religion, dressed in wide, white skirts.

[7] See DE ALMEIDA 2003, 341 *et passim*; see also DA SILVA 2007, 191-260, who shows similarities between Neo-Pentecostalism and African Brazilian religions even in the theology of prosperity.

[8] MACEDO 2004, 17. *Caboclos* are mestizos from indigenous and white parents; in Umbanda they are spirits represented by indigenous personalities. "Horses" refers to the idea that the divinities ride their initiated "son" or "daughter" like a horse.

[9] This is my expression following the reasoning of van de Kamp. It is notorious that the new South-South (and South-North) missionary movements tend not to use the notion of inculturation, nor to practice its content; see for instance O. VELHO 2007. On the other hand, "deculturation", in the sense of a perceptive, but critical stance towards local tradition and the struggle for its transformation, can have a liberating element, freeing from traditions that inhibit opportunities for women, for instance. In this sense, Velho speaks of "counter-inculturation" (ibid, 282), but also of "triumphant modernity" that paradoxically forms, he says, a pair with "paganized Christianity" (ibid, 284f.).

Brazilian Pentecostalism in Mozambique contributes towards a cultural
critical conscience and for a destabilization of cultural continuity, turning
people into 'strangers' within their own society.[10]

Ironically, some see the IURD as the first *evangélico* church in Brazil to
represent a real inculturation – others call it accommodation – given the
traditional anti-cultural stance of both historical Protestant and
Pentecostal churches. It is, as Gedeon de Alencar calls it, a "Tupiniquim
Protestantism".[11] Why would it be inculturated with such an aggressive
stance toward African Brazilian divinities? Because it is a full insertion
into that "religious matrix" – even if negatively, those forces are
acknowledged. At the same time, to be successful, one has to get liberated
from them. In a sociological reading, what is this struggle about? I shall
focus on this in the next section.

11.3 The struggle for power and wealth

Oro, Corten, and Dozon (2003, 35) affirm that "The theology of
prosperity, even before being an ideology of social ascension with the
tendency to produce fantasies [...] and mainly directed towards the
impoverished lower middle classes, is a discourse of rejecting
victimization". According to Corten, other prosperity gospel churches in
South Africa followed the 1979 implanted *Rhema Bible Church*, founded
originally in the 1960s by Kenneth Hagin in the USA. These churches,
like *Grace Bible Church, Zoe Bible Church,* and *Faithways Community
Church,* among others, are of a charismatic type and highly dependent on
USA influence. The IURD, however, the authors affirm, is not of a
charismatic type, and it is not middle class, neither does it use the USA
as a reference. Furthermore, it maintains a charity, the *Stop Suffering
Help Center,* and sees helping others as a first sign of social success.[12]

---

[10] VAN DE KAMP 2012, 63.75; see also ORO et al., 2003, 101 (Introduction to the section
on Africa): "In the Brazilian imagination, Africa continues to be a priviledged place for
the work of invisible forces".
[11] DE ALENCAR, 2005, esp. 83-117. "Tupiniquim" is an indigenous people in
Southeastern Brazil, but in everyday language is used as synonymous to "national".
[12] CORTEN 2003, 142-143. "Stop suffering" (*pare de sofrer*) is one of IURD's main
mottos.

The prosperity gospel and, with it, the success of the IURD in Brazil and in Africa can, thus, be seen as well located within the logic of striving for economic success and social ascension. It is "the most expressive accommodation of faith to the capitalist ideal of physical and material prosperity" (TIMM 2008, 966). Who could say this is not a legitimate desire for people held in poverty and oppression for far too long! On the radio, a believer affirmed: "I have already told God and the devil knows it, *I don't accept* poverty and misery; I have already *determined* for God, *I want to be prosperous* and nobody will take from me this right that I have" (CAMPOS 1999, 363, italics in original). The Brazilian *Dictionary of the Pentecostal Movement* summarises the position in this way: "The faith formula is: 1) say the thing; 2) do the thing; 3) receive the thing and 4) tell (or: count) the thing". Differently from *logos,* the term *rhema* (Romans 10:8) is taken to be "the word spoken by God in revelation and inspiration to a person at any time (…) In this way, the believer can repeat with faith any Biblical promise, applying it to his/her personal need, and claim its fulfilment" (DE ARAÚJO 2007, 617). Healing and prosperity are "rights" that can be "requested" from God "in the name of Jesus", with reference, for instance, to John 14:12: "Very truly, I tell you, the one who believes in me will also do the works that I do and, in fact, will do greater works than these, because I am going to the Father". The believer, it is said, can control things through such "positive confession". As Leonard Lovett affirms: "The logical conclusion […] is that we can purge the earth of sickness, sin, and even the 'demon of poverty'" (LOVETT 2002, 992). For Edir Macedo, Jesus "never was poor", because, as "king of kings", he "was rich".[13]

Rather than to a Weberian Protestant rational ethics fostering the spirit of capitalism, such belief and practice is close to magic, because it seeks to influence and, indeed, control God – even though, at the same time, it promotes a highly rational and highly capitalist religious marketing.[14] To this end, a price has to be paid, an investment is to be made so that retribution can be duly claimed.

---

[13] Interview of Edir Macedo to the weekly magazine *Veja*, 14/11/1990, quoted by MARIANO 2003, 248.

[14] As defended by CAMPOS 1999, passim, metaphorically represented by the three terms united in the title: the theatre (celebrations as in an arena, with all participating in the spectacle), the temple (the physical space as "the house of God", representing stability) and the market (a thoroughly capitalist practice in terms of finance and administration, understanding the needs of the religious consumer and attending to them).

> This heavy and enduring struggle is the price everyone has to pay to get the blessing. One cannot simply perform the prayer and remain waiting that things happen. No! It is necessary to make efforts, to persevere, to struggle or even to sacrifice for that which one wants do conquer! See, if Godself who is sovereign and Almighty had to sacrifice His Only Son to conquer me and you, just imagine what we, humans, must do! [...] Whoever wants to conquer something, of any kind, has to follow the path of sacrifice! (MACEDO 2000, 18).

Sacrifice is shown mainly through financial contributions to the church, tithes and other offerings. But not only a literal tithe, i.e. 10% of one's income. Some pastors call for a triple, trinitarian tithe: 10% for the Father, 10% for the Son, and 10% for the Holy Spirit (MARIANO 1999, 166f.). Beyond tithing, pastors encourage donations not based on the believers' actual income, but on their desired salary, which is invariably higher. The model is the poor widow of Luke 21:1-4 who gave all "she had to live on". Whoever does not contribute, is seen as "stealing from God" who, being the Lord of all existing riches, claims back 10% of the resources he provides for human beings. A survey carried out in 1994 showed that among the investigated churches, the faithful of the IURD were those who most frequently contributed above 10% (MARIANO 2004, 128).

In the early 1960s, Candido Procópio de Camargo (1961, 29; cf. HÖLLINGER 2007, 97-116) spoke of a "spiritualist continuum" of Kardecism and Umbanda which in times of rapid urbanisation and industrialisation had a therapeutic and socially integrative function. People were, then, simply "looking for a sacred solution for the hard burden of life". Pentecostal churches also appeared as an alternative: according to John Burdick (1993), like Umbanda they are "cults of affliction", in which people want to be relieved of their suffering and get strength for their life. The typical question in Brazil is, then, not whether there is a god and who this god might be, but what concrete difference in everyday life this or that god or divine mediator with its human mediators may be able to make, how to communicate with it and how to negotiate with it and expect reward. Such sacrifice can be the Eucharistic sacrifice; animal sacrifice (and other offerings) like in Candomblé; personal sacrifice to accumulate karma like in Kardecism; the self-sacrificing path of Christian sanctification; or money sacrifice as with Neo-Pentecostals. In such case, there is no salvation through grace alone; rather, this is a magical relationship of exchange, of delivery and counter-delivery.

11.4 The fight against grace

A first theological critique to be made, then, is precisely of a *magical manipulation of God.* It is certainly legitimate that persons, especially those in constant need of the even most basic items of life, those deprived of all benefits of modern capitalism, are seeking improvement, recognition, healing, and prosperity. The life transforming power of the Spirit is an important and truly biblical element. It represents the proximity and concrete experience of the presence of God. Through the Spirit, according to the Bible, demons are expelled, and thus persons restituted to their dominion over themselves, their dignity and their social inclusion (WELKER 2004). However, the idea that through investment and sacrifice God could be held accountable, goes against most of the biblical and theological tradition. Macedo contends that this is part of the promised "abundant life" (cf. John 10:10) – ironically a reference dear also to Liberation Theology and Christian NGOs, but in quite another sense – "God wishes to be our associate [...] The bases of our society with God are the following: what belongs to us (our life, our force, our money) shall belong to God; and what is His (blessings, peace, happiness, joy, and all that is good) shall belong to us" (MACEDO 1990, 85f.). In this contractual relationship, both God and the believer do have rights and duties with each other. From such a contractualised and monetarised relationship, it is not far for the believer-client to reclaim what has been invested, if God does not honour His part – it has already successfully happened.[15] On the other hand, pastors can always debit any lack in prosperity to the lack of faith (and, thus, of investment) and to the devil's action. Two problems, then, arise, with such a theology: For one, God's sovereignty as creator, redeemer, and sanctifier, as namely traditional Protestant theology has it, is abandoned, and the distance between the Creator and his creature diminished, which reduces both human and God's freedom. This is true despite all written (Edir Macedo's writings and church declarations) and built (the replica of Solomon's temple)

---

[15] Thus, a believer sold his car to give the 2,600 Reais he made of it to the IURD. A IURD pastor convinced him to get rid of all his material belongings and donate the revenue to the church, so that his life would take a positive turn. At the time, he was in deep financial trouble and at odds with his family. As what he had asked for did not materialise, he asked for the money back from the church. The court of appeal ruled in his favour; the court found he had been cunningly induced to make his donation; see VON SINNER 2012b.

statements that declare to give praise and honour to God. The other problem is that believers are induced to rather believe in a magical, miraculous improvement of their life than to do the right thing to achieve improvement and, thus, believe in the effect of their own efforts – even if they know that they have no "right" to be well, because the theology of cause and effect has ended emblematically with Job, the innocent sufferer. In this context, Ricardo Mariano (1999, 186) highlights the irony that the magic character of prosperity theology that rejects the old Protestant asceticism "could be smashing to the ground precisely the ethical element of Protestantism that might be, at least potentially, capable of promoting the realization of its first and foremost promise: the so much desired material prosperity". Indeed, such "Protestantism" is far from Weber's Protestant Ethics and inner-worldly asceticism. And the theology of prosperity only allows for success, not for failure. Such failure is, whenever it occurs, invariably attributed to failure of the believer, because he or she did not believe enough and did not give enough sacrifice – which causes even more suffering than the already critical situation out of which the believer did invest in faith. A theology of God's and human freedom which reckons with the existence of suffering is more apt to endure the ambiguities of life and still seek to make the best of it than a theology of retribution or prosperity.

A second theological critique is the total *abandonment of eschatology*. Even the IURD's motto, "Stop Suffering", indicates an immediatist view: now itself your life is to change, now you are to be liberated from all that holds you back from success, now you have to be healed, now you have to become victorious and get the blessings to which you are entitled. This is the message. To the contrary of much of classical Pentecostalism, which tends to be pre-millennial, expecting Christ to return soon and put things in order, establishing his reign of 1000 years (Revelation 20), and thus to put little faith in transformation here and now, the IURD preaches precisely this: transformation here and now. "God's Kingdom is today", says IURD Pastor Paulo De Velasco (as quoted by MARIANO 1999, 47). Again, the longing for a concrete transformation of life, for an end to poverty is more than legitimate. Liberation Theology also preached it, and also thought that the kingdom of God was to be realised in a "Christo-finalized" history, even if always under an eschatological reserve (GUTIÉRREZ 1988, 82-140). Still, the emphasis remains on God's free gift, and that the kingdom of God is not to be confounded with a human utopia.

Not to observe such eschatological reserve is to open doors to confuse God and human beings and, thus, to make human beings gods. Some representatives of a theology of prosperity have indeed claimed precisely that: according to Edir Macedo's brother-in-law Romildo Ribeiro Soares, leader of the Neo-Pentecostal *International Church of Grace,* "the believer has to act, to operate, as if he were a god"; others outrightly state that "you are God" (K. Copeland, quoted by MARIANO 1999, 155; cf. LOVETT 2002, 992). It, then, accommodates human beings completely within capitalism, without any critical distance. A God equal to humans, or subject to humans equal to Godself, cannot provide any critique of the reign of Mammon (cf. Lk 16:13). It is also no surprise that the IURD lowers moral standards normally claimed in Pentecostal churches, except for the rejection of prostitution, alcoholism and drug abuse, where it is in line with the more morally rigid *evangélicos.*[16] Social ethical standards are not on this list.

The third and arguably strongest theological argument against the theology of prosperity is that there is *no grace.*[17] Even though some churches, like R.R. Soares' *International Church of Grace* bear it in their name, there is no gratuity, gift, no *extra nos* that makes us receive faith and grace *mere passive*, as especially Lutheran theology has it. Rather, the stress is on human activity: whoever has enough faith and practices enough sacrifice can achieve human and divine goods. Whoever is unable to achieve this, is in disgrace, as Boff has described the situation of many people, especially the poor, already back in the 1970s. He has, at the same time, stressed that grace must be effective, concretely experienced (BOFF 2005).

Conversely, some contemporary Pentecostal theologians like Amos Yong precisely stress undeserved love and grace, and a truly Trinitarian and not only Spirit Theology. The word "prosperity" appears

---

[16] The IURD is more liberal in contrast to both Roman Catholicism and most of the *evangélico* field in terms of homosexuality – at least in a pragmatic and pastoral discourse so as to accept and receive in the church homosexual persons, in a kind of statement similar to Pope Francis on the plane back from the Rio Youth gathering in 2013: "if a person is gay and seeks God, who I am to judge?" – and also abortion, where Macedo defends the freedom of women to decide; see DE MORAES 2010; also NATIVIDADE and LEANDRO DE OLIVEIRA 2007, 261-302.

[17] In her popular comparison, ESPERANDIO 2013 compares theologies of retribution (Old Testament, while the book of Job definitively breaks with the causality of action and effect), prosperity (Neo-Pentecostalism), and grace and gratuity, based on Christ.

only once in his passionate book, and even there with caution: "The Spirit brings about blessings – sometimes in the form of material and financial prosperity – in transforming the lives of believers" (YONG 2012, 42). It is characteristic of Brazilian – and probably African – (Neo-)Pentecostalism, but such a pity that none of these sophisticated, dialogical, and ecumenical Pentecostal theologians are known in Brazil, nor are their books being translated into Portuguese. It is, however, also true that there is very little sophisticated theological discussion on a theology of prosperity, either in Brazil or elsewhere.[18] Such discussion is indeed necessary in view of the spread of the prosperity gospel in Brazil as in Africa.

---

[18] I came across, at least, a sophisticated treatment of "idols, powers and potentialities" (including the power of money) that connects to Neo-Pentecostal phenomena by initially describing visits to the IURD and to Umbanda; HAILER 2008, 9-13.

Chapter 12

Reformation Theology Between Migration and Mission In and From Brazil[*]

In his *Historia General de las Indias*, of 1552, Francisco Lopez de Gómara (1552/1918, 156) states the following: "The greatest thing aside from the creation of the world, excluding the incarnation and death of the one who created it, is the discovery of the Indies; and thus, they call it The New World. And they call it new not so much because it was found again, but because it was huge, and almost as big as the old world, which contains Europe, Africa and Asia". It was necessary to create new space for the New World in view of the prevalent conceptions at that time, because such a continent could not even exist according to the usual perceptions of a "geography of salvation". There were, of course, previous and fabulous ideas about what would be found on the other side of the ocean – we just need to recall Sir John Mandeville's popular travel story from the 14th century – and these imaginary impressions clearly influenced early descriptions of the New World. It was only possible to visualise the so-called savages as primordial and noble human beings sprung directly from paradise or as monsters, one or the other term being used depending upon the reception that European people came across when encountering the natives. The so-called cannibalism, or anthropophagy, was an existing pattern of expectations, which was confirmed, in its own way, by the first reports.

One is almost inclined to conclude that also Protestant and particularly Lutheran existence in Latin America still needs to find its place in the Christian "geography of salvation" and certainly also in its secular version. In any case, for some time it has become impossible not to realise that Latin America can no longer simply be called a "Catholic" continent. Meanwhile, the existence of *evangélicos* has become a discreet but recognisable presence in films and soap operas, which is a clear sign

---

[*] Originally published as: Reformatorische Theologie zwischen Migration und Mission in und aus Brasilien, in: Klaus Fitschen, Marianne Schröter, Christopher Spehr and Ernst-Joachim Waschke, eds., *Kulturelle Wirkungen der Reformation – Cultural Impact of the Reformation*. Kongressdokumentation Lutherstadt Wittenberg August 2017. Vol. II, pp. 33-49 (Leipzig: EVA, 2018). Used with permission. Translated by Alexander Busch and revised by the author.

that it is being noticed. It is known that the gravitational centre of Christianity as a whole has moved to the South and that currently not only the majority of Christians is found there, but also that this process brings about sweeping and rapid changes. About 14 years ago, in a lecture at Faculdades EST, Hans-Martin Barth (2007, 129) emphasised the need for a "deprovincialization" of Luther's theology, which elevates, among other things, "the possible relevance for the 'Third World'" to the condition of object of research. Was that goal achieved in the meantime? Certainly not, but, in this regard, there is already considerably more to be said.

While the Protestant and particularly Lutheran presence and reflection in Latin America is barely noticed in Europe, on the other hand, there are voices, also in Brazil, that claim that, despite great efforts over more than two centuries, "Luther's theology did not have a noticeable effect in Latin America, not even in Brazil" (BECK 2014, 629). The "not even" refers to the fact that by far the largest presence of Lutheran Christians is recorded in Brazil, namely, almost 1 million. Gedeon Freire de Alencar (2007), a sociologist and researcher of Pentecostal churches, raises, in his book on "Tupiniquim Protestantism", "Hypotheses about the (absent) *evangélico* contribution to Brazilian culture". In doing so, he starts from a tourism advertisement in which the components are introduced as representative of typical Brazilian culture. "The indigenous, Roman Catholic and Afro-Brazilian ethos is well defined and identified. But nothing, absolutely nothing, can be identified with Protestantism" (ibid, 11). Under "Protestantism" de Alencar here understands churches, theologies and forms of life that arose, in a very broad sense, from the 16th century Reformation and its resonances, including the nowadays clearly dominant and growing Pentecostal and Neo-Pentecostal churches – thus, the *evangélicos*. In his book *Protestantism and Brazilian Culture*, Presbyterian author Boanerges Ribeiro (1981) prominently idealised (missionary) Protestantism as a precursor to modernity. At the same time, Rubem Alves (1979) – who was ostracised by his Presbyterian Church when the same Boanerges Ribeiro was moderator of its Supreme Council – stigmatised Protestantism, in his book *Protestantism and Repression*, as its worst manifestation. Absence, modernity, repression – the cultural effects of the Reformation in Brazil and Latin America cannot be more than a tentative search for traces with varying results. The theology and Christianity arising from the Reformation did not permeate the whole society for reasons to be mentioned, and, where they did, it not rarely causes embarrassment because of its poorly reflected hegemonic pretensions (see Chapter 9 above) and, in my view, little consonance with the gospel. As elsewhere, the greater or smaller differences between the theology articulated by the academy or the official church and the actual living religion have to be taken into account. Therefore, I will include in my reflections perceptions of religious studies. On the other hand, it must be said that, in general in Brazil – in what follows I will focus on this country – theological knowledge and the academic study of theology have political, scientific and, therefore, cultural importance that go far beyond Lutheranism and Protestantism (cf. WACHHOLZ 2018). Indeed, one of the important contributions of Protestant and particularly Lutheran theology in Brazil, in addition to profound theoretical and practical contributions to diaconia and social justice (see Chapter 4 above), seems to be, at least from my perspective, the solid, methodological, and epistemologically responsible reflection that can and should be carried out with contextual creativity, academic freedom, evangelical commitment and awareness of public responsibility.

In my search for traces, I will first expose, in a global historical retrospective, the Protestant presence in 16th century America, in which resonances of Reformation theology can already be found (12.1). Then, I will address aspects of the Lutheran church and theology in Brazil from the 19th century onwards (12.2), and finally discuss, from the perspective of Reformation theology, the widespread prosperity gospel of Neo-Pentecostal churches (12.3).

12.1 Protestantism and America in the 16th century: a global historical retrospective

In his most recent work, *1517 – Weltgeschichte eines Jahres* [1517 – World History of One Year], Heinz Schilling (2017) undertook a comprehensive evaluation of that date in the world context. So he refers, for instance, to the fact that in the European spring of that year, a Spanish expedition arrived in the Yucatan Peninsula and encountered the Mayans who at the time dominated that region. The famous Indian rhinoceros – as well as the elephant Hanno – given as gifts by the Portuguese King Manuel I (1469-1521) to Pope Leo X (1475-1521), immortalised by Albrecht Dürer in 1515 in a woodcut based on sketches of a merchant from Nuremberg, emblematically reveals that Europe's expansion into new worlds was well known in the Old World. This was the same pope who excommunicated Luther. It seems, in turn, that the pope's love for elephants did not go unnoticed by Luther.[1]

Even more surprising is the fact that Luther – but also Emperor Charles V, his opponent – made virtually no reference to the New World.[2] They were too busy with the political and religious conflicts in Europe. In the following quotation, which deals with mission, Luther at least appears to refer to the discovery of America: "I would like, however, to say that this did not happen in the time of the apostles; after all, Germany was converted 800 years after the apostles, and recently many islands and lands have been discovered, [and should we therefore conclude that] now, 1,500 years later, nothing of this grace has been revealed?"[3] Moreover, Luther interpreted the diseases brought from overseas to Europe as signs of the end of the world – he did not, however, speak of the thousands of lives claimed by diseases taken from Europe to America. In short, Schilling (2016, 26) notes that Luther did not have, "beyond the historical-missionary and eschatological perspective [...], any interest in Europe's expansion to other continents". And the expansion of Lutheran territories outside Europe was not within his reach. Thus, the Reformation remained concentrated in Central Europe in both conceptual and political terms, and the Protestant presence in South America remained episodic until the 19th century. The religious field would only change in a truly revolutionary way in the second half of the 20th century because of the explosive growth of fully autochthonous Pentecostal churches.

---

[1] WA.TR3,54,19-22 [n° 2890 b] "[19] Elephantes sunt humanissima et docilia animalia. [20] – Et dixit quoddam papae donatum neminem laesisse et fuisse mansuetissimum. [21] Aiunt eos certis temporibus hominibus inservire in suis regionibus, [22] deinde discedere et redire ad sua officia". After "quoddam", the WA mentions in a footnote: "*scil.* animal. *The elephant was a gift from King Emanuel of Portugal to Leo X, 1514*" and refers to Ferdinand Gregorovius, Geschichte der Stadt Rom im Mittelalter. Vom V. bis zum XVI. Jahrhundert, Bd. 8, Stuttgart 1872, 178. I cordially thank my colleague Gury Schneider-Ludorff (Augustana-Hochschule Neuendettelsau) for her decisive help in locating the passage in Luther.

[2] See, on Charles V, REINHARD 2016, 607; regarding the whole issue see KOSCHORKE 1994.

[3] "Die Epistel zu der Messe in der Christnacht. Ti 2.11-15", in *Kirchenpostille* [1522], WA 10/I/1, 18-58, (quote on 21, 14-17).

The situation described for the 16th century, in which the Counter-Reformation also spread to the New World through Jesuit missionaries, gradually led to the realisation that, as it seemed, the North was reserved for the heretic Luther, and the South for the true Catholic faith. In fact, the interest of southern Europe for the New World was far greater than that of Central Europe. At that time, the Germans did not undertake their own expeditions. Still, they followed the new developments with interest. This was true not only regarding the banking houses of the Fuggers and Welsers, with whom the new colonial powers as well as the German Catholic princes were highly indebted and who, understandably, were interested in new economic opportunities. For Charles V to marry Isabela from Portugal, he resorted to the help of the Welsers and gave them, in return, Venezuela. There, from 1528 to 1546, a German colony was established, which, however, according to Jean-Pierre Bastian (1995, 48-50), could hardly have been designated, in its entirety, as Lutheran, even though most of the settlers came from Augsburg, which had recently become a Lutheran city.

Therefore, at that time, on the other side of the ocean there were practically no Lutherans or other Protestants. In the New World it was very difficult to have access to their writings. Inquisition proceedings against Protestants were extremely rare (BASTIAN 1995, 55; PRIEN 1978, 333-44). Still, the name "Luther" and the designation "Lutheran" became well known symbols of heresy, and even the greatest of them. Luther was regarded as "possessed, monster, leviathan, dragon, wolf, serpent, hydra" (MAYER 2004, 120). The Mexican Chronicles called Luther "*archihereticus maledictus in Germania*" [the cursed arch-heretic in Germany] (ibid, 123). The Franciscan Bernardino de Sahagún wrote, in his *Historia general de las Cosas de Nueva Espanã* (1577), "it seems that in these times, and in these places and with these people, our Lord wanted to restore to the church what the devil had stolen [in] England, Germany and France, in Asia and Palestine, so we are compelled to give thanks" (ibid, 124). The New World thus became the antonym of Central Europe impregnated with Lutheran heresy, the privileged acting place of divine providence, the America free from heresy. New Spanish paintings portrayed Luther, Calvin, and other reformers being run over by the Roman Curia's triumphant chariot or drowning in the sea before the victorious Roman vessel. Also, for this reason, Marian piety was deliberately promoted by extolling the Virgin of Guadalupe in Mexico and presenting Luther as her antipode. In this conception, Iberian culture, the South American soil and the Roman Catholic religion formed a unity. The notion that Protestants (and other false doctrines) constituted "sects" that were foreign to South America in religious, cultural, and political terms was disseminated well into the 20th century. At the time of Mexico's independence movement in the 19th century, the Inquisition even equated Luther with the leader of the rebels, priest Miguel Hidalgo, who, however, vigorously protested against this (SCHMIDT 2004, 151). Some liberal Mexicans saw in Protestantism the hope for economic growth and progress. Something similar applies to Brazilian republicanism in the late 19th century. Also, and precisely because of the alliance between liberal Roman Catholics, Positivists, Freemasons and Protestants, the secular states in South America were established – thus, well before the secularisation in Europe, at least from the legal point of view.

All these were rhetorical constructs advanced in the 16th century by Europeans who were upset with the new confessional situation in Europe. For the so-called common people, this contrast should not have been very significant; in any case, this understanding of "Luther" as evil was consolidated. Sometimes one still comes across it today. On the other hand, Luther was claimed by Leonardo Boff, for instance, in favour of the struggle against tutelage and oppression by church and state alike, and, at least for some people, Luther has become a symbol of freedom and liberation. Walter Altmann devoted himself to exploring this theme, with all the necessary academic rigor, in his work *Luther and Liberation*, recently published in a revised and expanded edition (2016); moreover, in 2008 a symposium discussed, in dialogue with Leonardo Boff, the relationship between his theology and Protestant theology, particularly Lutheran (VON SINNER, ed., 2010).

We know that one of the first Protestants to set foot in the southern region of the New World was Hans Staden (1525-1576), from Hesse, a mercenary hired by the Portuguese. Prior to his trip to America, he probably fought for Philip of Hesse in the Smalkaldic War. He also dedicated his book, published in 1557, to landgrave Philip, in which he described the nine months of his captivity among the Tupinambá under the title "Veritable History and Description of a Country Belonging to the Wild, Naked, Savage, Man-eating People, Situated in the New World America" (STADEN 1557/2008; cf. SCHMIDEL 1604/2010). The book became a best seller. Several times, Hans Staden escaped from being eaten by so-called cannibals. It is not possible to ascertain exactly why.

Brazilian anthropologist Darcy Ribeiro believes that Staden simply was not worthy as a sacrificial banquet: "[...] three times, he was taken to anthropophagy ceremonies and three times the indigenous refused to eat him, because he cried and wet himself, begging for mercy. You didn't eat a coward".[4] Staden himself reports that he feared constantly for his life, but he always managed to convince the Tupinambás that his God was stronger. Furthermore, according to his account, when he was afraid, he prayed and sang the hymn "From the depths I cry to thee, O Lord" (Staden 1557/2008, 60).

Certainly, the discourse about cannibalism suited the European prejudices and served to distinguish it from Christian civility. However, the Genevan Calvinist Jean de Léry (1536-1613), who, in turn, spent time among the Tupinambá and wrote an important travel account, establishes, in retrospect, a critical comparison between the Tupinambá cannibalism and the Massacre of Saint Bartholomew's Day in 1572: "the fat of human bodies [...] was it not publicly sold to the highest bidder? The livers, hearts, and other parts of these bodies – were they not eaten by the furious murderers, of whom Hell itself stands in horror?"[5] De Léry thus denounces the unilateral and hypocritical European disgust for cannibalism, since in European countries not only enemies were murdered, as among the Tupinambá, but also "kinsmen, neighbors, and compatriots" (ibid, 133).

A few months after the return of Staden, who had managed to escape from the Indigenous, a French expedition – under the command of Vice Admiral Nicolas Durand de Villegagnon, a former colleague of Calvin's, and with the support of Admiral Coligny, a Huguenot – left in 1555 to Guanabara Bay, in Rio de Janeiro, to establish the "Antarctic

---

[4] RIBEIRO 1995, 34. Ribeiro arrived at these conjectures based on the fact that anthropophagy does not serve for feeding, but is a ritual, in which the members of the tribe that were killed by the enemies are revenged and re-incorporated through devouring the defeated. As part of the ritual, before being killed and devoured, the enemies are well treated - this includes being scolded by the victors who remind their victims of how many enemies they have already killed and eaten. Therefore, it is not out of fear, but rather pride, according to the account of Jean de Léry, which was taken up and valued by LÉVI-STRAUSS (1978, 71-75; DE LÉRY 1992, 122-33. Lévi-Strauss (1978, 71) refers to de Léry's classic book as the *Ethnologist's breviary*. Staden repeatedly mentions his fear of being devoured, but he always stresses that he was saved by divine providence.

[5] DE LÉRY 1992, 132; cf. SCHMIDEL, 2010, 58f., who traces a parallel to the devouring of dead colleagues by hungry Spanish soldiers.

France" colony, that is, the French Southern colony.[6] It was difficult to get enough crew members for this, which is why rather dubious figures were also employed. After the arrival and foundation of Fort Coligny on the island of Serigipe ("Crab", today Villegagnon Island), the expedition requested support from their homeland in the form of reliable people – the expectation was to recruit them from the persecuted Huguenots in France. Villegagnon wrote to Calvin especially for this purpose. In fact, the Antarctic France had also been conceived as a place of refuge for Protestants, as "little Geneva". A group of people left for Brazil under the leadership of Pierre Richier (Peter Richter), a former Carmelite monk from Palatinate; On March 10, 1557, Richier preached the first Protestant sermon in Brazilian territory. This group also included the aforementioned Jean de Léry, then a student of theology. He reports extensively in his *History of a Voyage to the Land of Brazil*, published a year after Staden's book, about that first – and for many decades only – visible Protestant presence in the New World. But it was short-lived: Villegagnon turned more and more back to the old faith. According to de Léry's narrative, there were vehement discussions above all about the real presence of Christ in the Lord's supper, which, in another passage, he associates with the anthropophagy of the Tupinambá and the French Huguenot slayers, as a "brutal action of really (as one says) chewing and devouring human flesh" (DE LÉRY 1557/1995, 132). As the vessel that would take the Huguenots – including de Léry – back to France could not carry all of them, five men returned to Brazil on a rowboat. Villegagnon wanted to eliminate them immediately and demanded from the laymen a positioning on controversial theological issues to be written in a very short time, which led to the 1558 *Confessio Fluminensis*. It particularly rejected transubstantiation, but, for instance, also the use of priestly robes and the mixing of wine and water. This is the first Protestant confession of faith in the New World and one of the earliest of the Reformed tradition, which, unfortunately, is generally ignored in the collections of these confessions.[7] Three of the five Huguenot castaways, Jean Du

---

[6] In what follows, I refer mainly to BEGRICH 1957.

[7] See, for instance, MÜLLER, ed., 1999; ROHLS 1987. *Die Bekenntnisschriften der reformierten Kirche* [1903]. In any case, 300 hundred years later, Emile G. Léonard (1958) writes about the confession, comparing it with the usual European Reformed confessions and with Calvin and Luther, highlighting, among others, that predestination is understood, against Calvin, in an infralapsarian way. What is striking is precisely the

Bourdel, Matthieu Vermeil and Pierre Bourdon, were subsequently executed as heretics and made history as the first Protestant martyrs in the New World. André La Fon was spared because he was the only tailor in the colony. Jean Jacques Le Balleur, who had not signed the confession – he probably was a Lutheran – escaped at first, but was later arrested and hanged as a trophy for the "political and confessional victory over the French" (BEGRICH 1957, 195), in the presence of the Jesuit priest José de Anchieta, in what was then the country's capital, São Salvador da Bahia de Todos os Santos. In 1560, Fort Coligny was destroyed, and in 1567, the last Frenchmen were expelled. Presbyterians in Brazil took advantage of the commemorative year of 1917 to publicly bring forth and remember the First Protestant Reformed martyrs in the country. For Lutherans of German descent in Brazil, it was impossible to hold a public remembrance of Martin Luther during World War I. For reasons of space, unfortunately I must omit the important presence of the Dutch Reformed through the West India Company in the 17th century, from 1630 to 1654, on the coast of northeastern Brazil; in any case, those years went down in history as a time of great tolerance towards Jews and even Roman Catholics. Therefore, I now move on, as mentioned above, to discuss the Protestantism of immigration and mission of the 19th century.

12.2 Protestantism of immigration and mission in Brazil from the 19th century onwards

As very well described by José Míguez Bonino (2003) in his book *Faces of Latin American Protestantism*, there are on the continent several faces of Protestantism – liberal, evangelical, pentecostal, and ethnic – whereas in the constant growing Pentecostal and Neo-Pentecostal churches, once again, other faces can be seen. Initially, Protestant Christianity came to Brazil and America through immigration from Europe, especially from German-speaking regions: Hunsrück, Pomerania, Rhineland and Westphalia, but also Switzerland, Austria, and East Prussia. The Brazilian Empire, independent from Portugal from 1822 onwards, allowed and even encouraged this immigration to colonise and protect the territories in the south ceded by Spanish America not long before. The 1824 Constitution maintained the status of the state church of the Roman

---

knowledge of patristics these laymen had, especially the main author, Jean du Bourdel, as the confession invokes Augustine, Ambrose, and Cyprian.

Catholic Church, but authorised non-Catholic worship as long as it took place in private homes or in buildings that did not have the appearance of temples, e.g. no belfry. Many immigrants were Lutherans, Reformed, or members of the United Church; the clergy, in turn, came from Europe, for example, through missionary societies, which sent pastors specifically to work in immigrant communities, but not to do mission within the Roman Catholic population. Latin America was considered a Christian region, so it was also not represented at the Edinburgh Missionary Conference in 1910, despite the protest of American Protestant missionaries. Regardless of how it may be assessed, one effect of this process was that ethnic Protestantism remained enclosed in itself, which, until today, has given it a certain stability, but largely linked it to its ethnicity. This also applies, albeit to a lesser extent, to the Old Lutheran church, which emerged among German immigrants and their descendants from the beginning of the 20th century through the missionary work of the Missouri Synod based in the USA. The Missouri Synod, in turn emerged from German Lutheran immigrants who did not agree with the Prussian Union of 1817 and, specially, with the introduction of the Prussian worship manual.

It was determined, then, that European immigrants would dedicate themselves to agriculture and livestock on small properties, without the use of slave labour, meaning that large families were needed to do the work, which was also desirable in order to increase the white population. At that time, there were more black people than white people in Brazil, and the government feared that there could be an uprising of Afro-descendants, as in Haiti in 1804. Thus, a new model of land cultivation emerged: family farming instead of the large plantations that depended largely upon slave labour. For European countries, emigration in times of crop failures in agriculture and industrial shortcomings was very welcome, and was often supported with one-way tickets. In Brazil, however, immigrant families were second-class citizens: as there was no civil registration, nor civil marriages or public cemeteries – all of this was in the hands of the Roman Catholic Church – Protestant baptisms and marriages were, strictly speaking, non-valid, and the immigrants themselves had to organise their cemeteries. Only with the proclamation of the Republic in 1889 and the subsequent abolition of the state church and the patronage system did religious freedom in the full sense come about and the state was secularised. It is noteworthy to remember that all this still happened 30 years before the same took place in the homeland of the German immigrants.

The so-called Mission Protestantism arrived in Brazil through North American Mission Societies mainly from 1859 onwards, when the North American Presbyterian Ashbel Green Simonton (1833-1867) started his work. The missionaries had a strongly anti-Roman Catholic and countercultural stance, prohibiting, among others, the consumption of alcohol, smoking, and especially dancing, which was so very common in Brazil. This was probably one of the reasons why, for such a long time, Protestant Christianity was hardly perceived as a culturally significant phenomenon, but rather as a strange, foreign body. Especially through the missionary work coming from the southern USA, the Presbyterian, Methodist, Baptist, and Episcopal churches were established; and later, Mennonites, Adventists, Jehovah's Witnesses and Mormons also came to the country. The first Protestant histories in Brazil refer almost exclusively to these denominations; to this day, Lutherans are not perceived or taken seriously as Protestants by many of the others, because they seem to be restricted to their ethnic group, they do not act evangelistically, and liturgically and theologically they are perceived as being too close to Roman Catholics.[8] On the other hand, precisely for this reason – and also because of the coexistence with German immigrant Catholics, with whom, beyond religious controversy, there was cultural proximity – they are currently the most active church in the ecumenical movement. Lutheranism enjoys a high recognition in academic-theological circles, even far beyond the Lutheran church, so much that currently the Faculdades EST has, mainly in the graduate school, students from diverse churches and even from other religions, coming from all regions of Brazil. Ivone Gebara, a Catholic theologian and nun, describes the religious field in Brazil (rightly, as it seems) as follows:

> One can belong to the African Brazilian religion Candomblé and the Roman Catholic brotherhood of Senhor do Bonfim, join the third Franciscan order and the charismatic movement, be Roman Catholic, study theology with the Lutherans and consult with a spiritist or Buddhist

---

[8] Cf. LÉONARD 2002, 24, who explains, in a footnote (2), that he does not address the "German churches" because they would have a "mainly ethnic character".

guru. Here we come face to face with the complexity of the actual
religious phenomenon and our inability for closed approaches.[9]

We also carried out, as a team, empirical investigations in three
communities among new members or sympathisers of Lutheranism.[10]
One community had emerged originally in a very independent way, being
formed by ex-Pentecostal Christians dissatisfied with their church of
origin, who searched the Internet for an ecumenically open and morally
less rigid church and discovered the Lutheran church. Since 2005 there
has been a Lutheran community in São Luís do Maranhão that originally
has no connection with Germany or with Southern Brazil. In the
traditional Lutheran community of Rio de Janeiro, great importance is
still attached to its German origin. Still, the congregation is attracting
sympathisers who appreciate the Lutheran church for its great stress on
individual freedom and the well-prepared and demanding preaching. In
the Lutheran community in Sapucaia do Sul/RS, a colleague Oneide
Bobsin discovered a "religious underground" whose beliefs and practices
include notions of reincarnation and the search for other religious
activities that have, at most, a very weak link with Lutheran theology.
Bobsin (1997, cf. 2003) recalls the famous novel *Dona Flor and Her Two
Husbands*, by Jorge Amado (2006), and its characters Vadinho – a jack
of all trades that could not be trusted, but who was also attractive and
always surprising – and Dr. Teodoro Madureira – highly reliable and
traditional, but somewhat tedious and too predictable. Like Dona Flor,
the Lutheran pastor would have to function within two religious
universes, the confessional superstructure and the religious underground.
Nowadays, however, it can be said that this underground is no longer
hidden, but it displays itself quite clearly. When entering the home of a
Lutheran family, it is not uncommon to find, in addition to a statue of
Christ and a picture of a Lutheran pastor, also a witch on her broom and
a small statue of Buddha, among other figurines. This phenomenon was
not entirely unknown in Germany and elsewhere.

Now, in this regard, some researchers – in Germany, mainly the
religious scholar Fritz Heinrich, who knows Brazil well – defended the

---

[9] GEBARA 1997, 100. In this case, the term "inability" does not refer to the lack of
competence of the researchers, but to the impossibility of the enterprise towards the
highly complex religious field.
[10] Cf. VON SINNER et al., 2012, 497-504 (about Rio de Janeiro); BOBSIN and BARTZ 2011
(about all three).

existence of a religious matrix, a common and underground religious substrate, to which several religious systems, but also entire denominations, can appeal to. Especially the IURD, one of the Neo-Pentecostal churches, uses this matrix, which originally emerged from popular Catholicism, indigenous, African Brazilian and spiritist elements. Despite its exclusivist discourse, in practice the IURD makes use of elements of this matrix, insofar as it seeks, in a certain way and magical manner, to compel God to grant blessings in exchange for sacrifices – especially in the form of cash payments. This is similar to the "positive confession" of the prosperity gospel of Kenneth Hagin and many others who came after him, but yet, enriched through ritual elements, such as the Bible as an object of healing, whose content, on the other hand, is practically neglected. The Jordan River water, the Sinai sand, fig paste, a necklace or collar with Jesus' name and other objects serve as protective amulets to heal the body, build stronger marriages, and impel financial prosperity. Such religious practices and theology suit societies well, especially where large sections of the population desire and aim for social ascension. Thus, it is no accident that, in addition to Brazil, the IURD is particularly successful in South Africa, mainly among the poor and black people (see Chapter 11). On the other hand, Classic Pentecostal churches, such as the AD, seek to position themselves as evangelical Christians who prioritise experience, but also want to be taken seriously in regard to their theology. In its recently published 120-page declaration of faith, the General Convention of the Assemblies of God places itself, among other things, clearly in the tradition of the confessions of faith of the ancient church. The Amazonas State Convention requires from its more than 3,000 male (and now also female) pastors a bachelor's degree in academic theological studies – in the meantime, it is organising its own master's programme in theology. To this end, Lutheran academic teachers were training 12 PhD students of the AD Church. Thus, while the IURD, with its anti-Roman stance, makes use of elements originally from popular Catholicism, the AD, a traditionally anti-academic and experience-centred church, approaches the demanding Lutheran theology and clearly positions itself as heir to the Reformation. I now move on to the third part, a theological discussion of these new positions.

12.3 The prosperity gospel and the Reformation theology

It would be certainly possible for one to just observe an apparently hybrid, lived religion and its new configurations, which can be metaphorically described, with Lévi-Strauss (2021), as *bricolage*, or with Édio Soares (2009) as *butinage* (pollen gathering from different plants). Surely such empirical observation and scientific-religious interpretation is important and necessary to avoid proposing an abstract theological treatise *etsi religio non daretur*. At the same time, however, it is equally important to consider the new expressions of an increasingly diversified and rapidly changing Protestantism from a theological point of view. After all, these new denominations want to be seen as part of the evangelical Protestant Christianity. Even the IURD, on the occasion of the inauguration of its "Temple of Solomon", built with stones brought from Israel, placed Martin Luther in its multimedia presentation of salvation history. This is, in fact, a brilliant move to ensure lasting cultural visibility. The temple is already being praised as a tourist attraction. Theologically, the line would go from Abraham, passing through Solomon and Zorobabel, to Jesus, and then, with Constantine, the true faith would have been lost and the "apostatic" Catholic Church would have introduced a millennium of darkness. Only Luther would have rediscovered the Bible and true faith, which would have reached its true fulfilment in the IURD, as subtly hinted. The founder and supreme bishop of the Church, Edir Macedo, showed up with a long beard, wearing a tallit and a kippah, while the national anthem of Israel and other Israeli songs were sung, and an ark of the covenant was carried into the temple, whose walls, in turn, are painted with numerous representations of menorot, the seven-branched candlestick of the Jewish tradition. The Israeli General Consul, who was present at the inauguration, must have been embarrassed by the obvious replacement theology and appropriation of Jewish symbols.

As a typical expression of the Neo-Pentecostal prosperity gospel, we can quote the following statement from a believer made on a radio broadcast: "I already told God and the devil is aware of it: I *do not accept* poverty and misery. I have already *demanded* from God: I want to be *prosperous* and no one will take away my rights from me" (quoted by CAMPOS 1999, 363, italics in original). This is, therefore, the prosperity gospel, which abandons the centrality of a Reformation theology of grace because human beings determine and prescribe what God must do. There are critics who have already spoken of a new "trade of indulgences", with the difference, however, that what is at stake is precisely not the salvation of one's soul in eternity, but an immediacy without any eschatology. It is, moreover, a theology without a cross, a triumphalist *theologia gloriae*, which strongly recalls the controversies of the sixteenth century, particularly with Luther's theology of the cross (cf. COUREY 2016). It does not seem insignificant to me that, at that time, *theologia gloriae* was on the side of the powerful and *theologia crucis*, at least initially, on the side of the lower classes who were gradually rebelling, whereas today the situation is reversed: The poor are attracted to a *theologia gloriae*, while established theologians, although not necessarily on side of the powerful, propagate a *theologia crucis*.

If, from the point of view of the science of religion and above all of the sociology of religion, it is necessary, first of all, to recognise the existence and attractiveness of the Neo-Pentecostal prosperity gospel and the wishes and needs of the believers that are expressed in it, acknowledging that these churches that call themselves *evangélicos*, in one way or another belong to the history and theology of Reformation Christianity, and therefore, can be subject – in my opinion, must be subject – to theological inquiries precisely from this confessional tradition. I ventured into that in Chapter 11.

Therefore, the search for traces in the 16th and 19th centuries and in the present time did not indicate an absence, but several presences, recognised in different ways, both positive and problematic, of theology, life forms and churches rooted in the Reformation. In several ways they relate to Europe, but also to Africa and Asia – through colonisation, immigration, and mission in and from Brazil. Such theology participates and is involved in the secular state, in the achievement of religious freedom, in formation and diaconia, and, thus, in the advancement for – but, alas, also the oppression of – freedom in individual belief and academic thought. Thus, an exciting, diverse, and challenging picture, full of tensions, emerges. To conclude with a simultaneously humorous and serious observation: if a sign on a building indicates it is available for rental, but not for a bar, a brothel or a church – that is, everything that makes noise and attracts an unwanted audience – and, on the other hand, if a "fully furnished" evangelical church is being offered for rent, then there can certainly remain no doubt about its cultural and public presence, but also the need for a new Reformation.

BIBLIOGRAPHY

AHLSTRAND, Kajsa, 1993. *Fundamental Openness. An Enquiry into Raimundo Panikkar's Theological Vision and its Presuppositions.* Uppsala: Swedish Institute for Missiological Research.

AHMED, Akbar S. and Hastings DONNAN, eds., 2003. *Islam, Globalization and Postmodernity.* London and New York: Routledge.

ALTHAUS-REID, Marcella, 2000. *Indecent Theology.* London: Routledge.

———, Ivan PETRELLA and Luiz Carlos SUSIN, eds., 2007. *Another Possible World.* London: SCM.

ALTMANN, Walter, 2000. *Luther and Liberation: A Latin American Perspective.* Eugene, Or.: Wipf & Stock.

———, 2006. "Por um projeto para o Brasil". *Pastoral Letter* n° 121 of January 7, 2006.

———, 2016. *Luther and Liberation.* 2nd ed. Minneapolis: Fortress.

ALVES, Rubem, 1979. *Protestantism and Repression.* London: SCM.

AMADO, Jorge, 2006. *Dona Flor and Her Two Husbands.* New York: Vintage.

AMIGO, Ricardo, 2014. "New Religious Spaces in the Megacity: The Igreja Universal do Reino de Deus and its Temple of Solomon in São Paulo, Brazil". *Zeitschrift für junge Religionswissenschaft* 9, 5-21.

ANDRADE, Claudionor, 2008. "Bibliologia – a Doutrina das Escrituras", in Antonio GILBERTO et al., eds., *Teologia Sistemática Pentecostal,* pp. 17-48. Rio de Janeiro: CPAD.

AQUINAS, Thomas, 1997. *Summa Theologiae: A Concise Translation* [1265-1274], edited by Timothy MCDERMOTT. Allen, Tx.: Thomas More Publishing.

ARAÚJO, Glauber S., ed., 2017. *A Reforma Protestante: uma visão adventista.* Tatuí: Casa Publicadora Brasileira.

ASSMANN, Hugo, ed., 1972. *El pueblo oprimido. Señor de la historia.* Montevideo: Tierra Nueva.

———, 1994. *Crítica à lógica da exclusão.* São Paulo: Paulus.

———, 2000. "Por uma teologia humanamente saudável", in Luis Carlos SUSIN, ed., *O mar se abriu: trinta anos de teologia na América Latina,* pp. 115-30. Porto Alegre: SOTER; São Paulo: Loyola.

———, and Jung Mo SUNG, 2010. *Competência e sensibilidade solidária. Educar para a esperança.* 3rd ed. Petrópolis: Vozes.

AUGÉ, Marc, 2009. *Non-Places. An Introduction to Supermodernity.* 2nd ed. New York: Verso.

AUGUSTINUS, Aurelius, 1886. *The City of God* [413-26]. A Select Library of the Nicene and Post-Nicene Fathers of the Christian Church, vol. II, edited by Philip SCHAFF. Edinburgh: T & T Clark.

AVRITZER, Leonardo, 2002. *Democracy and the Public Space.* Princeton: Princeton University Press.

BAKER, Christopher and Elaine GRAHAM, 2017. "Urban Ecology and Faith Communities", in Sebastian KIM and Katie DAY, eds., *A Companion to Public Theology,* pp. 390-417. Leiden: Brill.

BARTH, Hans-Martin, 1990. *Einander Priester sein. Allgemeines Priestertum in ökumenischer Perspektive.* Göttingen: Vandenhoeck & Ruprecht.

_____, 2007. "A teologia de Martim Lutero num contexto global". *Estudos Teológicos*, 47(2), 123-144.

_____, 2008. *Dogmatik. Evangelischer Glaube im Kontext der Weltreligionen*, 3rd ed. Gütersloh: Gütersloher Verlagshaus.

BARTH, Karl, 1981. *Fides Quaerens Intellectum. Anselms Beweis der Existenz Gottes im Zusammenhang seines theologischen Programms* [1931], edited by Eberhard JÜNGEL and Ingolf U. DALFERTH. Zürich: TVZ.

BARTH, Ulrich, 2003a. *Religion in der Moderne*. Tübingen: Mohr Siebeck.

_____, 2003b. "Die Umformungskrise des modernen Protestantismus", in *Religion in der Moderne*, pp. 167-200. Tübingen: Mohr Siebeck.

_____, and Wilhelm GRÄB, eds., 1993. *Gott im Selbstbewußtsein der Moderne. Zum neuzeitlichen Begriff der Religion*. Gütersloh: Gütersloher Verlagshaus.

BARTSCH, Hans-Werner, 1983. "Freiheit. IV. Freiheit und Befreiung im Neuen Testament", in *Theologische Realenzyklopädie*, pp. 506-508. Vol. 11. Berlin: de Gruyter.

BASTIAN, Jean-Pierre, 1995. *Geschichte des Protestantismus in Lateinamerika*. Luzern: Exodus.

BECK, Nestor Luiz João, 2014. "Luther Studies in Latin America". In Robert KOLB, Irene DINGEL and L'ubomír BATKA, eds., *The Oxford Handbook of Martin Luther's Theology*, pp. 627-632. Oxford: Oxford University Press.

BECKA, Michelle, 2007. *Interkulturalität im Denken Raúl Fornet-Betancourts*. Nordhausen: Verlag Traugott Bautz.

BEDFORD-STROHM, Heinrich, 2015. *Liberation Theology for a Democratic Society*, collected and edited by Eva HARASTA. Münster: LIT.

BEGRICH, Martin, 1957. "Villegaignon und die Hugenotten in der Guanabarabucht". *Staden Jahrbuch* 5, 185-201.

BERGER, Peter L., ed., 1999. *The Desecularization of the World: Resurgent Religion and World Politics*. Washington: Ethics and Public Policy Center. Grand Rapids: Eerdmans.

BERNECKER, Walther L., et al., eds., 1994. *Handbuch der Geschichte Lateinamerikas*, Vol. 1. Stuttgart: Kohlhammer.

BERNHARDT, Reinhold, 1994. "Theologia Ludens", in Reinhold BERNHARDT, Martin HAILER, Gesine VON KLOEDEN and Ulrike LINK-WIECZOREK, eds., *Theologische Samenkörner: Dem Lehrer Dietrich Ritschl zum 65*, pp. 60-70. *Geburtstag*. Münster: LIT.

_____, and Klaus VON STOSCH, eds., 2009. *Komparative Theologie. Interreligiöse Vergleiche als Weg der Religionstheologie*. Zürich: TVZ.

_____, Martin HAILER, Gesine VON KLOEDEN and Ulrike LINK-WIECZOREK, eds., 1994. *Theologische Samenkörner: Dem Lehrer Dietrich Ritschl zum 65. Geburtstag*. Münster: LIT.

BEYER, Peter F., 1990. "Privatization and the Public Influence of Religion in Global Society, in Mike Featherstone, ed., *Global Culture? Nationalism, Globalization and Modernity*, pp. 373-396. London: Sage.

BHABHA, Homi, 2004. *The Location of Culture*. Milton Park: Routledge.

BIEHL, João, 2005. *Vita. Life in a Zone of Social Abandonment*. Berkeley: University of California Press.

BINGEMER, Maria Clara and Ivone GEBARA, 1989. *Mary, Mother of God and Mother of the Poor*, Maryknoll: Orbis.

BIRMAN, Patricia, ed., 2003. *Religião e espaço público*. São Paulo: Attar.

BITTENCOURT, Filho José, 2003. *Matriz religiosa brasileira: religiosidade e mudança social*. Petrópolis: Vozes.

BITTERLI, Urs, 1993. *Cultures in Conflict: Encounters between European and Non-European Cultures*. Stanford: Stanford University Press.

BITUN, Ricardo, ed., 2017. *A Reforma Protestante*, São Paulo: Hagnos.

BLEDSOE, David Allen, 2010. "Igreja Universal do Reino de Deus: A survey of selected areas". *Missionalia* 38(1), 69-98.

BOBSIN, Oneide, 1997. "O subterrâneo religioso da vida eclesial: intuições a partir das ciências da religião". *Estudos Teológicos* 37(3), 261-280.

_____, 2003. "Der dunkelhäutige Tod des weissen Protestantismus – Geister-Schmuggel an den religiösen Grenzen", in Wolfgang STEGEMANN, ed., *Theologische Akzente: Religion und Kultur – Aufbruch in eine neue Beziehung*, pp. 201-129. Stuttgart: Kohlhammer.

_____, Rogério Sávio LINK, Nivia Ivette Núñez DE LA PAZ, and Iuri Andréas REBLIN, eds., 2008. *Uma Religião Chamada Brasil*. São Leopoldo: Oikos.

_____, and Alessandro BARTZ, 2011. *Mobilidade religiosa e adesão em comunidades urbanas da IECLB:* relatório de pesquisa. São Leopoldo: Oikos.

BOFF, Clodovis, 1987. *Theology and Praxis: Epistemological Foundations*, Maryknoll: Orbis.

_____, 1993. "Epistemology and Method of the Theology of Liberation", in ELLACURIA and SOBRINO, eds., *Mysterium Liberationis: Fundamental Concepts of Liberation Theology*, pp. 57-85. Maryknoll, NY: Orbis Books.

BOFF, Leonardo, 1981. *Teologia à escuta do povo*. Petrópolis: Vozes.

_____, 1986. *Ecclesiogenesis: The Base Communities Reinvent the Church*. Maryknoll, NY: Orbis Books.

_____, 1987a. *Und die Kirche ist Volk geworden* [1986]. Düsseldorf: Patmos.

_____, 1987b. *The Maternal Face of God: The Feminine and its Religious Expressions*. San Francisco: Harper and Row.

_____, 1988. *Trinity and Society*. Exeter: Burns & Oates.

_____, 1989a. *Faith on the Edge: Religion and Marginalized Existence*. San Francisco: Harper and Row.

_____, 1989b. "Um balanço de corpo e alma", in Leonardo BOFF et al., eds., *O que ficou. Balanço aos 50*, pp. 9-29. etrópolis: Vozes.

_____, 1991. "O que significa teologicamente povo de Deus e igreja popular?" [1986], in *E a Igreja se fez povo. Eclesiogênese: A Igreja que nasce da fé do povo*, 3rd ed., pp. 39-57. Petrópolis: Vozes.

_____, 1995. *Ecology and Liberation: A New Paradigm*. Translated by John Cumming. Maryknoll, NY: Orbis. Books.

_____, 1997. *Cry of the Poor, Cry of the Earth*. Maryknoll: Orbis.

_____, 2005. *Liberating Grace*. Eugene, Or. Wipf & Stock.

_____, 2011a. *Church, Charism and Power*. Eugene, Or.: Wipf & Stock.

_____, 2011b. *Die Kirche neu erfinden* [2006]. Mainz: Grünewald.

BOFF, Leonardo and Clodovis BOFF, 1987, *Introducing Liberation Theology*. Maryknoll, NY: Orbis Books.

BONHOEFFER, Dietrich, 2010. *Letters and Papers from Prison.* Dietrich Bonhoeffer's Works English, vol. 8. Minneapolis: Fortress Press.

BOODOO, Gerald M., ed., 2016. *Religion, Human Dignity and Liberation.* São Leopoldo: Oikos.

BOUTENEFF, Peter and Dagmar HELLER, eds., 2001. *Interpreting Together. Essays in Hermeneutics,* Geneva: WCC.

BRAKEMEIER, Gottfried, 1989. *Eleições.* Carta Pastoral no. 11229/89, 24 August 1989.

_____, 1992. *Relatório do Pastor Presidente,* XVIII Concílio Geral.

_____, 1993. *O direito e o poder,* Carta da Presidência no. 17817/93, 23 November 1993.

_____, 1997. *Por Paz e Justiça: manifestos da presidência da Igreja Evangélica de Confissão Luterana no Brasil, 1986-1994,* Blumenau: Otto Kuhr.

BRANDT, Hermann, 1973. "Die evangelische Kirche lutherischen Bekenntnisses in Brasilien (EKLB) und die Feiern zum 150. Jahrestag der Unabhängigkeit Brasiliens am 7. September 1973". *Zeitschrift für Evangelische Ethik* 17(1), 43-49.

_____, 1982 "Vorwort - nicht nur zur Übersetzung," in Carlos MESTERS, ed., *Die Botschaft des leidenden Volkes,* pp. 9-17. Neukirchen-Vluyn.

_____, 2002. "Theologie II/5.2, Theologie der Befreiung". in *Theologische Realenzyklopädie,* Vol. 33, pp. 306-311. Berlin: De Gruyter.

BRASIL, 2014. Ministério da Educação. Parecer Conselho Nacional de Educação. Câmara de Educação Superior nº 60, de 12 de março de 2014: "Diretrizes Curriculares Nacionais para o curso de graduação em Teologia". Available at: http://portal.mec.gov.br/index.php?option=com_docman&view=download&alias=16071-pces060-14-1&Itemid=30192[accessed August 12, 2021].

_____, 2016. Ministério da Educação. Conselho Nacional de Educação. Câmara de Educação Superior. Resolução nº 4, de 16 de setembro de 2016: "Institui as Diretrizes Curriculares Nacionais para o curso de graduação em Teologia e dá outras providências". Available at: http://portal.mec.gov.br/index.php?option=com_docman&view=download&alias=48421-rces004-16-pdf&category_slug=setembro-2016-pdf&Itemid=30192 [accessed August 12, 2021].

BREITENBERG JR., E. Harold, 2003. "To Tell the Truth: Will the Real Public Theology Please Stand Up?" *Journal of the Society of Christian Ethics* 23(2), 55-96.

[BSLK] EVANGELISCHE KIRCHE IN DEUTSCHLAND, 2014. *Die Bekenntnisschriften der Evangelisch-Lutherischen Kirche,* ed. Irene DINGEL. Vollständige Neuedition. Göttingen: Vandenhoeck & Ruprecht.

BURDICK, John, 1993. *Looking for God in Brazil: The Progressive Catholic Church in Urban Brazil's Religious Arena.* Berkeley: University of California Press.

BURITY, Joanildo A., 2016. "Minoritization and Pluralization. What Is the 'People' That Pentecostal Politicization Is Building?" *Latin American Perspectives* 43(3), 116-132.

_____, 2020. "Conservative Wave, Religion and the Secular State in Post-Impeachment Brazil". *International Journal of Latin American Religions* 4, 83-107.

BUSCH, Eberhard, 2007. *Reformiert. Profil einer Konfession.* Zürich: TVZ.

BUSS, Paulo Wille, 2017a. "Igreja Evangélica de Confissão Luterana no Brasil (IECLB)", in Timothy J. WENGERT, ed., *Dictionary of Luther and the Lutheran Traditions,* p. 356-357. Grand Rapids: Baker Academic.

_____, 2017b. "Igreja Evangélica Luterana do Brasil (IELB)", in Timothy J. WENGERT, ed., *Dictionary of Luther and the Lutheran Traditions*, p. 357. Grand Rapids: Baker Academic.

BUTTELLI, Felipe Gustavo Koch; Clint LE BRUYNS and Rudolf VON SINNER, eds., 2014. *Teologia pública no Brasil e na África do Sul: Cidadania, interculturalidade e HIV/AIDS,* Teologia pública vol. 4. São Leopoldo: Sinodal.

CALDEIRA, Teresa P.R., 2000. *City of Walls: Crime, Segregation, and Citizenship in São Paulo*. Berkeley: University of California Press.

CALIMAN, Cleto, 2011. "Igreja, Povo de Deus, Sujeito da Comunhão Eclesial". *Horizonte* 9(24), 1047-1071.

CAMARGO, Candido Procópio de, 1961. *Kardecismo e Umbanda: uma Interpretação Sociológica.* São Paulo: Pioneira.

CAMPOS, Leonildo Silveira, 1999. *Teatro, templo e mercado: organização e marketing de um empreendimento neopentecostal.* 2nd ed. Petrópolis: Vozes; São Paulo: Simpósio/UMESP.

CARDOSO, Fernando Henrique and Enzo FALETTO, 1979. *Dependency and Development in Latin America.* Berkeley: University of California Press.

CASANOVA, José, 1994. *Public Religions in the Modern World.* Chicago: University of Chicago Press.

CASARA, Rubens, 2017. *Estado pós-democrático, neo-obscurantismo e gestão dos indesejáveis.* Rio de Janeiro: Civilização Brasileira.

CAVALCANTE, Ronaldo, 2017. *As relações entre Protestantismo e Modernidade*, São Paulo: Paulinas.

_____, and José Roberto BONOME, eds., 2017. *500 Anos da Reforma Protestante: História, Cultura e Sociedade.* São Paulo: Terceira Via.

_____, and Rudolf VON SINNER, eds., 2011. *Teologia pública em debate.* 2nd edition. São Leopoldo: Sinodal.

CHARADEAU, Patrick, 2014. *Le discours politique: les masques du pouvoir.* Limoges: Lambert-Lucas.

CHAUÍ, Marilena, 2000. *Brasil: Mito fundador e sociedade autoritária.* São Paulo: Perseu Abramo.

CHAVES, Gilmar Vieira, 2017. *Reforma Protestante: História, ensinos e legado.* Rio de Janeiro: Central Gospel.

CIPRIANI, Roberto, 2006. "Secularization or 'diffused religion'?", in FRANZMANN, Manuel, Christel GÄRTNER, and Nicole KÖCK, eds., 2006. *Religiosität in der säkularisierten Welt: Theoretische und empirische Beiträge zur Säkularisierungsdebatte in der Religionssoziologie*, pp. 123-140. Wiesbaden: VS Verlag für Sozialwissenschaften.

CNBB [Conferência Nacional dos Bispos do Brasil], 2006. *Eleições 2006: Orientações da CNBB.* Brasília: CNBB.

COLEMAN, Simon, 2000. *The Globalization of Charismatic Christianity. Spreading the Gospel of Prosperity.* Cambridge: Cambridge University Press.

_____, 2012. "The Protestant Ethic and the Spirit of Urbanism", in Rik PINXTEN and Lisa DIKOMITIS eds., *When God Comes to Town. Religious Traditions in Urban Contexts*, pos. 814-1093. New York: Berghahn Books. Kindle Edition.

COMBLIN, José, 1968. *Theólogie de la ville.* Paris: Éditions Universitaires.

_____, 1987. *Antropologia cristiana.* Madrid: Paulinas.

_____, 1991. *Teologia da cidade.* São Paulo: Edições Paulinas.

_____, 1996. *Viver na cidade.* Pistas para a pastoral urbana. São Paulo: Paulus.

_____, 1998. *Called For Freedom: The Changing Context of Liberation Theology.* Maryknoll, NY: Orbis Books.

COMMISSION ON FAITH AND ORDER, 1998. *A Treasure in Earthen Vessels: An Instrument for an Ecumenical Reflection on Hermeneutics.* Faith and Order Paper No. 182. Geneva: World Council of Churches.

CONTRERAS, Jaime and Rosa María MARTÍNEZ DE CODES, eds., 2013. *Trends of Secularism in a Pluralistic World.* Frankfurt: Verwuert.

COOPER, Thia, ed., 2013. *The reemergence of Liberation Theologies: Models for the Twenty-First Century.* New York: Palgrave Macmillan.

CORTEN, André, 1996. *Os pobres e o Espírito Santo. O pentecostalismo no Brasil.* Petrópolis: Vozes.

_____, 2003. "A Igreja Universal na África do Sul". In Ari Pedro ORO, André CORTEN and Jean-Pierre DOZON, eds., *Igreja Universal do Reino de Deus: os novos conquistadores da fé,* pp. 137-145. São Paulo: Paulinas.

COSTA, Sérgio, J. Mauricio DOMINGUES, Wolfgang KNÖBL, and Josué P. DA SILVA, eds., 2006. *The Plurality of Modernity: Decentring Sociology.* München, Mering: Rainer Hampp.

COUREY, David J., 2016. *What has Wittenberg to do with Azusa? Luther's Theology of the Cross and Pentecostal Triumphalism.* London: T & T Clark.

COX, Harvey, 1995. *Fire from Heaven. The Rise of Pentecostal Spirituality and the Reshaping of Religion in the 21st Century.* Cambridge: Da Capo Press.

_____, 2013. *The Secular City. Secularization and Urbanization in Theological Perspective* [1969]. Princeton: Princeton University Press.

CUNHA, Dilney, 2004. *Das Paradies in den Sümpfen. Eine Schweizer Auswanderungsgeschichte nach Brasilien im 19. Jahrhundert,* Zürich: Limmat.

CUNHA, Magali do Nascimento, 2006. "Um olhar sobre a presença pública das igrejas evangélicas no Brasil: análise crítica e possibilidades futuras", in Clovis Pinto DE CASTRO, Magali do Nascimento CUNHA and Nicanor LOPES, eds., *Pastoral Urbana. Presenca Publica das Igrejas em Areas Urbanas,* pp. 99-123. São Bernardo do Campo.

_____, 2007. *Explosão Gospel: um olhar das ciências humanas sobre o cenário evangélico no Brasil.* Rio de Janeiro: Mauad.

DAGNINO, Evelina, 1994. "Os movimentos sociais e a emergência de uma nova noção de cidadania', in Evelina DAGNINO ed., *Os anos 90: política e sociedade no Brasil,* pp. 103-115. São Paulo: Brasiliense.

DAHLING-SANDER, Christoph, 2003. Zur Freiheit befreit. Das theologische Verständnis von Freiheit und Befreiung nach Martin Luther, Huldrych Zwingli, James H. Cone und Gustavo Gutiérrez. Frankfurt: Lembeck Verlag.

DAMATTA, Roberto, 1991. *Carnivals, Rogues, and Heroes,* Notre Dame: Notre Dame University Press.

_____, 1995. "For an Anthropology of the Brazilian Tradition or 'A Virtude está no Meio'" in David J. HESS and Roberto A. DAMATTA, eds., *The Brazilian Puzzle. Culture on the Borderlands of the Western World*, pp. 270-291. New York: Columbia University Press.

_____, 1997. *A casa e a rua: espaço, cidadania, mulher e morte no Brasil.* 5th ed. Rio de Janeiro: Rocco.

DANZ, Christian, 2010. *Einführung in die evangelische Dogmatik.* Darmstadt: Wissenschaftliche Buchgesellschaft.

DAVIE, Grace, 1994. *Religion in Britain since 1945: Believing without Belonging.* Oxford: Blackwell.

DE ALENCAR, Gedeon Freire, 2007. *Protestantismo Tupiniquim: Hipóteses sobre a (não) Contribuicão Evangélica à Cultura Brasileira.* São Paulo: Arte Editorial.

DE ALMEIDA, Ronaldo, 2003. "A guerra das possessões", in Ari Pedro ORO, André CORTEN and Jean-Pierre DOZON, eds., *Igreja Universal do Reino de Deus: os novos conquistadores da fé,* pp. 321-342. São Paulo: Paulinas.

_____, 2019. "Bolsonaro Presidente: conservadorismo, evangelismo e a crise brasileira", in *Novos Estudos CEBRAP* 38/1, 185-213.

DE ARAÚJO, Isael, 2007. *Dicionário do movimento pentecostal.* Rio de Janeiro: CPAD.

DE AZEVEDO, Thales, 1981. *A religião civil brasileira: um instrumento politico.* Petrópolis: Vozes.

DE CARVALHO, José Murilo, 1989. *Os bestializados. O Rio de Janeiro e a república que não foi.* São Paulo: Companhia das Letras.

_____, 2001. *Cidadania no Brasil. O longo caminho.* Rio de Janeiro: Civilização Brasileira.

DE CASTRO, Clovis Pinto, 2000. *Por uma Fé Cidadã. A Dimensão Pública da Igreja. Fundamentos para uma Pastoral da Cidadania.* São Bernardo do Campo: UMESP; São Paulo: Loyola.

_____, Magali do Nascimento CUNHA, and Nicanor LOPES, eds., 2006. *Pastoral Urbana: Presença Pública da Igreja em Áreas Urbanas.* São Bernardo do Campo: EDITEO/UMESP.

DE GRUCHY, John W., 1991. *Liberating Reformed Theology. A South African Contribution to an Ecumenical Debate.* Grand Rapids: Eerdmans.

_____, 2001. *Christianity, Art and Transformation. Theological Aesthetics in the Struggle for Justice.* Cambridge: Cambridge University Press.

_____, 2004. "From Political to Public Theologies: The Role of Theology in Public Life in South Africa", in Willaim F. STORRAR and Andrew R. MORTON, eds., *Public Theology for the 21st Century. Essays in Honour of Duncan B. Forrester,* pp. 45-62. London: T & T Clark.

DEHN, Ulrich, 2011. *Interkulturelle Theologie als Wahrnehmungswissenschaft weltweiten Christentums.* Available at: <http://www.theologie.uni-hamburg.de/imoer/ download/grundlagentext_interkulturelle_theologie.pdf>. [accessed May 4, 2011]

DE LÉRY, Jean, 1992. *History of a Voyage to the Land of Brazil.* Translation and introduction by Janet Whatley. Berkeley, Los Angeles & London: University of California Press.

DELLA CAVA, Ralph, 1976. "Catholicism and Society in Twentieth-Century Brazil". *Latin American Research Review* 11(2), 7-50.

DE OLIVEIRA, David Mesquiati, Ismael DE VASCONCELOS FERREIRA and Maxwell Pinheiro FAJARDO, eds., 2017. *Pentecostalismos em perspectiva.* São Paulo: Terceira Via.

DE OLIVEIRA, Cláudio Ribeiro and Alessandro ROCHA (eds.), 2017. *Reforma e Ecumenismo*, São Paulo.

DE OLIVEIRA, Jorge Batista Dietrich, 2014. "Igreja nos lares. Ensaio sobre a capilaridade da igreja cristã no contexto urbano", in Roberto E. ZWETSCH, ed., *Cenários urbanos: Realidade e esperança. Desafios às comunidades cristãs*, pp. 13-57. São Leopoldo: Sinodal; EST.

DE OLIVEIRA, Pedro Ribeiro, 1984. "Was bedeutet analytisch betrachtet 'Volk'?" *Concilium* 20(6), 505-512.

DEMO, Pedro, 1995. *Cidadania Tutelada e Cidadania Assistida*. Campinas: Editora Autores Associados.

DE SANTA ANA, Julio, 1987. *Ecumenismo e libertação,* Petrópolis: Vozes.

DE SOUZA, Jessé, 2019. *A elite do atraso: da escravidão a Bolsonaro.* Rio de Janeiro: Estação Brasil.

DE SOUZA SANTOS, Boaventura, s.d. *Para uma sociologia das ausências e uma sociologia das emergências.* Available at: <http://www.boaventuradesousasantos.pt/ documentos/sociologia_das_ausencias.pdf> [accessed August 12, 2021].

DE THEIJE, Marjo, 2012. "Reading the City Religious: Urban Transformation and Social Recontstruction in Recife, Brazil", in Rik PINXTEN and Lisa DIKOMITIS, eds., *When God Comes to Town. Religious Traditions in Urban Contexts,* pos. 2154-2568. New York: Berghahn Books, Kindle Edition.

DIEHL, Paula, 2011. "Die Komplexität des Populismus. Ein Plädoyer für ein mehrdimensionales und graduelles Konzept". *Totalitarismus und Demokratie* 8, 273-291.

_____, 2019. "Twisting representation", in Carlos DE LA TORRE, ed., *Routledge Handbook of Global Populism,* pp. 129-143. London & New York: Routledge.

DOSTOYEVSKY, Fyodor, 1993. *The Grand Inquisitor, with related chapters from the Brothers Karamazov.* Hackett.

DREHER, Martin, 1978. *Kirche und Deutschtum in der Entwicklung der Evangelischen Kirche Lutherischen Bekenntnisses in Brasilien.* Göttingen: Vandenhoeck & Ruprecht.

_____, 1984. "Luteranismo e participação política", in *Reflexões em Torno de Lutero,* vol. 2, pp. 121-132. São Leopoldo: Sinodal.

_____, 2008. "Reflexões sobre os 60 anos da EST", in Lothar HOCH, Carlos Marga Janete STRÖHER and Wilhelm WACHHOLZ, eds., *ESTações da formação teológica. 60 anos de história da EST,* pp. 57-70. São Leopoldo: EST.

DUCCINI, Luciana and Miriam C.M. RABELO, 2013. "As religiões afro-brasileiras no Censo de 2010". In Faustino TEIXEIRA and Renata MENEZES, eds., *Religiões em movimento: o Censo de 2010,* pp. 219-234. Petrópolis: Vozes.

DUSSEL, Enrique, 1993. "Theology of Liberation and Marxism", in Ignácio ELLACURÍA and Jon SOBRINO, eds., *Mysterium Liberationis Fundamental Concepts of Liberation,* pp. 85-102. Maryknoll, NY: Orbis Books.

_____, 2003. *Philosophy of Liberation*. Eugene, OR: Wipf & Stock.

ECKHOLT, Margit and Stefan SILBER, eds., 2014. *Glauben in Mega-Citys. Transformationsprozesse in lateinamerikanischen Großstädten und ihre Auswirkungen auf die Pastoral*. Ostfildern: Matthias-Grünewald-Verlag.

EISENSTADT, Shmuel N., 2000. "Multiple Modernities", *Daedalus* 129(1), 1-29.

_____, ed., 2002. *Multiple Modernities*. Piscataway, NJ: Transaction Publishers.

ELLACURÍA, Ignácio, 1993a. "The Historicity of Christian Salvation", in Ignácio ELLACURÍA and Jon SOBRINO, eds., *Mysterium Liberationis Fundamental Concepts of Liberation,* pp. 251-89. Maryknoll, NY: Orbis Books.

_____, 1993b. "The Crucified People", in Ignácio ELLACURÍA and Jon SOBRINO, eds., *Mysterium Liberationis Fundamental Concepts of Liberation,* pp. 591-592. Maryknoll, NY: Orbis Books.

ELLACURÍA, Ignácio and Jon SOBRINO, eds., 1990. *Mysterium Liberationis:* conceptos fundamentales de la teología de la liberación. Madrid: Editorial Trotta. 2 vols.

_____, eds., 1993. *Mysterium Liberationis. Fundamental Concepts of Liberation Theology*. Maryknoll, NY: Orbis Books.

ESPERANDIO, Mary Rute Gomes, 2013. *Retribuição, prosperidade e graça. Teologias em um mundo em sofrimento*. São Leopoldo: CEBI.

ESTERMANN, Josef, 2006. *Teología Andina: el tejido diverso de la fe indígena.* 2 vols. La Paz: ISEAT, Plural Editores.

_____, 2012. *Apu Taytayku: Religion und Theologie im andinen Kontext Lateinamerikas*. Mainz: IKU.

ESTRADA, Juan Antonio, 1993. "People of God", in Ignácio ELLACURÍA and Jon SOBRINO, eds., *Mysterium Liberationis. Fundamental Concepts of Liberation Theology*, pp. 604-614. Maryknoll, NY: Orbis Books.

FACHGRUPPE "RELIGIONSWISSENSCHAFT UND MISSIONSWISSENSCHAFT" der Wissenschaftlichen Gesellschaft für Theologie/Verwaltungsrat der Deutschen Gesellschaft für Missionswissenschaft, 2005. *Mission als Interkulturelle Theologie und ihr Verhältnis zur Religionswissenschaft.* "Positionspapier" of September 21, 2005. Available at: <http://theologie.uni-hd.de/rm/publikationen/uebersicht> [accessed May 4, 2011].

FELDMEIER, Reinhard, 2008. *The First Letter of Peter. A Commentary on the Greek Text.* Waco, Texas: Baylor University Press.

FERREIRA, Jorge, 2017. "O nome e a coisa: o populismo na política brasileira", in id., ed., *O populismo e sua história,* 4th ed., pp. 59-124. Rio de Janeiro: Civilização Brasileira.

FERRY, Luc, 2002. *Man Made God: The Meaning of Life.* Chicago: University of Chicago Press.

FIEGENBAUM, Ricardo Zimmermann, 2006. *Midiatização do campo religioso e processos de produção de sentido: análise de um conflito anunciado. O caso do Jornal Evangélico da IECLB.* Master's Thesis in Media Science, São Leopoldo: Unisinos.

FIELD, David N., 2018. "Who are 'the People'? Populism, the 'Othered', and the Public Identity of a Minority Church in Europe". *International Journal of Public Theology* 12(1), 102-118.

FISCHER, Joachim, 1970. "Geschichte der Evangelischen Kirche Lutherischen Bekenntnisses in Brasilien", in Joachim FISCHER and Christoph JAHN, eds., *Es begann am Rio dos Sinos: Geschichte und Gegenwart der Ev. Kirche Lutherischen Bekenntnisses in Brasilien,* 2nd ed., pp. 83-204. Erlangen: Erlanger Verlag für Mission.

_____, 1983. "Luther in Brasilien". *Luther-Jahrbuch* 50, 150-165.

FITSCHEN, Klaus, 2001a. "Stadt II. Neues Testament", in *Theologische Realenzyklopädie,* vol. 32., pp. 92-93. Berlin: De Gruyter.

_____, 2001b. "Stadt III. Kirchengeschichte", in *Theologische Realenzyklopädie,* vol. 32., pp. 93-104. Berlin: De Gruyter.

FOLLMANN, José Ivo, 2001. *O mundo das religiões em São Leopoldo.* São Leopoldo: Unisinos.

FORNET-BETANCOURT, Raúl, 1997. *Lateinamerikanische Philosophie zwischen Inkulturation und Interkulturalität.* Frankfurt a.m.: IKO-Verlag.

_____, 2007. *Religião e interculturalidade.* São Leopoldo: Sinodal.

FORSTER, Dion, 2020. "State Theology and Political Populism? A Kairos Critique of Religious Populism in South Africa". *Journal of Church and State* 62(2), 316-333.

FRANK, André Gunder, 1967. *Capitalism and Underdevelopment in Latin America: Historical Studies of Chile and Brazil.* New York: Monthly Review Press.

FRANZMANN, Manuel, Christel GÄRTNER, and Nicole KÖCK, eds., 2006. *Religiosität in der säkularisierten Welt: Theoretische und empirische Beiträge zur Säkularisierungsdebatte in der Religionssoziologie.* Wiesbaden: VS Verlag für Sozialwissenschaften.

FREIRE, Paulo, 2000. *Pedagogy of the Oppressed.* London: Continuum.

FRESTON, Paul, 1994. *Evangélicos na Política Brasileira: História Ambígua e Desafio Ético.* Curitiba: Encontro.

_____, 2001a. *Evangelicals and Politics in Asia, Africa and Latin America.* Cambridge: Cambridge University Press.

_____, 2001b. "The Transnationalisation of Brazilian Pentecostalism", in André CORTEN and Ruth MARSHALL-FRATANI, eds., *Between Babel and Pentecost. Transnational Pentecostalism in Africa and Latin America,* pp. 196-215. Bloomington/Indianapolis: Indiana University Press.

_____, 2005. "The Universal Church of the Kingdom of God: A Brazilian Church Finds Success in Southern Africa". *Journal of Religion in Africa* 35(1), 33-65.

FUKUYAMA, FRANCIS, 1992. *The End of History and the Last Man.* New York: Avon.

_____, 1996. *Confiança: as virtudes sociais e a criação da prosperidade.* Rio de Janeiro: Rocco. [engl. ed.: Trust. The Social Virtues and the Creation of Prosperity. New York: Free Press, 1995].

GABRIEL, Karl, Christel GÄRTNER, and Detlef POLLACK, eds., 2014. *Umstrittene Säkularisierung: Soziologische und historische Analysen zur Differenzierung von Religion und Politik,* 2nd ed. Berlin: Berlin University Press.

GAEDE NETO, Rodolfo, 1998. "Teologia da Prosperidade e diaconia." In Rodolfo Gaede NETO, Laude Erandi BRANDENBURG and Evandro Jair MEURER, eds., *Teologia da Prosperidade e Nova Era,* pp. 5-20. São Leopoldo: IEPG.

GEBARA, Ivone, 1997. *Teologia ecofeminista.* São Paulo.

GERTZ, René E., 2004. "Die Lutheraner in der Gesellschaft und Kultur Brasiliens", in Hans MEDICK and Peer SCHMIDT, eds., *Luther zwischen den Kulturen.*

Zeitgenossenschaft - Weltwirkung, pp. 164-189. Göttingen: Vandenhoeck & Ruprecht.

GETUI, Mary N., Luiz Carlos SUSIN, and Beatrice W. CHURU, eds., 2008. *Spirituality for Another Possible World*. Nairobi: Twaweza.

GIBELLINI, Rosino, 1998. *A teologia do século XX*. Trad. João P. Netto. São Paulo: Loyola.

GILBERTO, Antonio, ed., 2008. *Teologia sistemática pentecostal*. Rio de Janeiro: CPAD.

GIL FILHO, Sylvio Fausto, 2013. "Geografia da Religião", in João Décio PASSOS and Frank USARSKI eds., *Compêndio de Ciência da Religião*, pp. 275-286. São Paulo: Paulinas; Paulus.

GIUMBELLI, Emerson, 2002. *O fim da religião: dilemas da liberdade religiosa no Brasil e na França*. São Paulo: Attar.

_____, 2003. "O chute na santa", in Patricia BIRMAN, ed., *Religião e espaço público*, pp. 169-199. São Paulo: Attar.

GMAINER-PRANZL, Franz, 2010. "'Relativer Sinn' und 'unbedingte Wahrheit'", in Mariano DELGADO AND Guido VERGAUWEN, eds., *Interkulturalität. Begegnung und Wandel in den Religionen,* pp. 129-160. Stuttgart: Kohlhammer.

_____, 2012. "Welt-Theologie. Verantwortung des christlichen Glaubens in globaler Perspektive". *Zeitschrift für Missionswissenschaft* 38, 408-432.

GMAINER-PRANZL, Franz and Eneida JACOBSEN, eds., 2016. *Desclocamentos: Verschiebungen theologischer Erkenntnis. Ein ökumenisches und interkulturelles Projekt.* Innsbruck/Wien: Tyrolia.

GMAINER-PRANZL, Franz and Sigrid RETTENBACHER, ed., 2013. *Religion in postsäkularer Gesellschaft: Interdisziplinäre Perspektiven*. Frankfurt: Peter Lang.

GOLDSTEIN, Horst, 1991. *Kleines Lexikon zur Theologie der Befreiung*. Düsseldorf: Patmos.

GÓMARA, Francisco Lopez de, 1918. *Historia general de las Indias* [1552]. Madrid.

GRÄB, Wilgelm, 2006. *Religion als Deutung des Lebens. Perspektiven einer Praktischen Theologie gelebter Religion*. Gütersloh: Gütersloher Verlagshaus.

GRAF, Friedrich Wilhelm, 1991. "Das Grundrecht auf Provinzialität. Interkulturelle Theologie und die multikulturelle Lage", *Lutherische Monatshefte* 30(4), 170-172.

_____, 2004. *Die Wiederkehr der Götter. Religion in der modernen Kultur*. München: C.H. Beck.

GREENBLATT, Stephen, 1992. *Marvellous Possessions: The Wonder of the New World*. Chicago: University of Chicago Press.

GROßHANS, Hans-Peter, 2011. "Gottesverhältnis und Freiheitsgefühl: Schleiermachers Theologie zwischen Neuzeit und Moderne", in Andreas ARNDT and Kurt-Victor SELGE, eds., *Schleiermacher: Denker für die Zukunft des Christentums?* pp. 11-30. Berlin: De Gruyter.

GUNN, T. Jeremy, 2013. "Secularism, the Secular, and Secularization", in CONTRERAS, Jaime and Rosa María MARTÍNEZ DE CODES, eds. *Trends of Secularism in a Pluralistic World*, pp. 59-105. Frankfurt: Verwuert.

GUTIÉRREZ, Gustavo, 1993. "Option for the Poor", in Ignácio ELLACURÍA and Jon SOBRINO, eds., *Mysterium Liberationis. Fundamental Concepts of Liberation,* pp. 235-250. Maryknoll, NY: Orbis Books.

_____, 1997. "Renewing the Option for the Poor", in DAVID BATSTONE et al., eds., *Liberation Theologies, Postmodernity, and the Americas,* pp. 69-82. London, New York: Routledge.

_____, 1988. *A Theology of Liberation: History, Politics, and Salvation* [1972]. Revised Edition with a New Introduction. Maryknoll: Orbis.

_____, 2004. *The Power of the Poor in History* [1979]. Eugene, Or.: Wipf & Stock.

HABERMAS, Jürgen and Joseph RATZINGER, 2007. *The Dialectics of Secularization: on Reason and Religion.* San Francisco: Ignatius Press.

HAGOPIAN, Frances and Scott MAINWARING, eds., 2005. *The Third Wave of Democratization in Latin America. Advances and Setbacks.* Cambridge: Cambridge University Press.

HAILER, Martin, 2007. "Wie viel Magie verträgt der Glaube? Systematisch-theologische Reflexionen," in Gabriele LADEMANN-PRIEMER, Rüdiger SCHMITT and Bernhard WOLF, *Alles fauler Zauber? Beiträge zur heutigen Attraktivität von Magie,* pp. 103-36. Münster: Ugarit-Verlag.

_____, 2008. *Götzen, Mächte und Gewalten.* Göttingen: Vandenhoeck & Ruprecht.

HANKE, Ezequiel, 2020. *Do que são feitos os sapatos do estado laico?* Liberdade religiosa versus direitos dos animais. Unpublished Doctoral Dissertation. Faculdades EST: Programa de Pós-Graduação em Teologia, São Leopoldo.

HÄRLE, Wilfried, 1995. *Dogmatik.* Berlin: De Gruyter.

HASLER, Eveline, 1988. *Ibicaba. Das Paradies in den Köpfen,* München: DTV.

HAVEA, Sione, 1986. "Relevant Pacific Theology", in PACIFIC COUNCIL OF CHURCHES, *Towards a Relevant Pacific Theology,* pp. 21-31. Suva: PCC.

HEGEL, Georg Wilhelm Friedrich, 1970. Vorlesungen über die Philosophie der Geschichte [1822], in: *Werke in zwanzig Bänden.* Vol. 12. Frankfurt a. M.: Suhrkamp.

HEINE, Steven, and Charles S. PREBISH, eds., 2003. *Buddhism in the Modern World. Adaptations of an Ancient Tradition.* Oxford: Oxford University Press.

HEINE, Susanne, Hermann BRANDT, Klauspeter BLASER and Julius J. LIPNER, 2002. "Theologie II/5. Theologie in der entstehenden Weltgesellschaft", in *Theologische Realenzyklopädie,* vol. 33, pp. 300-323. Berlin: De Gruyter.

HEUSER, Andreas, ed., 2015. *Pastures of Plenty: Tracing Religio-Scapes of Prosperity Theologies in Africa – and Beyond.* Frankfurt et al.: Peter Lang.

HICK, John, 2005. *An Interpretation of Religion.* Human Responses to the Transcendent, 2nd ed. New Haven: Yale University Press.

HINKELAMMERT, Franz J., 1986. *The Ideological Weapons of Death: a Theological Critique of Capitalism.* Maryknoll, NY: Orbis Books.

HOBBES, Thomas, 2000. *Leviathan* [1651], Stuttgart: Reclam [engl. ed. London, Penguin Books, 1982].

HOCH, Lothar Carlos, 2001. "Healing as a Task of Pastoral Care among the Poor", *Intercultural Pastoral Care and Counselling* 7, 32-38.

_____, Marga Janete STRÖHER and Wilhelm WACHHOLZ, eds., 2008. *EStações da formação teológica. 60 anos de história da EST.* São Leopoldo: EST.

HOCK, Klaus, 2011. *Einführung in die Interkulturelle Theologie.* Darmstadt: Wissenschaftliche Buchgesellschaft.

HOFFMANN, Martin, Daniel C. BEROS and Ruth MOONEY, eds., 2017. *Radicalizando a Reforma: Outra teologia para outro mundo.* São Leopoldo: Sinodal, EST.

HÖHNE, Florian und Torsten MEIREIS, eds., 2020. *Religion and Neo-Nationalism in Europe.* Berlin: Nomos.

_____, and Frederike VAN OORSCHOT, eds., 2015. *Grundtexte Öffentliche Theologie.* Leipzig: Evangelische Verlagsanstalt.

HOLENSTEIN, Elmar, 1998. "Ein Dutzend Daumenregeln zur Vermeidung interkultureller Missverständnisse", in *Kulturphilosophische Perspektiven,* pp. 288-312. Frankfurt a.M.: Suhrkamp.

HOLLENWEGER, Walter J., 1988. *Geist und Materie: Interkulturelle Theologie,* vol. 3. München: Chr. Kaiser.

HÖLLINGER, Franz, 2007. *Religiöse Kultur in Brasilien: Zwischen traditionellem Volksglauben und modernen Erweckungsbewegungen.* Frankfurt: Campus Verlag.

HÖLSCHER, Lucian, 1990. "Die Religion des Bürgers. Bürgerliche Frömmigkeit und protestantische Kirche im 19. Jahrhundert". *Historische Zeitschrift* 250, 595-630.

HOLSTON, John, and Teresa CALDEIRA, 1998. "Democracy, Law, and Violence: Disjunctions of Brazilian Citizenship", in Felipe AGÜERO and Jeffrey STARK, eds., *Fault Lines of Democracy in Post-Transition Latin America,* pp. 263-296. Miami: North-South Center Press, University of Miami.

HONNETH, Axel, 1996. *The Struggle for Recognition. The Moral Grammar of Social Conflicts.* Boston: MIT Press.

HORTON, Stanley., ed., 1994. *Systematic Theology.* Springfield: Logion Press.

HUBER, Wolfgang, 1991. *Kirche und Öffentlichkeit,* 2nd ed. München: Kaiser.

_____, 2003. "Volkskirche I: Systematisch-theologisch," in *Theologische Realenzyklopädie* vol. 35, pp. 249-254. Berlin: De Gruyter.

IECLB [Evangelical Church of the Lutheran Confession in Brasil], 2004. "Mensagem do XXIV Concílio da IECLB", *Boletim Informativo* 185.

ILLICH, Ivan, 1989. *Tools for Conviviality.* Berkeley: Heyday.

INGLEHART, Ronald, 1999. "Trust, Well-being and Democracy", in Mark E. WARREN, ed., *Democracy and Trust,* pp. 88-120. Cambridge: Cambridge University Press.

IONESCU, Ghiţa and Ernest GELLNER, eds., 1969. *Populism: Its Meaning and National Characteristics.* London: Macmillan.

IRELAND, Rowan, 1991. *Kingdoms Come. Religion and Politics in Brazil.* Pittsburgh: Pittsburgh University Press.

_____, 1998. "Pentecostalism, Conversions, and Politics in Brazil", in Edward L. CLEARY and Hannah W. STEWART-GAMBINO, eds. *Power, Politics, and Pentecostals in Latin America,* pp. 123-137. Boulder: Westview Press.

JACOBSEN, Eneida, Rudolf VON SINNER and Roberto E. ZWETSCH, eds., 2013. *Public Theology in Brazil: Social and Cultural Challenges.* Münster: LIT.

JEFFERS, Chike Nathan Jelani, 2010. *The Black Gift: Cultural Nationalism and Cosmopolitanism in African Philosophy,* PhD Dissertation submitted to Northwestern University, Evanston, IL.

JENKINS, Philip, 2006. *The New Faces of Christianity. Believing the Bible in the Global South*. New York: Oxford University Press.

_____, 2007a. *The Next Christendom. The Coming of Global Christianity*. Revised and expanded edition. New York: Oxford University Press.

_____, 2007b. "Christianity Moves South", in Frans WIJSEN and Robert SCHREITER eds., *Global Christianity. Contested Claims*, pp. 15-33. Amsterdam: Rodopi.

_____, 2007c. *God's Continent. Christianity, Islam, and Europe's Religious Crisis*. New York: Oxford University Press.

JOAS, Hans, 2014. "Gefährliche Prozessbegriffe. Eine Warnung vor der Rede von Differenzierung, Rationalisierung und Modernisierung", in Karl GABRIEL, Christel GÄRTNER, and Detlef POLLACK, eds., 2014. *Umstrittene Säkularisierung: Soziologische und historische Analysen zur Differenzierung von Religion und Politik*, pp. 603-622. 2nd ed. Berlin: Berlin University Press.

JOEST, Wilfried, 1989. *Dogmatik*. Vol. I: *Die Wirklichkeit Gottes*. 3rd ed. Göttingen: Vandenhoeck & Ruprecht.

JOHNSON, Todd M., and Kenneth R. ROSS, 2009. *Atlas of Global Christianity 1910-2010*. Edinburgh: Edinburgh University Press.

KALTWASSER, Cristobal Rovira, Paul A. TAGGART, Paulina Ochoa ESPEJO, and Pierre OSTIGUY, eds., 2020. *The Oxford Handbook of Populism*. Oxford: Oxford University Press. Kindle Edition.

KANT, Immanuel, 1989. *Foundations of the Metaphysics of Morals* [1785], 2nd ed. Prentice Hall.

_____, 2015. *Critique of Practical Reason,* Revised ed. Cambridge: Cambridge University Press.

KARNAL, Leandro, 2017. *Todas contra todos: o ódio nosso de cada dia*. Rio de Janeiro: Leya.

KIM, Sebastian and Kirsteen KIM, 2007. *Christianity as a World Religion*. London: Continuum.

KITAMORI, Kazoh, 2005. *Theology of the Pain of God* [1972]. Eugene, OR: Wipf & Stock.

KLIEWER, Gerd Uwe, 2005. "Effervescent Diversity: Religions and Churches in Brazil Today". *The Ecumenical Review* 57(3), 314-321.

KNITTER, Paul F., 1996. "Cosmic Confidence or Preferential Option?" in Joseph PRABHU, ed., *The Intercultural Challenge of Raimon Panikkar*, pp. 177-191. Maryknoll, NY: Orbis. Books

KOMULAINEN, Jyri, 2005. *An Emerging Cosmotheandric Religion? Raimon Panikkar's Pluralistic Theology of Religions*. Leiden, Boston: Brill.

KOOPMAN, Nico, 2003. "Some Comments on Public Theology Today". *Journal of Theology for Southern Africa* 177, 3-19.

KOSCHORKE, Klaus, 1994. "Konfessionelle Spaltung und weltweite Ausbreitung des Christentums". *Zeitschrift für Theologie und Kirche*, 91, 10-24.

_____, 2009. "Veränderte Landkarten der globalen Christentumsgeschichte". *Kirchliche Zeitgeschichte* 22, 187-210.

_____, 2010. "Christliche Missionen und religiöse Globalisierung im 19. Jahrhundert", in Walter DEMEL and Hans-Ulrich THAMER, eds., *WBG Weltgeschichte*, vol. 5: *Entstehung der Moderne 1700-1914*, pp. 195-208. Darmstadt: Wissenschaftliche Buchgesellschaft.

KOYAMA, Kosuke, 1999. *Water Buffalo Theology* [1974]. Maryknoll, NY: Orbis Books.

KRECH, Volkhard, 2014. "Über Sinn und Unsinn religionsgeschichtlicher Prozessbegriffe", in Karl GABRIEL, Christel GÄRTNER, and Detlef POLLACK, eds., 2014. *Umstrittene Säkularisierung: Soziologische und historische Analysen zur Differenzierung von Religion und Politik*, pp. 565-602. 2nd ed. Berlin: Berlin University Press

KUNDERT, Lukas, 2014. *Die reformierte Kirche. Grundlagen für eine reformierte Schweizer Ekklesiologie*. Zürich: TVZ.

KÜNG, Hans, 1998. *A Global Ethic for Global Politics and Economics*. Oxford: Oxford University Press.

_____, 2011. *Ist die Kirche noch zu retten?* München: Piper.

KUNERT, Augusto E., 1982. "Aspectos da relação IECLB e Estado, em uma compreensão histórica e teológica". *Estudos Teológicos* 22(3), 215-242.

KUSMIERZ, Katrin and James COCHRANE, 2006. "Öffentliche Kirche und öffentliche Theologie in Südafrikas politischer Transformation", in Christine LIENEMANN-PERRIN and Wolfgang LIENEMANN, eds., *Kirche und Öffentlichkeit in Transformationsgesellschaften*, pp. 403-431. Stuggart: Kohlhammer.

KÜSTER, Volker, 1996. *Jesus und das Volk im Markusevangelium. Ein Beitrag zum interkulturellen Gespräch in der Exegese*. Neukirchen-Vluyn: Neukirchener.

_____, 1999. *Die vielen Gesichter Jesu Christi. Christologie interkulturell*. Neukirchen-Vluyn: Neukirchener.

_____, 2001. "Interkulturelle Theologie", in Hans-Dieter BETZ, Don S. BROWNING, Bernd JANOWSKI, and Eberhard JÜNGEL, eds., *Die Religion in Geschichte und Gegenwart*, 4th ed., vol. 4, pp. 198-199. Tübingen: Mohr Siebeck.

_____, 2011, *Einführung in die interkulturelle Theologie*. Göttingen: Vandenhoeck & Ruprecht.

LACLAU, Ernesto, 2004. "Glimpsing the Future", in Simon CRITCHLEY and Oliver MARCHART, eds., *Laclau – A Critical Reader,* pp. 279-328. London & New York: Routledge.

_____, 2005. *On Populist Reason.* London & New York: Verso.

_____, and Chantal MOUFFE, 2014. *Hegemony and Socialist Strategy. Towards a Radical Democratic Politics.* 2nd edition. London: Verso.

LAMPORT, Mark, ed., 2017. *Encyclopedia of Martin Luther and the Reformation.* Lanham, MD: Rowman & Littlefield.

LANGE, Armin and Zlatko PLEŠE, 2014. "Derveni – Alexandria – Qumran. Transpositional Hermeneutics in Jewish and Greek Culture", in Sydney H. AUFRÈRE, Philip S. ALEXANDER and Zlatko PLEŠE in association with CYRIL JACQUES BOLOUX, eds., *On the Fringe of Commentary. Metatextuality in Ancient Near Eastern and Ancient Mediterranean Cultures*. Leuven: Peeters.

LAS CASAS, Bartolomé de, 1996. "Traktat über die Indiosklaverei", in Mariano DELGADO ed., *Sozialethische und staatsrechtliche Schriften*. Werkauswahl, 3/1. Paderborn-München-Wien: Schöningh.

LATINOBARÓMETRO, 2003. *Informe 2003.* Santiago de Chile: Latinobarómetro.

_____, 2010. *Informe 2010.* Santiago de Chile: Latinobarómetro.

_____, 2014. "Las religiones en tiempos del Papa Francisco", document of April 16, 2014. Available at: http://www.latinobarometro.org/latNewsShop.jsp [April 21, 2014].

_____, 2018. *Informe 2018.* Santiago de Chile: Latinobarómetro.

LAUSTER, Jörg, 2005. *Religion als Lebensdeutung. Theologische Hermeneutik heute.* Darmstadt: Wissenschaftliche Buchgesellschaft.

LEFEBVRE, Henri, 1991. *The Production of Space* [1974]. Translated by D. Nicholson-Smith. Oxford & Cambridge, Blackwell.

LEIBNIZ, Gottfried Wilhelm, 1996. *Die Theodizee I. Philosophische Schriften 2.1*, in French and German. Frankfurt a.M.: Suhrkamp.

LÉONARD, Émile G, 2002. *O protestantismo brasileiro* [1963]. 3rd ed. São Paulo.

LÉVI-STRAUSS, Claude, 1978. *Traurige Tropen.* Frankfurt am Main: Suhrkamp.

_____, 2021. *Wild Thought.* A New Translation of La Pensée Sauvage. Chicago: University of Chicago Press.

LEWGOY, Bernardo, 2012. "Entre herança europeia e hegemonia brasileira: notas sobre o novo kardecismo transnacional", in Ari Pedro ORO, Carlos Alberto STEIL and João RICKLI, eds., *Transnacionalização religiosa: fluxos e redes*, pp. 101-121. São Paulo: Terceiro Nome.

LICHTENBERG, Georg Christoph, 1985. "Lichtenberg, Von den Kriegs- und Fast-Schulen der Schinesen, neben einigen andern Neuigkeiten von daher" [1796], in ADRIAN HSIA, ed., *Deutsche Denker über China,* pp. 103-116. Frankfurt a. M.: Insel.

LIEDHEGENER, Antonius, 2014. "Säkularisierung als Entkirchlichung. Trends und Konjunkturen in Deutschland von der Mitte des 19. Jahrhunderts bis zur Gegenwart", in Karl GABRIEL, Christel GÄRTNER, and Detlef POLLACK, eds., 2014. *Umstrittene Säkularisierung: Soziologische und historische Analysen zur Differenzierung von Religion und Politik*, pp. 481-531. 2nd ed. Berlin: Berlin University Press.

LIENEMANN-PERRIN, Christine, and Mee-Hyun CHUNG, 2006. "Vom leidenden Volk zur Staatsbürgerschaft. Koreanische Kirchen zwischen *Minjung* und *Shimin*", in Christine LIENEMANN-PERRIN and Wolfgang LIENEMANN, eds., *Kirche und Öffentlichkeit in Transformationsgesellschaften*, pp. 301-31. Stuttgart: Kohlhammer.

LIENEMANN, Wolfgang, 2010. "Wahrheit und Freiheit der Religionen", in Walter DIETRICH and Wolfgang LIENEMANN, eds., *Religionen – Wahrheitsansprüche – Konflikte*, pp. 9-42. *Theologische Perspektiven.* Zürich: TVZ.

LIMA, Eduardo Campos, 2021. "L'oecuménisme brésilien mis en péril", in *Réformés.ch,* 11 March, 2021. Available at: https://www.reformes.ch/eglises/2021/03/ loecumenisme-bresilien-mis-en-peril-bresil-monde-oecumenisme-polarisation-de-la. [accessed May, 9 2021].

LISSNER, Jørgen, and Arne SOVIK, eds., 1978. *A Lutheran Reader on Human Rights.* Geneva: Lutheran World Federation.

LITS, Marc, 2009. "Présentation Générale. Populaire et populisme: entre dénigrement et exaltation", in Marc LITS ed., *Populaire et Populisme,* pp. 9-27. Paris: CNRS Éditions.

LITTLE, David, 2013. "The Global Challenge of Secularism to Religious Freedom", in CONTRERAS, Jaime and Rosa María MARTÍNEZ DE CODES, eds., *Trends of Secularism in a Pluralistic World*, pp. 31-58. Frankfurt: Verwuert.

LOVETT, Leonard, 2002. "Positive Confession Theology", in Stanley M. BURGESS and Eduard M. VAN DER MAAS, eds., *The New International Dictionary of*

Pentecostal and Charismatic Movements, pp. 992-994. Revised and expanded edition. Grand Rapids, MI: Zondervan.

LUCKMANN, Thomas, 2014. *A religião invisível.* São Paulo: Olho d'Água; Loyola.

LUHMANN, Niklas, 1971. "Die Weltgesellschaft". *Archiv für Rechts- und Sozialphilosophie* 57, 1-35.

_____, 2000. *Vertrauen. Ein Mechanismus der Reduktion sozialer Komplexität* [1968], 4ᵗʰ ed. Stuttgart: Lucius & Lucius.

_____, 2001. "Vertrautheit, Zuversicht, Vertrauen, Probleme und Alternativen", in MARTIN Hartmann and Claus OFFE, eds., *Vertrauen. Die Grundlage sozielen Zusammenhalts* pp. 143-160, Frankfurt: Campus Verlag.

LUTHER, Martin. Die Epistel zu der Messe in der Christnacht. Ti 2.11-15. In: *Kirchenpostille* [1522], WA 10/I/1, 18-58.

_____, 1959. The Large Catechism, in *The Book of Concord,* translated and edited by Theodore G. TAPPERT. Philadelphia: Fortress Press.

LUTHERAN WORLD FEDERATION, 1971. *Sent into the World: The Proceedings of the Fifth Assembly of the Lutheran World Federation, Evian, France, July 14-24, 1970,* edited by LaVern K. GROSC. Minneapolis: Augsburg.

MACEDO, Edir, 1990. *Vida com abundância.* Rio de Janeiro: Editora Gráfica Universal.

_____, 2000. *Aliança com Deus.* 2ⁿᵈ ed. Rio de Janeiro: Editora Gráfica Universal.

_____, 2003. *O poder sobrenatural da fé.* Rio de Janeiro: Editora Gráfica Universal.

_____, 2004. *Orixás, Caboclos & Guias: deuses ou demônios?* Rio de Janeiro: Editora Gráfica Universal.

MACHADO, Carly, 2013. "'É muita mistura': projetos religiosos, políticos, sociais, midiáticos, de saúde e segurança pública nas periferias do Rio de Janeiro". *Religião & Sociedade* 33(2), 13-36.

MACLEAN, Iain S. 1999. *Opting for Democracy? Liberation Theology and the Struggle for Democracy in Brazil.* New York: Peter Lang.

MADURO, Otto, 2006. "Once Again Liberating Theology? Towards A Latin American Liberation Theological Self-Criticism", in Marcella ALTHAUS-REID, ed., *Liberation Theology and Sexuality,* pp. 19-31. Aldershot: Ashgate.

MARIANO, Ricardo, 1999. *Neopentecostais: sociologia do novo pentecostalismo no Brasil.* São Paulo: Loyola.

_____, 2003. "O reino da prosperidade da Igreja Universal." In Ari Pedro ORO, André CORTEN and Jean-Pierre DOZON, eds., *Igreja Universal do Reino de Deus: os novos conquistadores da fé,* pp. 237-58. São Paulo: Paulinas.

_____, 2004. "Expansão pentecostal no Brasil: o caso da Igreja Universal". *Estudos Avançados* 18(52), 121-138.

_____, 2008. "Usos e limites da teoria da escolha racional da religião". *Tempo Social:* Revista de Sociologia da USP, São Paulo 20(2), 41-66.

MARIZ, Cecília L. and Paulo GRACINO JR., 2013. "As igrejas pentecostais no Censo de 2010." In Faustino TEIXEIRA and Renata MENEZES, eds., *Religiões em movimento: o Censo de 2010,* pp. 161-174. Petrópolis: Vozes.

MARSHALL, Thomas H., 1965. *Class, Citizenship, and Social Development.* Garden City: Anchor Books.

MARTIN, David, 2006. "Comparative Secularisation North and South", in Manuel FRANZMANN, Christel GÄRTNER, and Nicole KÖCK, eds., *Religiosität in der säkularisierten Welt: Theoretische und empirische Beiträge zur*

Säkularisierungsdebatte in der Religionssoziologie, pp. 105-122. Wiesbaden: VS Verlag für Sozialwissenschaften.

MARTINS, Antônio Henrique Campolina, 2010. "Um comentário sociológico-político sobre a cidade de Deus de Agostinho". *Revista Ética e Filosofia Política* 2(12), 276-278.

MARTINS, José de Souza, 2020. "A fé do Brasil dividido", *Cidadania 21*, published on January 24, 2020. Available at https://cidadania23.org.br/2020/01/24/jose-de-souza-martins-a-fe-do-brasil-dividido/ [accessed February 23, 2020].

MARZO, GIUSEPPE DE, 2010. *Buen vivir: para una democracia de la Tierra*. La Paz.

MAUSS, Marcel, 1990. *The Gift: The Form and Reason for Exchange in Archaic Societies*. London: Routledge.

MAYER, Alicia, 2004. "'The Heresiarch that Burns in Hell': The Image of Martin Luther in New Spain", in Hans MEDICK and Peer SCHMIDT, eds., *Luther zwischen den Kulturen. Zeitgenossenschaft – Weltwirkung*, pp. 119-140. Göttingen: Vandenhoeck & Ruprecht.

MBITI, John, 1969. *African Religions and Philosophy*. London: Heinemann.

MCLEAN, Iain S., 1999. *Opting for Democracy? Liberation Theology and the Struggle for Democracy in Brazil*. New York: Peter Lang.

MCLEOD, Hugh, 2014. "Separation of Church and State: An Elusive (Illusive?) Ideal", in Karl GABRIEL, Christel GÄRTNER, and Detlef POLLACK, eds., 2014. *Umstrittene Säkularisierung: Soziologische und historische Analysen zur Differenzierung von Religion und Politik*, pp. 460-480. 2nd ed. Berlin: Berlin University Press.

MEDICK, Hans and Peer SCHMIDT, eds., 2004. *Luther zwischen den Kulturen: Zeitgenossenschaft – Weltwirkung*. Göttingen: Vandenhoeck & Ruprecht.

MEEKS, Wayne A., 2003. *The First Urban Christians. The Social World of the Apostle Paul*. New Haven and London: Yale University Press.

MESTERS, Carlos, 1983. *Von der Bibel zum Leben - vom Leben zur Bibel. Ein Bibelkurs aus Brasilien für uns*, 2 vols. Mainz & München: Grünewald.

MIGNOLO, Walter D., 2012. *Local Histories, Global Design: Coloniality, Subaltern Knowledges, and Border Thinking*. Reissue with a new preface. Princeton: Princeton University Press.

MÍGUEZ BONINO, José, 2003. *Rostos do protestantismo latino-americano*. São Leopoldo: Sinodal, EST.

_____, 2004. "From Justice to Law and Back: An Argentinian Perspective", in William F. STORRAR and Andrew R. MORTON, eds., *Public Theology for the 21st century. Essays in Honour of Duncan B. Forrester,* pp. 63-74. London: T & T Clark.

_____, 2006. "Latin America", in John PARRATT ed., *An Introduction to Third World Theologies,* pp. 16-43. Cambridge: Cambridge University Press.

MIN, Anselm Kyonsuk, 2002. "From the Theology of Minjoong to the Theology of the Citizen: Reflections on Minjoong Theology in 21st Century Korea", *Journal of Asian and Asian American Theology* 5(Spring), 11-35.

_____, 2004. "Towards a Theology of Citizenship as the Central Challenge in Asia". *East Asian Pastoral Review* 41(2), 136-59.

MINISTÉRIO PÚBLICO FEDERAL/RJ, 2014. *Pedido de Agravo de Instrumento,* 9 May, 2014, Available at: https://s.conjur.com.br/dl/agravo-instrumento-interposto-mpf-rj.pdf [accessed July 30, 2021].

MOLTMANN, Jürgen, 1993a. *The Trinity and the Kingdom.* Minneapolis: Fortress.

_____, 1993b. *Theology of Hope: On the Ground and the Implications of a Christian Eschatology.* Minneapolis: Fortress.

_____, 1999. *God for a Secular Society: The Public Relevance of Theology.* Minneapolis: Fortress.

MONTERO, Paula, 2006. "Religião, pluralismo e esfera pública no Brasil". *Novos Estudos do CEBRAP* 74, 47-65.

_____, 2011. "Religião e esfera pública: a reinvenção do pluralismo religioso no Brasil", in Ronaldo CAVALCANTE and Rudolf VON SINNER, eds., *Teologia pública em debate,* pp. 145-157. São Leopoldo: Sinodal; EST.

MORAES, Gerson Leite de, 2010. "Neopentecostalismo – um conceito-obstáculo na compreensão do subcampo religioso Pentecostal brasileiro", in *Rever* 2. Available at: http://www.pucsp.br/rever/rv2_2010/t_moraes.htm [accessed August 12, 2021].

MOUFFE, Chantal, 2003. "Democracia, cidadania e a questão do pluralismo". *Política e Sociedade: Revista de Sociologia Política* 1(3), 11-26.

_____, 2005. "Por um modelo agonístico de democracia". *Revista de Sociologia e Política* 25, 11-23.

_____, 2013. *Agonistics. Thinking the World Politically.* London & New York: Verso.

_____, 2018. *For a Left Populism.* London & New York: Verso. (Kindle Edition)

MUDDE, Cas, 2004. "The populist zeitgeist," *Government and Opposition* 39(4), 542-63.

_____, 2020. "Populism: An Ideational Approach", in Cristóbal Rovira KALTWASSER, Paul TAGGART, Paulina Ochoa ESPEJO, AND Pierre OSTIGUY, eds., *The Oxford Handbook of Populism,* pp. 27-47. UK: Oxford University Press.

MÜLLER, Achim, 2001. "Dietrich Ritschl – Der Mensch ist, was er von sich erzählen kann," in Lothar BAUEROCHSE and Klaus HOFMEISTER, eds., *Wie sie wurden was sie sind: Zeitgenössische Theologinnen und Theologen im Portrait,* pp. 178-193. Gütersloh: Gütersloher Verlagshaus.

MÜLLER, Andreas, 2010. "'All das ist Zierde für den Ort...' Das diakonisch-karitative Großprojekt des Basileios von Kaisareia," *Zeitschrift für Antikes Christentum* 13(3), 452-474.

MÜLLER, E. F. K., ed., 1999. *Die Bekenntnisschriften der reformierten Kirche* [1903]. Waltrop: Hartmut Spenner.

MÜLLER, Jan-Werner, 2017. *Was ist Populismus?* Ein Essay, 5th edition. Frankfurt: Edition Suhrkamp.

NATIVIDADE, Marcelo and Leandro DE OLIVEIRA, 2007. "Religião e intolerância à homossexualidade. Tendências contemporâneas no Brasil", in Vagner Gonçalves DA SILVA, ed., *Intolerância religiosa. Impactos do neopentecostalismo no campo religioso afro-brasileiro,* pp. 261-301. São Paulo: Edusp.

NEHRING, Andreas, 2010. "Das 'Ende der Missionsgeschichte'", *Berliner Theologische Zeitschrift* 27(1), 161-193.

NEUTZLING, Inácio, ed., 2006. *Teologia pública.* São Leopoldo: Unisinos. (*Cadernos IHU em formação* 2/8)

NITSCHE, Bernhard, ed., 2005. *Gottesdenken in interreligiöser Perspektive.* Raimon Panikkars Trinitätstheologie in der Diskussion. Frankfurt am Main/Paderborn: Verlag Otto Lmbeck/Bonifatius Verlag.

NITSCHE, Bernhard, 2008. *Gott – Welt – Mensch: Raimon Panikkars Gottesdenken – Paradigma für eine Theologie in interreligiöser Perspektive.* Zürich: TVZ.

O'DONNELL, Guillermo, 2005. "Polyarchies and the (Un)Rule of Law in Latin America: A Partial Conclusion", in Hauke BRUNKHORST and Sérgio COSTA, eds., *Jenseits von Zentrum und Peripherie: Zur Verfassung der fragmentierten Weltgesellschaft,* pp. 53-79. München/Mering: Rainer Hampp Verlag.

OEVERMANN, Ulrich, 2006. "Modernisierungspoteniale im Monotheismus und Modernisierungsblockaden im fundamentalistischen Islam", in Manuel FRANZMANN, Christel GÄRTNER, and Nicole KÖCK, eds., *Religiosität in der säkularisierten Welt: Theoretische und empirische Beiträge zur Säkularisierungsdebatte in der Religionssoziologie,* pp. 395-428. Wiesbaden: VS Verlag für Sozialwissenschaften

OFFE, Claus, 1999. "How can we trust our fellow citizens?" in Mark WARREN, ed., *Democracy and Trust,* pp. 42-87. Cambridge: Cambridge University Press.

_____, 2001. "Wie können wir unseren Mitbürgern vertrauen?" in Martin HARTMANN and Claus OFFE, eds., *Vertrauen. Die Grundlage sozialen Zusammenhalts,* pp. 241-294. Frankfurt: Campus.

OLSON, Nels Lawrence, 1994. *O plano divino através dos séculos.* 10 ed. Rio de Janeiro.

OMENYO, Cephas N., 2012. "'I Have Seen the Light': The Changing Trends in Conversion in Ghanaian Christianity", in Christine LIENEMANN-PERRIN and Wolfgang LIENEMANN, eds., *Crossing Religious Borders: Studies on Conversion and Religious Belonging,* pp. 523-537. Wiesbaden: Harrassowitz.

OOSTERBAAN, Martijn, 2009. "Sonic Supremacy: Sound, Space and Charisma in a Favela in Rio de Janeiro". *Critique of Anthropology,* 29, 81-104.

ORO, Ari Pedro, André CORTEN and Jean-Pierre DOZON, eds., 2003. *Igreja Universal do Reino de Deus: os novos conquistadores da fé.* São Paulo: Paulinas.

OSTERHAMMEL, Jürgen, 2001. *Geschichtswissenschaft jenseits des Nationalstaats: Studien zu Beziehungsgeschichte und Zivilisationsvergleich,* Göttingen: Vandenhoeck & Ruprecht.

_____, 2009. *Die Verwandlung der Welt: Eine Geschichte des 19. Jahrhunderts,* München: Beck.

OSTIGUY, Pierre, 2020. "Populism: A Social-Cultural Approach", in Cristóbal Rovira KALTWASSER, Paul TAGGART, Paulina Ochoa ESPEJO, AND Pierre OSTIGUY, eds., *The Oxford Handbook of Populism,* pp. 73-97. UK: Oxford University Press.

PANIKKAR, Raimon, 1978. *The Intra-Religious Dialogue.* New York: Paulist Press.

_____, 1979. *Myth, Faith and Hermeneutics. Cross-cultural Studies.* New York: Paulist Press.

_____, 1985. "The Invisible Harmony: A Universal Theory of Religion or a Cosmic Confidence in Reality?" in Leonard SWIDLER, ed., *Towards a Universal Theology of Religion,* pp. 118-153. Maryknoll: Orbis Books.

_____, 1988. "The Jordan, the Tiber, and the Ganges. Three Kairological Moments of Christic Self-Consciousness", in John HICK and Paul F. KNITTER, eds., *The Myth of Christian Uniqueness*, pp. 89-116. London: SCM.

_____, 1993. *La nueva Inocencia.* Estella: Verbo Divino.

_____, 1996. "A Self-Critical Dialogue", in Joseph PRABHU, ed., *The Intercultural Challenge of Raimon Panikkar*, pp. 227-291. Maryknoll, NY: Orbis Books.

_____, 1998. "Religion, Philosophie und Kultur". *Polylog*, 1(1), 13-37.

PANNENBERG, Wolfhart, 1967. *Erwägungen zu einer Theologie der Religionsgeschichte.* Göttingen: Vandenhoeck & Ruprecht.

PANOTTO, Nicolás, 2016. *Religión, política y poscolonialidade em América Latina.* Hacia una teologia posfundacional de lo público. Buenos Aires, Madrid: Miño e Dávila.

PARRATT, John, ed., 2006. *An Introduction to Third World Theologies.* Cambridge: Cambridge University Press.

PASSOS, João Décio, 2012. "Teologia e cidade: panorama histórico e interrogações atuais". *Perspectiva Teológica* 44(123), 257-274.

_____, and Frank USARSKI, eds., 2013. *Compêndio de Ciência da Religião.* São Paulo: Paulinas/Paulus.

PAULY, Evaldo Luis, 1995. *Cidadania e pastoral urbana.* São Leopoldo: Sinodal.

PERLATTO, Fernando, 2016. "Adeus ao populismo? Reviravoltas de um conceito e de uma política no Brasil do tempo presente", in Fernando PERLATTO and Daniel CHAVES, eds., *Repensar os populismos na América do Sul: debates, tradições e releituras,* pp. 70-94. Macapá/Rio de Janeiro: Editora da Universidade Federal do Amapá/Autografia.

PETRELLA, Ivan, 2006. *The Future of Liberation Theology: An Argument and Manifesto.* London: SCM.

PLÜSS, David, Matthias D. WÜTHRICH, and Matthias ZEINDLER, eds., 2016. *Ekklesiologie der Volkskirche. Theologische Zugänge in reformierter Perspektive.* Zürich: TVZ.

POLLACK, Detlef, 2006. "Explaining religious vitality; Theoretical considerations and empirical findings in Western and Eastern Europe", in Manuel FRANZMANN, Christel GÄRTNER, and Nicole KÖCK, eds., *Religiosität in der säkularisierten Welt: Theoretische und empirische Beiträge zur Säkularisierungsdebatte in der Religionssoziologie,* pp. 83-103. Wiesbaden: VS Verlag für Sozialwissenschaften.

_____, 2012. *Säkularisierung - ein moderner Mythos?* Studien zum religiösen Wandel in Deutschland. 2nd ed. Tübingen: Mohr Siebeck.

_____, and Gergely ROSTA, 2015. *Religion in der Moderne: Ein internationaler Vergleich.* Frankfurt: Campus Verlag.

PRANDI, Reginaldo, 2001. *Mitologia dos orixás,* 10th ed. São Paulo: Companhia das Letras.

_____, 2013. "As religiões afro-brasileiras em ascensão e declínio", in Faustino TEIXEIRA and Renata MENEZES, eds., *Religiões em movimento: o Censo de 2010,* pp. 203-18. Petrópolis: Vozes.

PRIEN, Hans-Jürgen, 1977. "Identity and Problems of Development: The Evangelical Church of Lutheran Confession in Brazil", in Ulrich DUCHROW, ed., *Lutheran Churches – Salt and Mirror of Society? Case Studies on the Theory and*

Practice of the Two Kingdoms Doctrine, pp. 192-242. Geneva: Lutheran World Federation.

———, 1978. *Die Geschichte des Christentums in Lateinamerika.* Göttingen: Vandenhoeck & Ruprecht.

———, 1989. *Evangelische Kirchwerdung in Brasilien. Von den deutsch-evangelischen Gemeinden zur Evangelischen Kirche Lutherischen Bekenntnisses in Brasilien.* Gütersloh: Gütersloher Verlagshaus.

PRIESTER, Karin, 2012. *Rechter und linker Populismus. Annäherung an ein Chamäleon.* Frankfurt/New York: Campus.

QUEIRUGA, Andrés Torres, 1997. *O diálogo das religiões.* São Paulo: Paulus.

———, 2007. *Autocompreensão cristã: diálogo das religiões.* São Paulo: Paulinas.

RADLER, Karola, 2013. "Theology as Politics versus 'Political Theology'", in Kirsten Busch NIELSEN, Ralf Karolus WÜSTENBERG, and Jens ZIMMERMANN, eds., *A Spoke in the Wheel. The Political in the Theology of Dietrich Bonhoeffer*, pp. 270-286. Gütersloh: Gütersloher Verlagshaus.

REBLIN, Iuri Andréas, 2012. "Waves of Liberation Theology: God non-science since Rubem Alves". *Protestantismo em Revista* 27, 3-8.

———, and Rudolf VON SINNER, eds., 2012. *Religião e Sociedade: desafios contemporâneos*, São Leopoldo: Sinodal; EST.

REINHARD, Wolfgang, 2016. *Die Unterwerfung der Welt: Globalgeschichte der europäischen Expansion 1415-2015.* 2nd ed. München: Beck.

RENZ, Andreas, Mohammed GHARAIBEH, Anja MIDDELBECK-VARWICK and Bülent UCAR, 2012. *"Der stets größere Gott": Gottesvorstellungen im Christentum und Islam.* Regensburg: Pustet.

RIBEIRO, Boanerges, 1981. *Protestantismo e cultura brasileira: aspectos culturais da implantação do protestantismo no Brasil.* São Paulo: Casa Editora Presbiteriana.

RIBEIRO, Darcy, 1995. *O povo brasileiro: a formação e o sentido do Brasil.* 2nd ed. São Paulo: Companhia das Letras.

RIBEIRO, João Ubaldo, 1984. *An Invincible Memory.* HarperCollins Publishers.

RICOEUR, Paul, 1965. *De l'interprétation: essai sur Freud.* Paris: Seuil.

———, 1969. *Le conflit des interprétations.* Paris: Seuil.

RIEGER, Jörg, Jung Mo SUNG and Nestor MÍGUEZ, 2009. *Beyond the Spirit of Empire.* London: SCM.

RIESEBRODT, Martin, 2001. *Die Rückkehr der Religionen. Fundamentalismus und der "Kampf der Kulturen"*, 2nd ed. München: Beck.

———, 2007. *Cultus und Heilsversprechen: Eine Theorie der Religionen.* München: C.H. Beck.

RITSCHL, Dietrich, 1957. The Concept of Union with Christ in the Early Catholic Church. Ann Arbor: University Microfilms.

———, 1962, *Nur Menschen: Zur Negerfrage in den amerikanischen Südstaaten.* Berlin: Käthe Vogt Verlag.

———, 1981, *Theologie in den Neuen Welten: Analysen und Berichte aus Amerika und Australasien.* München: Chr. Kaiser.

———, 1984. *Zur Logik der Theologie: Kurze Darstellung der Zusammenhänge theologischer Grundgedanken.* München: Chr. Kaiser. [English translation: *The Logic of Theology.* London: SCM, 2012]

_____, 1986a. *Konzepte: Ökumene, Medizin, Ethik: Gesammelte Aufsätze*. München: Chr. Kaiser.

_____, 1986b. "How to Be Most Grateful to Karl Barth Without Remaining a Barthian," in Donald K. MCKIM, ed., *How Karl Barth Changed My Mind*, pp. 86-93. Grand Rapids: Eerdmans.

_____, 1986c. "Wege ökumenischer Entscheidungsfindung", in Wolfgang HUBER, Dietrich RITSCHL and Theo SUNDERMEIER, eds., *Ökumenische Existenz heute*, pp. 11-48. München: Chr. Kaiser.

_____, 1990. "Lehre", in *Theologische Realenzyklopädie*, Vol. 20, pp. 608-621. Göttingen: Vandenhoeck & Ruprecht.

_____, 1994. "Ökumenische Theologie", in Dietrich RITSCHL and Werner USTORF, eds., *Ökumenische Theologie – Missionswissenschaft*, pp. 7-97. Stuttgart: Kohlhammer.

_____, 1998. "Dietrich Ritschl", in Christian HENNING and Karsten LEHMKÜHLER, eds., *Systematische Theologie der Gegenwart in Selbstdarstellungen*, pp. 3-23. Tübingen: Mohr Siebeck.

_____, 2003. *Theorie und Konkretion in der Ökumenischen Theologie: Kann es eine Hermeneutik des Vertrauens inmitten differierender semiotischer Systeme geben?* Münster: LIT.

_____, 2008. *Bildersprache und Argumente:* Theologische Aufsätze. Neukirchen-Vluyn.

_____, 2017. *Dietrich Ritschl: Bibliographie 1949 bis 2016*. Reigoldswil.

_____, and Hugh O. JONES, 1976. *Story als Rohmaterial der Theologie*. München: Chr. Kaiser.

_____, and Martin HAILER, 2010. Grundkurs Christliche Theologie. Diesseits und jenseits der Worte. 3rd ed. Neukirchen-Vluyn: Neukirchener.

ROBECK, JR., Cecil M., and Amos YONG, eds., 2014. *The Cambridge Companion to Pentecostalism*. New York: Cambridge University Press.

ROBERT, Dana L., 2000. "Shifting Southward. Global Christianity since 1945". *International Bulletin of Missionary Research* 24(2), 50-57.

ROHLS, Jan, 1987. *Theologie refomierter Bekenntnisschriften: von Zürich bis Barmen*. Göttingen.

ROSA, Hartmut, 2016. *Resonanz. Eine Soziologie der Weltbeziehung.* Frankfurt a.M.: Suhrkamp. [English edition: *Resonance. A Sociology of Our Relationship to the World.* Cambridge: Polity, 2021].

_____, 2017. "Gelingendes Leben in der Beschleunigungsgesellschaft. Resonante Weltbeziehungen als Schlüssel zur Überwindung der Eskalationsdynamik der Moderne", in Tobias KLÄDEN and Michael SCHÜSSLER, eds., *Zu schnell für Gott? Theologische Kontroversen zu Beschleunigung und Resonanz*, pp. 18-51. Freiburg: Herder.

_____, 2019. *Aceleração. A transformação das estruturas temporais na modernidade*. São Paulo: UNESP.

ROSANVALLON, Pierre, 2020. *Le siècle du populisme*. Paris: Seuil.

ROUSSEAU, Jean-Jacques, 2019. *On the Social Contract,* 2nd ed. Indianapolis: Hackett.

SAID, Edward W., 1979, *Orientalism*. New York: Vintage.

SANCHES, Regina Fernandes, 2009. *Teologia da Missão Integral: História e método da teologia evangélica latino-americana*. São Paulo: Reflexão.

SANCHEZ, Wagner Lopez, 2013. Teologia da cidade. Relendo a Gaudium et Spes. Aparecida: Santuário.

SANDER, Hans-Joachim, 2015. "Os sinais dos tempos e o Deus que mora na cidade: sobre a topologia urbana da fé crista", in Franz GMAINER-PRANZL and Eneida JACOBSEN eds., *Teologia pública: deslocamentos da teologia contemporânea.* Teologia pública vol. 5, pp. 123-140. São Leopoldo: Sinodal.

SANNEH, Lamin, 2003. *Whose Religion is Christianity? The Gospel beyond the West.* Grand Rapids, MI: Eerdmans Publishing Company.

SCHÄFER, Heinrich, 2005. "Identität als Netzwerk. Ein Theorieentwurf am Beispiel religiöser Bewegungen im Bürgerkrieg Guatemalas". *Berliner Journal für Soziologie* 15(2), 259-282.

SCHILLING, Heinz, 2016. *Martin Luther: Rebell in einer Zeit des Umbruchs:* Eine Biographie. 4th München: Beck.

_____, 2017. *1517: Weltgeschichte eines Jahres.* München: Beck.

SCHLAG, Thomas, 2012. *Öffentliche Kirche. Grunddimensionen einer praktisch-theologischen Kirchentheorie.* Zürich: TVZ.

SCHLEIERMACHER, Friedrich Daniel Ernst, 2000. *Sobre a religião. Discursos aos seus menosprezadores eruditos.* Trad. Daniel Costa. São Paulo: Novo Século.

_____, 1999. *Die christliche Sitte nach den Grundsätzen der evangelischen Kirche im Zusammenhang dargestellt* [1843]. Waltrop: Spenner.

SCHMIDEL, Ulrich, 2010. *Wahrhafte Historie einer wunderbaren Schifffahrt welche Ulrich Schmidel von Straubing von 1534-1554 in Amerika oder Neue Welt bei Brasilia oder Rio della Plata getan* [1604]. Ed. Fernando Amado AYMORÉ. Wiesbaden: Edition Erdmann.

SCHMIDT, Karsten, 2014. "Säkularisierung und die Weltreligionen", in Thomas M. SCHMIDT and Annette PITSCHMANN, eds., *Religion und Säkularisierung: Ein interdisziplinäres Handbuch,* p. 356-369. Stuttgart: J. B. Metzler.

SCHMIDT, Peer, 2004. "'Der Rabe aus Deutschland'. Luther, Mexiko und die Entstehung 'Lateinamerikas' (c. 1808-c. 1860)", in Hans MEDICK and Peer SCHMIDT, eds., *Luther zwischen den Kulturen. Zeitgenossenschaft – Weltwirkung,* pp. 141-163. Göttingen: Vandenhoeck & Ruprecht.

SCHMIDT, Thomas M., and Annette PITSCHMANN, eds., 2014. *Religion und Säkularisierung: Ein interdisziplinäres Handbuch.* Stuttgart: J. B. Metzler.

SCHMITT, Carl, 2006. *Political Theology. Four Chapters on the Concept of Sovereignty.* Chicago: University of Chicago Press.

SCHREITER, Robert J., 1985. *Constructing Local Theologies.* Maryknoll, NY: Orbis Books.

SCHRÖTER, Susanne, 2006. "Politisierung von Religion und Sakralisierung von Politik. Lokale und nationale Konflikte zwischen Moslems und Christen in Indonesien", in Manual FRANZMANN, Christel GÄRTNER, and Nicole KÖCK, eds., 2006. *Religiosität in der säkularisierten Welt: Theoretische und empirische Beiträge zur Säkularisierungsdebatte in der Religionssoziologie,* pp. 357-374. Wiesbaden: VS Verlag für Sozialwissenschaften.

SCHÜNEMANN, Rolf, 1992. *Do gueto à participação: o surgimento da consciência sócio-política na IECLB entre 1960 e 1975.* São Leopoldo: EST.

SCHWÖBEL, Christoph, 2004. "Systematische Theologie", in *Die Religion in Geschichte und Gegenwart,* 4th ed., vol. 7, pp. 255-266. Tübingen: Mohr Siebeck, 2011-2018.

_____, 2005. "Theologie", in Hans-Dieter BETZ, Don S. BROWNING, Bernd JANOWSKI, and Eberhard JÜNGEL, eds., *Die Religion in Geschichte und Gegenwart,* 4th ed., vol. 8, pp. 255-306. Tübingen: Mohr Siebeck.

SEGUNDO, Juan Luis, 1976. *Liberation of Theology.* Maryknoll, NY: Orbis.

SELBAROLI, Daniel. *Hartmut Rosa.* Estudo Introdutório sobre a Ressonância. s.l./s.d. Edição Kindle.

SENGHOR, Léopold Sédar, 1962. *Pierre Teilhard de Chardin et la Politique Africaine.* Paris: Éditions du Seuil.

SHAULL, Richard, 1966. *As transformações profundas à luz de uma teologia evangélica.* Petrópolis: Vozes.

_____, 1967. "Die revolutionäre Herausforderung an Kirche und Theologie", in Ökumenischer RAT DER KIRCHEN (Hg.), *Appell an die Kirchen der Welt. Dokument der Welkonferenz für Kirche und Gesellschaft,* pp. 91-99. Berlin: Stuttgart.

_____, and Waldo CESAR, 1999. *Pentecostalismo e futuro das Igrejas cristãs: promessas e desafios.* Petrópolis, RJ: Vozes, São Leopoldo: Sinodal.

SHENK, Wilbert R., ed., 2002. *Enlarging the Story. Perspectives on Writing World Christian History.* Maryknoll, NY: Orbis Books.

SILVA, Vagner Gonçalves da, 2007. "Entre a gira de fé e Jesus de Nazaré", in Vagner Gonçalves DA SILVA, ed., *Intolerância religiosa. Impactos do neopentecostalismo no campo religioso afro-brasileiro,* pp. 191-260. São Paulo: Edusp.

SILVEIRA, Hendrix, 2019. *Afroteologia: Construindo uma teologia das tradições de matriz Africana.* Doctoral Dissertation in Theology. Postgraduate Programme in Theology, Faculdades EST, São Leopoldo.

SOARES, Afonso Maria Ligorio, 2003. *Interfaces da revelação:* pressupostos para uma teologia do sincretismo religioso no Brasil. São Paulo: Paulinas.

_____, and João Décio PASSOS, eds., 2011. *Teologia pública: reflexões sobre uma área de conhecimento e sua cidadania acadêmica.* São Paulo: Paulinas.

SOARES, Édio, 2009. *Le butinage religieux: pratices et pratiquants au Brésil.* Paris: Karthala.

SONG, Choan-Seng, 2002. *Third-Eye Theology: Theology in Formation in Asian Settings* [1979]. Eugene, OR: Wipf & Stock.

South African Truth and Reconciliation Commission (TRC), 2002. *Truth and Reconciliation Commission of South Africa Report.* Vol 1. Palgrave Macmillan.

SOUZA, Alzirinha, 2014. "A teologia da cidade segundo José Comblin". *Revista Eclesiástica Brasileira* 74(295), 564-598.

SPLIESGART, Roland, 2006. *"Verbrasilianisierung" und Akkulturation: Deutsche Protestanten im brasilianischen Kaiserreich am Beispiel der Gemeinden in Rio de Janeiro und Minas Gerais (1822-1889).* Wiesbaden: Harrassowitz.

SPIVAK, Gayatri Chakravorty, 1988. "Can the Subaltern Speak?", in Cary NELSON and Lawrence GROSSBERG, eds., *Marxism and the Interpretation of Culture,* pp. 271-313. Urbana: University of Illinois Press.

STACKHOUSE, Max, 1997. "Public Theology and Ethical Judgment". *Theology Today* 54(2), 165-79.

STADEN, Hans, 2008. *Hans Staden's True History: An Account of Cannibal Captivity* [1557]. Durham: Duke University Press.

STEGEMANN, Ekkehard W., and Wolfgang STEGEMANN, 2001. *The Jesus Movement: A Social History of its First Century.* Minneapolis: Fortress.

STOCK, Konrad, 2002. "Theologie III./4.4. Systematische Theologie", in *Theologische Realenzyklopädie* vol. 33, pp. 334-337. Berlin: De Gruyter.

SUNDERMEIER, Theo, 1986. "Konvivenz als Grundstruktur ökumenischer Existenz", in Wolfgang HUBER, Dietrich RITSCHL, and Theo SUNDERMEIER, eds., *Ökumenische Existenz heute,* pp. 49-100. München: Chr. Kaiser.

_____, 2007. *Christliche Kunst – weltweit. Eine Einführung.* Frankfurt a.M.: Lembeck.

_____, 2010. "Interkulturalität als Kategorie zur Interpretation christlicher Kunst in Afrika und Asien", in Mariano DELGADO and Guido VERGAUWEN, eds., *Interkulturalität. Begegnung und Wandel in den Religionen,* pp. 71-98. Stuttgart: Kohlhammer.

SUSIN, Luiz Carlos, 2014. "Die Stadt, die Gott will: Ein Platz und ein Tisch für alle", in Margit ECKHOLT and Stefan SILBER, eds., *Glauben in Mega-Citys: Transformationsprozesse in lateinamerikanischen Grossstädten und ihre Auswirkungen auf die Pastoral,* pp. 275-287. Matthias Grünewald Verlag.

SÜSS, Paulo, 1978. *Volkskatholizismus in Brasilien. Zur Typologie und Strategie gelebter Religiosität.* München/Mainz: Chr. Kaiser.

SZTOMPKA, Piotr, 1999. *Trust: A Sociological Theory.* Cambridge: Cambridge University Press.

TAMEZ, Elsa, 1993. *The Amnesty of Grace. Justification by Faith from a Latin American Perspective.* Nashville: Abingdon.

_____, 2016. "Justiça de Deus e graça sem revanchismo", in Iuri Andréas REBLIN and Rudolf VON SINNER, eds., *Reforma: tradição e transformação,* pp. 105-116. São Leopoldo: Sinodal.

TANNER, Matthias, Felix MÜLLER, Frank MATHWIG and Wolfgang LIENEMANN, eds., 2009. *Streit um das Minarett. Zusammenleben in der religiös pluralistischen Gesellschaft.* Zürich: TVZ.

TEIXEIRA, Faustino, 2013. "O Censo 2010 e as religiões no Brasil: esboço de apresentação", in Faustino TEIXEIRA and Renata MENEZES, eds., *Religiões em movimento: o Censo de 2010,* pp. 17-35. Petrópolis: Vozes.

THEISSEN, Gerd, 1999. *A Theory of Christian Primitive Religion.* London, SCM Press.

THORNTON, John, 1984. "The Development of an African Catholic Church in the Kingdom of Congo 1506-1543". *Journal of African History* 25, 147-167.

TIMM, Alberto R., 2008. "Teologia da prosperidade", in Fernando BORTOLLETO, ed., *Dicionário brasileiro de teologia,* pp. 966-896. São Paulo: ASTE.

TODOROV, Tzvetan, 1999. *The Conquest of America: The Question of the Other.* Oklahoma: University of Oklahoma Press.

TOMITA, Luiza E., José M. VIGIL, and Marcelo BARROS, eds., 2006. *Teologia latino-americana pluralista da libertação.* São Paulo: Paulinas.

UNGER, Roberto Mangabeira, 1996. *What Should Legal Analysis Become?* New York: Verso.

_____, 1998. *Democracy Realized: The Progressive Alternative.* New York: Verso.

URBINATI, Nadia, 2020. "Populism and the Principle of Majority", in Cristóbal Rovira KALTWASSER, Paul TAGGERT, Paulina Ochoa ESPEJO and Pierre OSTIGUY, eds., *The Oxford Handbook of Populism,* pp. 571-589. Oxford: Oxford University Press.

USTORF, Werner, 1994. "Missionswissenschaft", in *Theologische Realenzyklopädie* vol. 23, pp. 88-98. Berlin: De Gruyter.

USTORF, Werner, 2007. "Global Christianity, New Empire, and Old Europe", in Frans WIJSEN and Robert SCHREITER, eds., *Global Christianity. Contested Claims,* pp. 35-49. Amsterdam: Rodopi.

_____, 2008. "The Cultural Origins of 'Intercultural Theology'". *Mission Studies* 25, 229-251.

_____, 2010. "'The Beast from the South' und das 'Ende des liberalen Christentums'". *Berliner Theologische Zeitschrift* 27(1), 39-69.

_____, 2011. "The Cultural Origins of 'Intercultural Theology'", in Mark J. CARTLEDGE and David CHEETHAM, eds., *Intercultural Theology. Approaches and Themes,* pp. 11-28. London: SCM.

VAN DE KAMP, Linda, 2012. "Pentecostalismo brasileiro, 'macumba' e mulheres urbanas em Moçambique", in Ari Pedro ORO, Carlos Alberto STEIL and João RICKLI, eds., *Transnacionalização religiosa: fluxos e redes*, pp. 59-76. São Paulo: Terceiro Nome.

VELHO, Gilberto, 2003. *Projeto e metamorphose: antropologia das sociedades complexas.* 3rd ed. Rio de Janeiro: Zahar.

VELHO, Otávio, 2007. "Missionization in the post-colonial world". *Anthropological Theory* 7(3), 273-293.

VIANA, Ronaldo, 2017. *Reforma Protestante: "A Revolução". Puritanos, separatistas batistas.* Rio de Janeiro: Discere.

VICENTINI, Amanda Juliane, 2021. *A Teologia do Santo Daime a perspectiva de uma teologia pública.* Master's Thesis in Theology, Postgraduate Programme in Theology, Pontifícia Universidade Católica do Paraná, Curitiba.

VIGIL, José María, 2013. *Theologie des religiösen Pluralismus. Eine lateinamerikanische Perspektive.* Innsbruck: Tyrolia. [English translation: *Theology of Religious Pluralism.* Münster: LIT, 2008]

VITAL DA CUNHA, Cristina, 2015. *Oração de traficante:* uma etnografia. Rio de Janeiro: Garamond.

_____ and Renata MENEZES, 2017. "Editorial: reconfigurações do religioso na paisagem urbana". *Religião & Sociedade* 37(2), 9-12.

VÖGELE, Wolfgang, 1994. *Zivilreligion in der Bundesrepublik Deutschland.* Gütersloh: Kaiser, Gütersloher Verlagshaus.

VOIGT, Emílio, 2014. *Contexto e surgimento do Movimento de Jesus.* São Paulo: Loyola.

VOLF, Miroslav, 1997. *After our Likeness: The Church as the Image of the Trinity.* Grand Rapids: Eerdmans.

VOLZ, Rainer, 2001. "Volkskirche", in Martin HONECKER et al. *Evangelisches Soziallexikon.* Neuausgabe, p. 1709-1710. Stuttgart: Kohlhammer.

VON SINNER, Rudolf, 2001. "Ecumenical Hermeneutics: Suspicion versus Coherence?", in Peter BOUTENEFF and Dagmar HELLER, eds., *Interpreting Together: Essays in Hermeneutics,* pp. 111-121. Geneva: WCC.

_____, 2002. "Ecumenical Hermeneutics for a Plural Christianity. Reflections on Contextuality and Catholicity". *Bangalore Theological Forum* 34(2), 89-115.

_____, 2003. *Reden vom dreieinigen Gott in Brasilien und Indien. Grundzüge einer ökumenischen Hermeneutik im Dialog mit Leonardo Boff und Raimon Panikkar.* Tübingen: Mohr Siebeck.

_____, 2005. "Trust and Convivência: Contributions to a Hermeneutics of Trust in Communal Interaction". *The Ecumenical Review,* 5(3), 322-341.

_____, 2007. "Leonardo Boff – a Protestant Catholic", *Cultural Encounters* 3(2), 9-25.

_____, ed., 2010. *Leonardo Boff und die protestantische Theologie.* Frankfurt am Main: Lembeck.

_____, 2012a. *The Churches and Democracy in Brazil: Towards a Public Theology Focused on Citizenship.* Eugene, Or.: Wipf & Stock.

_____, 2012b. "Pentecostalism and Citizenship in Brazil: Between Escapism and Dominance". *International Journal of Public Theology* 6(1), 99-117.

_____, 2017. "Public Theology as a Theology of Citizenship", in Sebastian KIM and Katie DAY, eds., *A Companion to Public Theology,* pp. 231-250. Leiden & Boston: E.J. Brill.

_____, 2016. "Diatopische Ökumene", in Franz GMAINER-PRANZL and Eneida JACOBSEN, eds., *Deslocamentos – Verschiebungen theologischer Erkenntnis. Ein ökumenisches und interkulturelles Projekt,* pp. 477-499. Innsbruck/Wien: Tyrolia.

_____, 2018. *Teologia pública num estado laico: ensaios e análises.* Teologia Pública vol. 7. São Leopoldo: Sinodal.

_____, 2020. "The Diaconal Church in the Public Sphere in the Brazilian Context Today", in Godwin AMPONY, Martin BÜSCHER, and Beate HOFMANN, eds., *International Handbook of Ecumenical Diakonia,* pp. 477-499. Fortress Press.

_____, and Celso GABATZ, 2021. "Populism and 'People': Precarities and Polarizations as a Challenge and Task for a Public Theology". *International Journal of Public Theology* 15(3) [forthcoming].

_____, and Euler Renato WESTPHAL, 2018. "Lethal Violence, the Lack of Resonance and the Challenge of Forgiveness in Brazil". *International Journal of Public Theology* 12(1), 38-55.

_____, José Carlos ZANETTI and Marco GONDIM, eds., 2002. *3ª Consulta sobre Cidadania e Diaconia.* Gente Nova Construindo Novo Mundo - Tô Nessa! Salvador, Bahia: CESE.

_____, Oneide BOBSIN and Alessandro BARTZ, 2012. "Religiöse Mobilität in Brasilien", in Christine LIENEMANN-PERRIN and Wolfgang LIENEMANN, eds., *Religiöse Grenzüberschreitungen. Studien zu Bekehrung, Konfessions- und Religionswechsel – Crossing Religious Borders. Studies on Conversion and Religious Belonging,* pp. 477-505. Wiesbaden: Harrassowitz.

VOSLOO, Robert, 2020. "Afrikaner Nationalism, Religion and the Sacralization of the Past: Revisiting some Discourses on Nationalism and its Discontents in South Africa in a Changing Political Landscape", in Florian HÖHNE and Torsten MEIREIS, eds., *Religion and Ne-Nationalism in Europe,* pp. 347-358. Germany: Nomos Verlag.

WACHHOLZ, Wilhelm, 2018. "Spuren der Reformation und ihrer Wirkungen in Brasilien", in Klaus FITSCHEN, Marianne SCHÖTER, Christopher SPEHR, and Ernst-Joachim WASCHKE, eds., *Kulturelle Wirkungen der Reformation* Kongressdokumentation Lutherstadt Wittenberg August 2017. Vol. II, pp. 311-319. Leipzig: Evangelische Verlagsanstalt.

_____, and André D. REINKE, 2020. "Pela paz em Jerusalém? A origem do sionismo cristão, sua influência na igreja protestante brasileira e sua atuação no Congresso Nacional". *Revista Brasileira de História das Religiões* 13(37), 253-273.

WÄHRISCH-OBLAU, Claudia, 2009. *The Missionary Self-Perception of Pentecostal/Charismatic Church Leaders from the Global South in Europe.* Leiden: Brill.

WALDENFELS, Hans, 2005. *Kontextuelle Fundamentaltheologie*, 4th ed. Paderborn: Schöningh.

WALTHER, Christian, 2006. *Religionsverfassungsrecht in vergleichender und internationaler Perspektive.* Tübingen: Mohr Siebeck.

WEBER, Burkhard, 1999. *Ijob in Lateinamerika. Deutung und Bewältigung von Leid in der Theologie der Befreiung.* Mainz: Grünewald.

WEBER, Hans-Ruedi, 1982. *Und kreuzigten ihn. Bilder und Meditationen aus zwei Jahrtausenden*, 2nd ed. Göttingen: Vandenhoeck & Ruprecht.

_____, 1984, *Immanuel: The Coming of Jesus in Art and the Bible.* Grand Rapids: Eerdmans.

_____, 1995. *The Book that Reads Me. A Handbook for Bibles Study Enablers.* Genf: WCC.

WEINGÄRTNER, Lindolfo, 2001. A responsabilidade pública dos cristãos, exemplificado no Manifesto de Curitiba. Blumenau: Otto Kuhr.

WELKER, Michael, 2004, *God the Spirit.* Augsburg: Fortress Press.

WESTHELLE, Vítor, 1990. "Os sinais dos lugares: as dimensões esquecidas", in Martin Norberto DREHER, ed., *Peregrinação,* pp. 255-268. São Leopoldo: Sinodal.

_____, 2010a. *After Heresy: Colonial Practices and Post-Colonial Theologies.* Eugene, Or.: Cascade.

_____, 2010b. *The Church Event: Call and Challenge of a Church Protestant.* Minneapolis: Fortress Press.

_____, 2012. *Eschatology and Space: The Lost Dimension in Theology Past and Present.* New York: Macmillan.

WEYLAND, Kurt, 2020. "Populism: A Political-Strategic Approach" in Cristóbal Rovira KALTWASSER, Paul TAGGART, Paulina Ochoa ESPEJO and Pierre OSTIGUY, eds., *The Oxford Handbook of Populism,* pp. 48-72. United Kingdom: Oxford Universoty Press.

WIEDENHOFER, Siegfried, 1992. "Ekklesiologie", in Theodor SCHNEIDER, ed., *Handbuch der Dogmatik*, vol. 2, pp. 47-154. Düsseldorf: Patmos.

WILDBERGER, Hans, 1984. *"'mn"*, in Ernst JENNI and Claus WESTERMANN, eds., *Theologisches Handwörterbuch zum Alten Testament,* vol. 1, pp. 178-209. 4th ed. München, Zürich: Chr. Kaiser, Theologischer Verlag.

WIMMER, Franz Martin, 2003. *Globalität und Philosophie. Studien zur Interkulturalität.* Wien: Turia & Kant.

_____, 2004. *Interkulturelle Philosophie. Eine Einführung.* Wien: WUV Facultas.

WITHERINGTON III, Ben, 1995. *Conflict and Community in Corinth.* A Socio-Rhetorical Commentary on 1 and 2 Corinthians. Grand Rapids: Carlisle.

WITTRECK, Fabian, 2010. "Die Religionsfreiheit im Grundgesetz", in Astrid REUTER and Hans G. KIPPENBERG, eds., *Religionskonflikte im Verfassungsstaat,* pp. 66-92. Göttingen: Vandenhoeck & Ruprecht.

WROGEMANN, Henning, 2012. *Interkulturelle Theologie und Hermeneutik: Grundfragen, aktuelle Beispiele, theoretische Perspektiven.* Gütersloh: Gütersloher Verlagshaus.

YONG, Amos, 2012. *Spirit of Love: A Trinitarian Theology of Grace.* Waco, Tx.: Baylor University Press.

ZABATIERO, Júlio Paulo Tavares, 2008. "Religião e esfera pública". *Cadernos de Ética e Filosofia Política,* 12(1), 139-159.

_____, 2012. *Para uma teologia pública.* 2nd ed. São Paulo: Fonte Editorial.

ZIBORDI, Ciro Sanches, 2008. "Escatologia – a Doutrina das Últimas Coisas", in Antonio GILBERTO et al., *Teologia sistemática pentecostal,* pp. 483-560. Rio de Janeiro: CPAD.

ZWETSCH, Roberto E., 2008. *Missão como compaixão. Por uma teologia da missão em perspectiva latino-americana.* São Leopoldo: Sinodal; Quito: CLAI.

_____, ed., 2014. *Cenários urbanos: realidade e esperança:* desafios às comunidades cristãs. São Leopoldo: Sinodal, EST.

_____, 2015. "Pobreza e riqueza diante dos cenários urbanos: deslocamentos na teologia latino-americana a partir da perspectiva intercultural", in Franz GMAINER-PRANZL and Eneida JACOBSEN, eds., *Teologia pública: deslocamentos da teologia contemporânea.* Teologia pública vol. 5, pp. 79-122. São Leopoldo: Sinodal.

_____, ed., 2015. *Conviver: ensaios para uma teologia intercultural latino-americana.* São Leopoldo: Sinodal.

SUBJECT INDEX

INDEX OF NAMES

Niebuhr, H. Richard 155

Oevermann, Ulrich 133
Olson, Nels Lawrence 65
Oosterbaan, Martijn 148

Padilla, René 56
Panikkar, Raimon 25
Pannenberg, Wolfhart 61
Pathil, Kuncheria 63
Pauly, Evaldo Luis 42, 43
Petrella, Ivan 38, 39, 40
Philip of Hesse 75, 214
Pitschmann, Annette 129
Pollack, Detlef 129-133, 141
Prien, Hans-Jürgen 84

Rahner, Karl 50
Ratzinger, Joseph 140
Rauschenbusch, Walter 153
Reder, Michael 130
Ribeiro, Boanerges 210
Ribeiro, Darcy 51, 215
Richier, Pierre [Peter Richter] 216
Ricoeur, Paul 22, 24
Riesebrodt, Martin 129
Ritschl, Dietrich 3, 10, 24, 115, 116, 119
Robert, Dana 95
Robinson, Gene 97
Romero, Oscar A. 35
Rosa, Hartmut 145, 150, 158
Rosta, Gergely 136
Rousseau, Jean-Jacques 129, 169

Sander, Hans-Joachim 60
Sanneh, Lamin 93
Schilling, Heinz 211, 212
Schleiermacher, Friedrich Daniel Ernst 88, 107, 127, 158, 186
Schmitt, Carl 128, 169, 170, 174
Schreiter, Robert J. 101
Schröter, Susanne 133
Schwöbel, Christoph 109, 110, 111
Segundo, Juan Luis 32
Senghor, Leopold Sédar 93
Shaull, Richard 31, 79
Simonton, Ashbel Green 219
Soares, R. R. [Romildo Ribeiro] 207

Theology in the Public Square
Theologie in der Öffentlichkeit
edited by/hrsg. von Prof. Dr. Heinrich Bedford-Strohm (München/Bamberg, Germany),
Prof. Dr. James Haire (Canberra, Australia), Prof. Dr. Helga Kuhlmann (Paderborn, Germany),
Prof. Dr. Rudolf von Sinner (Curitiba, Brazil) und Prof. Dr. Dirkie Smit (Stellenbosch, South Africa)

Pascal Bataringaya; Claudia Jahnel; Traugott Jähnichen; Penine Uwimbabazi (Eds.)
Overcoming Violence
Challenges and Theological Responses in the Context of Central Africa and Europe
On the occasion of the 25th anniversary of the genocide in Rwanda and coinciding with the intensification of violent attacks on the civilian population in the East Kivu region of the Democratic Republic of Congo scholars and students from Rwanda, the Democratic Republic of Congo, Kenia, Cameroon, South Africa, Germany, Austria, Bosnia-Hercegovina and Switzerland joined together in Rwanda to discuss the topic "Overcoming violence". This volume is a documentation of the lectures of this conference, organised by the Protestant Institute of Arts and Social Sciences (PIASS) in Butare, the Presbyterian Church of Rwanda (EPR) and the Faculty of Protestant Theology of the Ruhr-University Bochum (RUB).
Bd. 14, 2021, 272 S., 34,90 €, br., ISBN 978-3-643-91207-7

Minseok Kim
Public Theology in Korea?
Rereading John Calvin
Public Theology is one of the most important topics in the field of theology across the world but not in Korea. There are several historical and theological reasons for this indifference of Korean Reformed Christianity as the mainstream in Korea. In order to dispel doubts of Korean Reformed Christianity to the public theological approaches it is necessary to demonstrates a coherence between some characteristics of public theology and Reformed theology. This study analyses and utilises the six characteristics of public theology presented by Heinrich Bedford-Strohm as a lens to engage aspects of John Calvin's theology and the period of the Reformation in Geneva. Based on this work, the author re-examines the history of Korean Christianity with a public theological point of view and asserts the justification for Korean Reformed Christianity to actively embrace public theological approaches.
Bd. 13, 2021, 372 S., 39,90 €, br., ISBN 978-3-643-91348-7

Christophe Chalamet; Hyun-Shik Jun (Eds.)
Main Challenges for Christian Theology Today
Religious Pluralism / Transhumanism / Ecotheology. Consultations between Yonsei University's College of Theology (Seoul) and the University of Geneva's Theological Faculty, 2016–2019
In this volume, on the basis of three consultations which took place in Seoul and Geneva (2016, 2017, 2018), theologians from Yonsei University College of Theology in Seoul, South Korea, and from the Theological Faculty at the University of Geneva reflect together on three of the main challenges facing Christian theology today. First, questions related to religious pluralism and multiple religious belonging are addressed. Second, the 'promise' of an enhanced human being through technology and other means is discussed. Third, the reality of the threat humanity represents to our ecosystem is considered. Each of these themes is examined from a Korean as well as from a Western European perspective, for Christian theology, in our day, can no longer afford to remain limited to is own geographical context.
vol. 12, 2021, ca. 288 pp., ca. 39,90 €, br., ISBN-CH 978-3-643-91329-6

Traugott Jähnichen; Pascal Bataringaya; Olivier Munyansanga; Clemens Wustmans (Eds.)
Dietrich Bonhoeffer
Life and Legacy
Bd. 11, 2019, 190 S., 29,90 €, br., ISBN 978-3-643-91106-3

LIT Verlag Berlin – Münster – Wien – Zürich – London
Auslieferung Deutschland / Österreich / Schweiz: siehe Impressumsseite

Heinrich Bedford-Strohm; Tharcisse Gatwa; Traugott Jähnichen;,
Elisée Musemakweli (Eds.)
African Christian Theologies and the Impact of the Reformation
Symposium Plass Ruanda February 18 – 23, 2016
Bd. 10, 2017, 460 S., 39,90 €, br., ISBN 978-3-643-90820-9

Heinrich Bedford-Strohm; Pasal Bataringaya; Traugott Jähnichen (Eds.)
Reconciliation and Just Peace
Impulses of the Theology of Dietrich Bonhoeffer for the European and African Context
Bd. 9, 2016, 242 S., 29,90 €, br., ISBN 978-3-643-90557-4

Katrin Kusmierz
Theology in Transition
Public Theologies in Post-Apartheid South Africa
Bd. 8, 2016, 360 S., 54,90 €, br., ISBN 978-3-643-80101-2

Heinrich Bedford-Strohm
Liberation Theology for a Democratic Society
Essays in Public Theology. Collected by Michael Mädler and Andrea Wagner-Pinggéra
Bd. 7, 2018, 344 S., 39,90 €, br., ISBN 978-3-643-90458-4

Eneida Jacobsen; Rudolf von Sinner; Roberto E. Zwetsch (Eds.)
Public Theology in Brazil
Social and Cultural Challenges
Bd. 6, 2013, 160 S., 29,90 €, br., ISBN 978-3-643-90409-6

Wolfgang Huber
Christian Responsibility and Communicative Freedom
A challenge for the future of pluralistic societies. Collected essays, edited by Willem Fourie
Bd. 5, 2012, 216 S., 29,90 €, br., ISBN 978-3-643-90239-9

Heinrich Bedford-Strohm; Florian Höhne; Tobias Reitmeier (Eds.)
Contextuality and Intercontextuality in Public Theology
(Proceedings from the Bamberg Conference 23. – 25. 06. 2011)
Bd. 4, 2013, 368 S., 39,90 €, br., ISBN 978-3-643-90189-7

Willem Fourie
Communicative Freedom
Wolfgang Huber's Theological Proposal
Bd. 3, 2012, 240 S., 24,90 €, br., ISBN 978-3-643-90145-3

Helga Kuhlmann (Hg.)
Fehlbare Vorbilder in Bibel, Christentum und Kirche
Von Engeln und Propheten bis zu Heiligen, Päpsten und Bischöfinnen
Bd. 2, 2010, 240 S., 24,90 €, br., ISBN 978-3-643-10749-7

Heinrich Bedford-Strohm; Etienne de Villiers (Eds.)
Prophetic Witness
An Appropriate Contemporary Mode of Public Discourse?
Bd. 1, 2012, 200 S., 19,90 €, br., ISBN 978-3-643-90044-9

LIT Verlag Berlin – Münster – Wien – Zürich – London
Auslieferung Deutschland / Österreich / Schweiz: siehe Impressumsseite

Entwürfe zur christlichen Gesellschaftswissenschaft

hrsg. von Prof. Dr. Günter Brakelmann, Prof. Dr. Traugott Jähnichen (Bochum), Prof. Dr. Karl-Wilhelm Dahm Prof. Dr. Hans-Richard Reuter (Münster) und Prof. Dr. Arnulf von Scheliha (Münster)

Dimitrij Owetschkin
Religion, Politik und solidarisches Handeln
Kirchliche Jugendarbeit und Dritte-Welt-Engagement im Spannungsfeld von Verband und Bewegung (1970 – 1990)
Kirchliche Jugendarbeit und ihre verbandlichen Träger spielen eine wesentliche Rolle in Prozessen der religiösen und kirchlichen Sozialisation. In den 1970er und 1980er Jahren war die Jugendarbeit in beiden großen Kirchen einem tiefgreifenden Wandel unterworfen. In der Studie wird dieser Wandel und insbesondere seine Bedeutung für das Verhältnis von Religion und Politik, von kirchlicher Organisation und sozialer Bewegung anhand der Selbstverständnisdiskussionen um die Jugendarbeit sowie am Beispiel des Dritte-Welt-Engagements der konfessionellen Jugenddachverbände AEJ und BDKJ analysiert.
Bd. 42, 2020, 350 S., 49,90 €, gb., ISBN 978-3-643-14716-5

Sungsoo Kim
Menschenrechte sichern durch gerechten Frieden
Zur Grundlegung der Sozialethik bei Wolfgang Huber
Sungsoo Kim rekonstruiert in seiner Dissertationsschrift eindrucksvoll die grundlegende Bedeutung der Ekklesiologie für die Sozialethik Wolfgang Hubers. Dabei wird deutlich, wie bei Huber theologische Theorie und kirchliche Praxis – etwa im Blick auf die Denkschriften der EKD – einen einheitlichen Bezugsrahmen für die christliche Verantwortung für den Schutz der Menschenrechte und die Entwicklung eines gerechten Friedens bilden. Kim zeigt, dass Hubers Friedenskonzept den starren Gegensatz von Gewaltfreiheit und Gewalt in der Friedensethik überwindet mit dem Ziel der Durchsetzung und Sicherung der Menschenrechte.
Bd. 41, 2020, 198 S., 29,90 €, br., ISBN 978-3-643-14654-0

Roland Mierzwa
Gutes Arbeiten, das Zukunft hat
Eine Arbeitsethik
Bd. 40, 2020, 126 S., 24,90 €, br., ISBN 978-3-643-14553-6

Clemens Wustmans; Maximilian Schell (Hg.)
Hermeneutik
Fundamentaltheologische Abwägungen – materialethische Konsequenzen
Bd. 39, 2019, 208 S., 34,90 €, br., ISBN 978-3-643-14473-7

Günter Brakelmann
Kirche, Protestantismus und Soziale Frage im 19. und 20. Jahrhundert
Band 2: Beiträge zur Theologie, Anthropologie und Ethik der Arbeit – Zukunft der Arbeit – Gestaltung der „Sozialen Marktwirtschaft"
Bd. 38, 2018, 286 S., 39,90 €, gb., ISBN 978-3-643-14185-9

Günter Brakelmann
Kirche, Protestantismus und Soziale Frage im 19. und 20. Jahrhundert
Band 1: Personen und Positionen in der Geschichte des sozialen Protestantismus – Kirche und Arbeiterbewegung – Ruhrgebietsprotestantismus
Bd. 37, 2018, 412 S., 49,90 €, gb., ISBN 978-3-643-14184-2

Nina Behrendt-Raith
Diakonisches Handeln von Kirchengemeinden am Beispiel des Ruhrgebiets
Eine qualitative Studie zu Einflussfaktoren und Handlungsperspektiven der Gemeindediakonie
Bd. 36, 2018, 240 S., 29,90 €, br., ISBN 978-3-643-14055-5

LIT Verlag Berlin – Münster – Wien – Zürich – London
Auslieferung Deutschland / Österreich / Schweiz: siehe Impressumsseite

Religion – Geschichte – Gesellschaft
Fundamentaltheologische Studien
begründet von Prof. Dr. Dr. Johann Baptist Metz (†), Prof. Dr. Jürgen Werbick,
Prof. Dr. Johann Reikerstorfer
hrsg. von Prof. Dr. Ulrich Engel OP (Institut M.-Dominique Chenu, Berlin), Prof. Dr. Judith Gruber
(KU Leuven), Dr. Michael Hoelzl (University of Manchester)

Leonardo Boff

Gottes Leidenschaft für die Armen –
Der Gott der kleinen Leute

Zwischenbilanz 50 Jahre Theologie der Befreiung

Mit einem Vorwort von Jürgen Moltmann

Religion – Geschichte – Gesellschaft
Fundamentaltheologische Studien Bd. 55

LIT

Leonardo Boff
Gottes Leidenschaft mit den Armen – Der Gott der kleinen Leute
Zwischenbilanz 50 Jahre Theologie der Befreiung. Deutsche Übersetzung Bruno Kern.
Mit einem Vorwort von Jürgen Moltmann
Es ist ein einmaliger Vorgang innerhalb der mehr als zweitausendjährigen Geschichte der christlichen
Kirchen: Zum ersten Mal entsteht ein grundlegender theologischer Neuansatz, ein neues Paradigma
für das theologische Denken insgesamt, an der Peripherie der Weltgesellschaft und der Kirche. Die
eigentlichen Subjekte dieser Theologie sind die Armen, ihre Gemeinden und Selbstorganisationen.
Nach 50 Jahren beschreibt einer der Väter dieser neuen Theologie, Leonardo Boff, diesen radikalen
Standortwechsel und zeigt anhand zweier zentraler Herausforderungen auf, wie sich die Befreiungs-
theologie selbst weiterentwickelt hat.
Bd. 55, 2021, 108 S., 19,90 €, br., ISBN 978-3-643-91307-4

LIT Verlag Berlin – Münster – Wien – Zürich – London
Auslieferung Deutschland / Österreich / Schweiz: siehe Impressumsseite